Nine Irish Plays for Voices

Nine Irish Plays
for Voices

Eamon Grennan

Fordham University Press   New York   2023

Fordham University Press has no responsibility for the persistence or accuracy of URLs for external or third-party Internet websites referred to in this publication and does not guarantee that any content on such websites is, or will remain, accurate or appropriate.

Fordham University Press also publishes its books in a variety of electronic formats. Some content that appears in print may not be available in electronic books.

Visit us online at www.fordhampress.com.

Library of Congress Cataloging-in-Publication Data available online at https://catalog.loc.gov.

25 24 23   5 4 3 2 1

First edition

for Rachel, as always

with love and unbounded thanks
for all her love and support

and for her great gift to me of time
in which I was able to keep working
on these plays

and for her invaluable energy, practical help, and editorial advice
during the final stages of this collection

&

for Ros and Seán, my dear colleagues in Curlew Theatre Company

whose friendship and talents
prompted me to start work
on these plays for voices
in the first place
and without whom
they would never have been created and staged

Contents

The following nine short "plays for voices" were composed originally for Curlew Theatre Company, a small, three-person company formed in Renvyle, Connemara, by two actors— Seán Coyne and Ros Coyne (whose stage name is Tegolin Knowland)—and myself. I wrote and directed, Ros acted, while Seán acted and did most of the stage and tech work. Our first production (*J. M. Synge's The Aran Islands*) was in 2009, and we have done almost a play a year since then. In this brief introduction I don't intend to offer a critical commentary on each play, since I hope, in either reading or performance, each play implicitly demonstrates its own purpose and point. The following paragraphs simply contain a few general thoughts that may be of some help and/or interest to the reader, in addition to the brief background information provided in the introduction to each play.

My general title notes the fact that the plays deal with material drawn from Irish history in Part One: *Hunger*; *Emigration Road*; and *History!: Reading the Easter Rising*; and Irish literature in Part Two: *The Muse and Mr. Yeats*; *NoraMollyAnnaliviaLucia: The Muse and Mr. Joyce*; *J. M. Synge's The Aran Islands*; *The Loves of Lady Gregory*; and *Peig: An Ordinary Life*. Naturally those centered on literary figures deal with their public (i.e., historical) as well as private personae. The play called *Ferry*, though not directly based on Irish history or literature, has also drawn on material from both and serves as a kind of coda to the collection. In the composition of all of these, I've used many primary and secondary sources and materials in order to compose in each case my own many-voiced "audio collage." Since the plays are neither works of scholarship nor works of literary criticism, I have not burdened the scripts with references. Since, however, *J. M. Synge's The Aran Islands* and *Peig: An Ordinary Life* are adaptations (one from Synge's own prose book on the islands, and the other from Bryan MacMahon's English translation of the Peig Sayers original autobiography), I have noted this fact in my introduction to each. In addition, I should say that *The Muse and Mr. Yeats* was directly prompted by the critical work *WB Yeats and the Muses*, by Joseph Hassett.

When one turns from writing lyric poems to writing plays, certain adjustments have obviously to be made in the way the language is handled. The common thread, of course, is that in both the language itself is of paramount importance. For the poet, however, the language of any poem is always, in a crucially determining sense, part of the subject. The language is obliged to be—without necessarily seeming to be—self-conscious, without being self-regarding. Language, in a sense, is the master. The language in a play, on the other hand, reveals plot, reveals narrative, reveals character, and is, it could be said, the servant of these external facts and forces. Even in plays that have a distinctly "poetic" quality, language remains enlisted in causes other than its own. I learned this lesson as well as I could in working on each of these texts/scripts.

Having said that, my writing most of these pieces in lines that give the impression of verse needs a brief comment. I chose to do that, not because I think of these as "verse plays" but rather because I use the lines for myself as writer to keep me rhythmically more supple than I might be if I were writing prose sentences, sentences set out as prose. And I use the line-mode to be also of some assistance to the actors, because—written and presented thus—they assist in some way the memorizing of the script.

I might also add here that by choosing to call these pieces "Plays for Voices" (enacted in many voices either, in most cases, by two actors—one female and one male—or by a single woman performing alone), I'm calling attention to the presence and persuasive power of the human voice itself. Its power, that is (in small space and brief time), to tell a story, reveal a character, offer a little picture of the world with which the audience can sympathize, and by which—if the play works—it can be briefly illuminated. It might even be said that in their various ways all these plays are intent upon giving voice to silence, bringing dead voices—whether "literary" or "historical"—to life.

Finally, as far as length is concerned, my attempt as both writer and director was to keep each one to just about an hour, either a little over or a little under. Beyond that, I imagine I'd have taxed—more than I wanted to—not only my audience but also (given the burden of being onstage and speaking without a break for an hour or more) my two patient, talented, always willing, many-voiced players—Tegolin Knowland and Seán Coyne.

Eamon Grennan
January 2021

Note 1: These plays were first performed by Curlew Theatre Company's Tegolin Knowland and Seán Coyne. The director in each was Eamon Grennan.

Note 2: While three of these pieces were originally entitled "dramatic recitals for two voices," I have also always considered them and their successors as being "plays for voices" and adaptable to other forms—radio plays, for example, or stage events with more than two actors. For this reason I have, in most of the plays, removed many of the stage directions regarding movement I'd included for my two actors in performance, leaving only some more general directions, including those regarding voice, where they might be necessary for the purposes of clarification. In addition: directions regarding songs, as well as their music, can (where not already determined) be decided by a director.

Part One

HUNGER

A dramatic recital for two voices

performed by

Tegolin Knowland & Sean Coyne

devised and directed by Eamon Grennan

music by Arne Richards

Tue., 4/14/15, at 11 am
Nafe Katter Theatre,
UConn Storrs Campus

Co-sponsored by Irish Studies and Dramatic Arts

Hunger

Introduction

Hunger is a "play for two voices" and many characters. It draws on songs, poems, oral histories, letters, books, and government documents, all dealing with the catastrophe of the Great Irish Famine, *An Gorta Mór*, that convulsed the island and radically changed it between 1845 and 1850. By giving spoken, many-voiced life to the terrible events of the Famine—events that were followed by a century of near silence on the subject, the whole country stunned by trauma—*Hunger* hopes to bring home some of the human truths behind the terrible, mind-numbing statistics of probably the single most determining event in the making of "modern Ireland."

Through immersion in what the "living" dead voices of the period say, our sense of some of the features of the Famine landscape will become clearer. The play aims to create a "living history," a tableau that grants the audience some sense of what those times were like, and what they meant to many of those who lived and died in them.

The Great Famine was most immediately caused by a potato blight, with its distinctive smell of rotting potatoes, that destroyed crops throughout Europe during the 1840s. A third of the Irish population was entirely dependent on potatoes for nourishment. The devastation caused by the loss of the potato crops was intensified by a number of other factors, political, social, and economic. The result of all these contributing factors was one to one and a half million people dead and a massive wave of emigration that scattered one and a half to two million Irish people across the globe.

While the main concentration of the piece is the Great Famine itself, the first part serves as a kind of "historical prologue," sweeping from the sixteenth to the end of the eighteenth century and using snippets from such writers as Spenser and Swift and Goldsmith to show the presence of famine in Ireland prior to the terrible events of the Great Famine. In order to make out of all this material a "play for two voices," I decided to compose a patchwork out of the words of some of those directly involved in the catastrophe itself: men and women, ordinary people at all levels in society, politicians, priests, poets, Irish, English, American, Catholic, Protestant, Quaker, and so on.

In composing this patchwork I made use of documentary evidence, mostly by direct quotation. I sewed together these quotations, sometimes slightly altered, with linking passages of my own creation. I consulted and used as a source for speeches, poems, and songs contemporary with the Famine the following books and essays:

William Carleton, *The Black Prophet: A Tale of Irish Famine*. Irish University Press, 1972.

Oliver Goldsmith, *The Deserted Village*. Gallery Books, 2002.

Joan Johnson, *James & Mary Ellis: Background and Quaker Famine Relief in Letterfrack*. Historical Committee of the Religious Society of Friends in Ireland, 2000.

Ellen Shannon Mangan, *James Clarence Mangan: A Biography*. Irish Academic Press, 1996.

James Clarence Mangan, *The Collected Works of James Clarence Mangan Poems V2: Poems: 1838–1844; V4: Poems: 1848–1912*. Irish Academic Press, 1996, 1999.

Roger McHugh, "The Famine in Irish Oral Tradition." In *The Great Famine, Studies in Irish History, 1845–52*, ed. R. Dudley Edwards and T. Desmond Williams. Irish Committee of Historical Sciences, 1956.

Stuart McLean, *The Event and Its Terrors: Ireland, Famine, Modernity*. Stanford University Press, 2004.

Asenath Nicholson, *Annals of the Famine in Ireland*. Ed. Maureen Murphy. Lilliput Press, 1998.

Liam O'Flaherty, *Famine*. Random House, 1937.

Robert Scally, *The End of Hidden Ireland: Rebellion, Famine, & Emigration*. Oxford University Press, 1995.

Cecil Woodham Smith, *The Great Hunger, 1845–49*. Penguin Publishing Group, 1962.

Elizabeth Smith, *The Irish Journals of Elizabeth Smith, 1840–1850*. Ed. David Thomson and Moyra McGusty. Clarendon Press, 1979.

Edmund Spenser, *A View of the Present State of Ireland*. Vol. 4 of *The Complete Works of Edmund Spenser*, ed. W. L. Renwick. Scholartis Press, 1934.

Jonathan Swift, *A Modest Proposal* in *Irish Political Writings after 1725: A Modest Proposal and Other Works*, ed. D. W. Hayton and Adam Rounce. Cambridge University Press, 2019.

Liam Swords, *In Their Own Words: The Famine in North Connacht, 1845–1849*. Columba Press, 1999.

The play was originally performed by Curlew Theatre Company at the Clifden Arts Festival in September 2010. For this and subsequent productions the music for the following songs was composed by Arne Richards: "Brave Walter Raleigh"; "I wish that we were geese"; "Oh God! Great God!"; "The Lord of the plains"; "There is many a brave heart here, mother"; "To thee I'll return"; "The island it is silent now"; and "I am of Ireland" (based on The Wessex Carol).

For the original production

PROPS
    2 chairs, 2 stools
    2 shawls—1 black, 1 red
    1 white apron
    1 white scarf/cravat
    1 flowered scarf
    1 crucifix pendant

DRESS
    Black polo necks, black pants, black shoes

SET
    Bare stage except for the 2 chairs, 2 stools

Note: While this piece was originally written for two voices (male and female) it may be played—for stage or radio—by more than two.

The main voices are those of a Countryman and a Countrywoman who serve as Narrators. As other voices appear, they will be identified, and may be played by either one of the actors.

Historical Prologue *[narrators speak, antiphonally]*

Countryman:	*Tá siad go léir imithe anois. Is mór an trua.*
Countrywoman:	They're all gone now. More's the pity.
Countryman:	*Tá siad go léir imithe anois. Is mór an trua.*
Countrywoman:	They're all gone now. More's the pity.
Countryman:	*Tá siad go léir imithe anois. Is mór and trua.*
Countrywoman:	They're all gone now. More's the pity.

Countryman:	Out of silence have we come.
Countrywoman:	Out of what was once our home.
Countryman:	Voices . . .
Both:	Voices from the tomb.
Singer:	*The brave Walter Raleigh,*
	Queen Bess's own knight,
	Brought here from Virginia
	The root of delight.
	By him it was planted
	At Youghal so gay,
	An' sure Munster praties
	Are famed to this day.
Countryman:	Listen to me. In the 1580s
	wasn't Munster a rich country full of corn and cattle?
	But after a year of war and plantation
	weren't we brought to such wretchedness
	even a heart of stone would have wept at it?
Countrywoman:	*[quoting Edmund Spenser]* Out of every corner of the woods and glens they came,
	creeping forth upon their hands
	for their legs could not bear them.
	They looked like anatomies of death.
	They spoke like ghosts crying out of their graves.
	They ate carrion animals, and were happy to find them.
	And soon after, they'd eat one another,
	scraping the carcasses out of their graves.
	If they found a plot of watercress or shamrocks
	they'd flock to it as to a feast.
Countryman:	In a short time, so,
	a most populous and plentiful country
	was suddenly void of man and beast.
	In those wars not many perished by the sword,
	but all by the extremity of famine.
	Let go by a hundred years or more, then,
	and what would you find?

Countrywoman:	*[quoting an authority]* If a stranger visited Ireland in those times
	he'd think himself in the wilds of Lapland or Iceland,
	not in a country as favoured by nature as ours,
	for fruitful soil and temperate weather.
Countryman:	*[quoting]* For all you'll find there
	is the miserable dress and diet and dwelling of the people.
	General desolation in most parts of the Kingdom.
	Old seats of the gentry all in ruins.
	Families of farmers
	living in filth and nastiness on buttermilk and potatoes.
	And they without a shoe or a stocking to their feet.
	Or a house so convenient as a . . . an English hog-sty! to receive them.
	And there's more, much more. More than enough
	to make even Dean Swift himself mad.
	Seeing—as he said—
Dean Swift:	. . . the streets and roads and cabin doors
	crowded with beggars of the female sex.
	Followed by five or six children in rags,
	all begging every passerby for alms.
	Mothers who couldn't work for an honest living
	forced to spend all their time
	begging food for their helpless infants.
Countryman:	And seeing the failure of other expedients,
	he would make, himself, a *modest proposal*
	to save such a country from itself . . .
	[enumerating]
	So *landlords* would learn a little mercy.
	Shopkeepers learn to be a little more honest.
	So "*ladies*" would be cured of pride, vanity, idleness, gaming.
	And so *men* would be as fond of their pregnant wives
	as they were of . . . of their mares in foal . . .
	So there'd be a cure for want, for hunger, for famine.

	'Twas a *modest proposal* indeed! Listen
Dublin Protestant voice:	*[very practical]* I have been assured
	by a very knowing American of my acquaintance

'Twas a *modest proposal* indeed! Listen

Dublin Protestant voice: *[very practical]* I have been assured

by a very knowing American of my acquaintance

that a young healthy child, well nursed, is, at a year old,

a most delicious, nourishing, and wholesome food,

whether stewed, roasted, baked, or broiled.

And, indeed, I make no doubt

it will serve as well in a fricassee, or a ragout.

I grant that this food will be somewhat dear,

[voice shift to angry] and therefore very proper for
landlords—

who, as they have already devoured most of the *parents*,

seem to have *best title* to the children.

Countryman: That was in 1729. And sure wasn't *1741 itself* a year of
famine—

Blian an áir, they called it—the year of the slaughter.

The ordinary burial grounds weren't enough

for all those who died by the roadside,

or were taken from the abandoned cabins.

Schoolteacher: *[quoting Goldsmith]* And so on, and on, and on.

A poet's eye falls on one more deserted village:

Sweet smiling village, loveliest of the lawn,

Thy sports are fled, and all they charms withdrawn;

Amidst they bowers the tyrant's hand is seen,

And desolation saddens all thy green:

Countryman: *[angry, not "poetical"] One only master grasps the whole
domain,*

And half a tillage stints thy smiling plain;

No more thy glassy brook reflects the day,

But choked with sedges, works its weedy way;

Along thy glades a solitary guest,

The hollow-sounding bittern guards its nest;

Amidst thy desert walks the lapwing flies,

And tires their echoes with unvaried cries.

Sunk are thy bowers, in shapeless ruin all,

Schoolteacher:	*And the long grass o'ertops the mouldering wall,*
	And trembling, shrinking from the spoiler's hand,
	Far, far away thy children leave the land.

PAUSE

[sound of fiddle; a lament]

Countryman:	Much is said about "Years of Famine."
Schoolteacher:	Yet every year, *every year*
	since the potato came into this country
	there's been famine in some remote corner or other,
	bringing with it sickness and death.
	What, then, of the potatoes themselves,
	the beloved, necessary, fertile, fatal "spud"
	that Raleigh planted?
	What was it like in the years of plenty?
Countryman:	Meat was only for Christmas and Easter.
	Otherwise 'twas potatoes, potatoes, potatoes.
	Out of a rush-basket we'd ate 'em—
	with salt and water, or a little milk, maybe.
	"Dab at the stool," we'd call it.
	The gossons would take them cold to school.
	They'd save the biggest spud for the master.
	Fishing-men would have 'em and they out fishing—
	mashed up, like, in a woollen bag,
	or cooked over a fire of turf on the boat.
	Spade labourers, spalpeens abroad in the fields,
	would roast 'em over an open fire.
	And sure weren't the animals too reared on potatoes—
	the pigs, the hens, the cattle even.
Countrywoman:	Year after year we'd put down the seed
	in the same stretch of ground. Year after year
	the soil would get thinner, poorer.
	Sure in no time 'twas all used up and useless.
	Nothing would grow in it, or poor stuff only.

	But Lord above, the loads and loads of them,
	before the Hunger came! Too much for eating.
	Wouldn't we leave them in ditches, in gaps in the wall.
	We even, God forgive us, burned them!
Countrywoman:	But sure didn't other people, English and the like,
	think we were born slaves:
	us so attached to the potato,
	and they hardly touching one at all.
	Wouldn't you see it in their newspapers, in their pictures,
	in the superior way they'd talk about us in the big world?
Schoolteacher:	Here is the Litany of the Sacred Potato:

Countryman & Countrywoman: *[chant the litany antiphonally]*

Rocks and Cups and Champs and Lumpers,
Pray for us.
Pink Eyes, Leathercoats, Skerry Blues,
Pray for us.
Codders, Minions, Thistlewhippers,
Hear our prayer.
Scotch Downs, Green Tops, Bulls and Bucks,
Have mercy on us.

Countryman:	But no—come '46, then '47, Black '47!—
	there was no mercy in it.
Countrywoman:	You'd go to bed one night and your fields green as holly.
	You'd wake up next morning, they'd be black as soot.
	Were you ever abroad at night
	you'd know a potato field was near by the smell.
	And the fields a space of withered stalks.
	Not a thing could we do about it.
Countryman:	Sprinkle the field with holy water. No good.
	Cut away, dig up, shake out, clear. No good.
	Pile stones, scraws, or sods of turf itself, over them.
	Not a bit of good in the world.
Countrywoman:	All no use.
	A "hunger demon" it was, blackening the land.

They heard a fairy host in the sky over Connacht,
screeching *Black potatoes, black potatoes! Now we have them!*
And the blight swept over us, a fright to the world.
Like a thick brown cloud or a storm at sea.

Countryman: *Craosdeamhan a bhí ann, agus é ag dúchan na tíre.*
A hunger demon it was, blackening the land. . . . Aye.
And what'd we be eating then?
Anything we could find . . . 'twas never enough.

Countryman & Countrywoman: *[chant another list, one line each]*
Turnips pignuts cabbage-leaves grass.
Roots of dandelion and fern.
All kinds of berries and nuts.
Bark of holly, crab-apple, laurel, beech.
Cresses sorrel charlock dock.
Borage, nettles, carrageen moss.
Cow-blood seaweed shellfish frogs.
Snails and hedgehogs.
Crows and eggs of cormorants and gulls.
Foxes. Dogs.
Some lived entirely on fish and poteen.

Singer: *O, I wish that we were geese,*
night and morn, night and morn,
O, I wish that we were geese,
For they fly and take their ease,
And they live and die in peace,
Eating corn, eating corn.
O, we're trampled in the dust,
over here, over here,
O, we're trampled in the dust,
But the Lord in whom we trust,
will give us crumb for crust,
over here, over here.

PAUSE

[roll of bodhrán; fiddle music]

Young Irishman:	*Go mbeannaí Dia dhuit, a dhuine uasail.*
	Nach tú atá faoi bhláth, bail ó Dhia ort!
English visitor:	And pray what language is that, Sir,
	in which you have just addressed me?
Young Irishman:	It's the vernacular, sir, of a certain country . . .
	A country, sir,
	whose inhabitants live upon a meal a month:
	keep very little—for sound reasons—
	between themselves and the elements,
	and where abstinence from food is the national diversion.
English visitor:	God bless me! How very odd, very odd indeed!
	I shall take note of that.
	How very like . . . Ireland!

PAUSE

[merry fiddle music]

Countryman:	But the blight itself. Where did it come from?
	Many's the story.
	From God maybe. Or from man.
	John Mitchel it was who said
	"God sent the blight, but the English made the Famine."
	But blame is easy. God and England, is it?
	You're in trouble when that pair is agin you.
	Not to mention the weather.
	Not to mention Mother Nature!
	Aye, Mother Nature and her fallen angel, *Phytophthora Infestans.*
	That was the little devil done all the damage!
Preacher priest:	*[intense]* Isn't the Almighty in his wrath this moment
	proclaiming it through the heavens and the earth?
	Look about you, and say what is it you see
	that doesn't foretell famine—famine—famine!

Doesn't the dark wet day, and the rain, rain, rain, foretell
   it!
Doesn't the rotting crops, the unhealthy air,
and the green damp foretell it?
Doesn't the sky without a sun, the heavy clouds,
and the angry fire of the West foretell it?
Isn't the earth a page of prophecy,
and the sky a page of prophecy,
where every man may read of famine, pestilence, and
   death?
The earth now is softened for the grave,
and in the black clouds of heaven
you may see the death-hearse moving slowly along—
funeral after funeral—funeral after funeral—
and nothing to follow them but lamentation and woe—
the widow and orphan—the fatherless, the motherless, the
   childless—
woe and lamentation—lamentation and woe.

Countryman: Yes, and the children
were little living skeletons, wan and yellow,
and the very dogs couldn't as much as bark,
being nothing but ribs and skin,
though at night their hungry howlings
could be heard all over the country,
and they mixed in with the wailings of the people.

Schoolteacher: So all over the country
reports and letters were being written.
Parsons perturbed. Parish Priests in a panic.
Civil servants astonished.

Sympathetic Irish official: We regret we must confirm the rumour
of a very general failure of the potato crop in this county.
One-third of the crop is entirely lost.
If the failure were local,
the contributions of benevolent individuals
might save the peasantry from starvation,

but it is, alas, universal.
Yet the *grain* is leaving the country
as fast as it can be exported,
so the tenants can meet the demands of the *landlords*.
All very distressing, but we must only hope
that *Providence* will not desert the people
in their extremity.

Singer: *[hymn] O God! Great God! Thou knowest, seest, Thou!*
  All-blessed be thy name! This work is Thine—
  To Thy decrees, Thy laws, Thy will, we bow—
  We are but worms, and Thou art THE DIVINE . . .

Countryman: So much for the Divine. As for the *human*.
  As for *Man*. Man in the shape of the *Government*.
  Sure, the less said the better.
  Some did their best. Their names are on record.
  Some even resigned. One sympathetic English official
    said:
  I believe the destitution in Ireland
  and the indifference of the House of Commons to it
  is so manifest,
  that I can no longer be a fit agent of a policy
  which must be one of extermination.

Countryman: Others did little to help, a lot to hinder.
  Charles Edward Trevelyan, for example:
  Honourable Secretary, God help us, to the Treasury.
  The man in charge.
  He had his own point of view, parroting that *Malthus*.
  The Famine, says he,

Trevelyan: *[cold, "Oxford" accent]* Is a mechanism for reducing
    surplus population.
  Since it is the judgement of God
  that sent the calamity to teach the Irish a lesson,
  that calamity must not be *too much mitigated*. . . .
  The real evil with which we have to contend
  is not the *physical* evil of the *Famine*,

	but the moral evil of the selfish, perverse
	and turbulent character of the *people*.
Countryman:	Grand! So welcome Hunger. Céad míle fáilte!
	Being miles away in London, well fed and all,
	it must have been hard for the poor man
	to feel, or even imagine,
	all that suffering, misery, and death.
	Imagination. It's a dangerous business.
	You'd maybe have to act from your heart not your head.
	Providing of course you had a heart.
Trevelyan:	This false principle of giving public money in relief
	eats like a canker
	into the moral health and physical prosperity of the people.
	All classes "make a poor mouth"
	(as it is expressively called in Ireland).
	But now, by the occurrence of the most frightful calamities,
	Ireland has awakened from this dream
	that the government will hold its hand in any difficulty,
	and it has at last begun to be understood
	that the proper business of a Government
	is not to undertake the business
	of landowner, merchant, money-lender,
	or any other function of social life.
Countryman:	And sure didn't he add,
	"*What hope is there for a nation that lives on potatoes?*"
	Rubbing salt in the wound, like.
	But I once read in the paper that
	"*Racist and sectarian views of the Irish were common enough within the English governing classes . . .*
	Trevelyan's views, they said, *reflected*
	the prevailing Whig economic and social opinion
	and that of the Prime Minister, Lord John Russell."
	And sure didn't one fine government economist declare,

	[prissy official English voice] I fear the famine of 1848
	will not kill more than a million people,
	and that will scarcely be enough to do much good.
Countryman:	Mind you, that's a fine use of the word "good."
	But hungry as they were, the people—says he—
	shouldn't get used to depending on the state.
	Not for work. Not for food.
	Because think now where that could lead.
	Laissez-faire, says he. Leave things be.
	And didn't he order tons of grain
	to be taken from the land, exported like,
	and the people starving.
Trevelyan:	The Government must *not* interfere with free trade.
	I know you think this a serious evil.
	But you are merely administrators.
	I shall never, I repeat never,
	consider banning such exports.
	And yes, there may be riots.
	But we have two thousand troops standing by, at the ready.
Countryman:	And didn't he send them in too, two thousand of them,
	and every man-jack of them well fed
	with beef and pork and biscuits.
	And, Lord above, didn't he declare the Famine over in 1847.
	It's over, says he. *Over. Now go along with yiz.*
	And him so quick to have God on his side.
	Hard to say what class of God that'd be, now, wouldn't it?
	And didn't he repeat what that Edmund Spenser said
	(poet and civil servant, God help us)
	in the Munster disaster near three hundred years before—
Trevelyan:	*[quoting Spenser] They say it is the fatal destiny of that land,*
	that no purposes whatever that are meant for her good,
	will prosper or take good effect;
	which whether it proceed from the very genius of the soil,

or that Almighty God hath not yet appointed
the time of their reformation,
or that he reserveth her in this unquiet state still
for some secret scourge,
which by her shall come to England,
it is hard to be known, but much to be feared.

Countryman: Sure it shows you how much over the years, centuries
    even,
official policy, as they say, towards our crowd changed.
But what could you do with that class of thinking?
Guilty, before any trial is held at all.

Trevelyan: Our humble but sincere conviction is
that the appointed time of Ireland's *regeneration* is at last
    come . . .
laid bare by a direct stroke
of an all-wise and all-merciful *providence—*
and all beyond
the unassisted power of man.

Countryman: *Providence,* is it! Ireland's *regeneration,* is it!
God almighty! Would they never learn!

PAUSE

[a snatch of rebel music]

Countryman: And oh the landlords! . . . landlords too!
Landlords, is it?
Landlice, more like it. Land leeches!
Stonehearted bloodsuckers pure and simple.
A bad lot most of them. Present or absent! *Irish* or not!

Singer: *The Lord of the plains where that stream wanders on,—*
Oh! he loved not the Celtic race—
By a law of the land cast out fellow man,
And he feeds the fat ox in his place.
The hamlet he levelled, and issued commands,
Preventing all human relief,

> *And out by the ditches, the serfs of his lands,*
> *Soon perished of hunger and grief.*
> *He knew they should die—as he ate and he drank*
> *Of the nourishing food and wine;*
> *He heard the death cries of the famish'd and lank*
> *And fed were his dogs and his swine.*

Countryman:
As for agents and bailiffs? Don't be talking!

Worse than the landlords,

and near all the landlords was a bad bunch.

Not all, mind you, there was good ones among 'em,

trying their best they were.

But bailiffs and agents! Irish all! Locals too!

They'd steal the milk and you givin' it to the baby.

Grabbers too. Right scaldcrows they were.

Swooping down after an eviction.

Getting the place for half nothing.

Countrywoman:
The landlord might have been in London or some other place.

Or he lived in this house up on top of the hill.

And there was agents appointed then for to collect the rents.

And there was another fella . . . the bailia—

a man that would be in every district, like,

that used to watch the tenants, do ye see,

and not let them be abusin' the land or doin' any harm.

The bailia—or bailiff—they weren't liked at all.

They were hated; they were hated.

Old Countryman:
[angry] Evictions, clearances, that class of thing everywhere.

The people, most of 'em, too weak to resist.

Landlords, agents, bailiffs, soldiers, sheriffs, police, what have you—

they'd clear the land . . . oh they'd rightly *cleanse* it.

Knocking the cabins, chasing the people.

Off to hell with them!

To the workhouse, onto the roads, into the ditches.

[remembering; intense, controlled] I seen a tumbling myself
    once, as a boy.

I seen the sheriff and the policemen and the crowbar
    brigade,

fierce-looking fellows the lot of them,

and they dragging the people out who lived in this one
    cottage.

Then they tore the thatch down

and battered at the earthen walls with crowbars.

Then it was the screaming of the women I remember,

and the half-naked children.

And then I seen the grandmother and she paralysed,

and the tottering poor grandfather himself,

and weren't they hauled out and thrown by the roadside.

I was only twelve at the time,

but I think if a loaded gun had been put in my hands that
    time

I'd have fired into that crowd of villains

and they at their devil's work.

Countrywoman: Hordes of poor people on the roads every day.

No homes, no shelter for the night.

They'd sleep in barns if they were lucky, on an armful of
    straw,

with a sack or something to cover them.

And as soon as one horde of homeless poor people—

all naked the lot of them—

died off and were dead,

or some provided for in the workhouse itself,

another clearance doubled the number.

And so they in their turn, think of it,

go wandering from house to house,

or go burrowing in bogs or behind ditches

till they'd be broken down by the hunger and the cold

and seek out the workhouse, or die by the roadside.

But 'tis true, half the country was living underground—
living in the bog itself they were.
Listen:

Lecturer: The wall of the bog
forms two or three sides of the dwelling.
Sods form the remainder and the roof.
Windows none, chimneys not known.
A hole in front three or four feet high
serves as door window chimney.
Light, smoke, pigs, and children
all pass through this hole.
There might be a chest.
A few earthenware vessels.
All the inhabitants, it was said, "wild and all but naked,
scarcely human in appearance."
Yes, and the dying the living and the dead
lying on the same floor together.
Nothing between them and the cold earth,
save the few miserable rags they had on them.
Four square walls and an old straw roof.
No straw at all for their bedding.
A shower of liquid soot falling from the thatch
and a foetid fog rising from their filthy wet rags.
All a result, you see, of the *evictions* policy.
Of course the landlord's rights were defended.

Trevelyan: Undoubtedly it is the landlord's right to do as he pleases .
. .
the tenants must be taught by the strong arm of the law
that they have no power to oppose or resist.
Property will be valueless,
and capital no longer invested in cultivation of the land
if it is not acknowledged
that it is the landlord's undoubted and most sacred right
to deal with his property as he wishes.

Countryman: So *laws* were passed.

Grand, charitable laws they were too.

People got forty-eight hours' notice, forty-eight, mind you,

forty-eight hours' notice of an eviction.

And wasn't it a . . . a . . . a *misdemeanour*

to demolish a dwelling and the tenants still inside in it!

Then—(and this one they called

"the grandest gesture of goodwill")—

[imitate English voice] no evictions at all can take place
on Good Friday or on Christmas Day.

So I reckon 'twasn't Christmas Day, or Good Friday itself,

that the good Quaker, James Tuke of York,

was talking about:

James Tuke: *[provincial English voice]* I saw one old tottering grey-
        headed man

who bore in his arms his bedridden wife

and put her down at our feet.

Then he pointed in silent agony to her,

and then to his roofless dwelling,

the charred timbers of which

were scattered in all directions around about.

He had lived in this one village

which had been the home of his forefathers

all his life.

What prospects *are* there for these miserable outcasts?

Countryman: None, Friend James.

[to himself] None.

PAUSE

Countryman: There *were good* landlords, of course there were.

Their names are known.

But even they couldn't get a right hold on it,

on all the distress and death and desperation.

When all was said and done, they lived in a different
        world.

In truth they couldn't understand the people:

people they saw daily, people suffering in ways beyond words.

Wasn't there a gulf between them

wide and deep as the Roundstone Bog.

Listen to this lady, now wife of a landlord, not a bad one.

A lady of good character and charitable intention.

Landlord's wife: *[polite Anglo-Irish voice]* Went up Blackamore Hill, a large party,

to eat our cold dinner on the top, and then come down again.

One of the pleasantest sights of the day

was our group of attendants eating up the leftover fragments—

men who never taste meat twice in a year

truly enjoying what we had left of our luxuries.

The saddest sight was one the Doctor

and young John Hornidge called me to look at.

A little ragged frightened boy,

who had collected on a stone the shakings out of the tablecloth,

was piling up crusts of bread with one hand

and holding bare bones to his mouth with the other.

The very *impersonation* of famine.

Need I say that we added more substantial morsels to his store—

enough too for the morrow.

And the Doctor slipped sixpence into that poor thin hand

for milk thereafter.

Countryman: *[sympathetic]* Two different worlds, don't you see.

Later, though, in a winter of snow and freezing cold, she'd say:

Landlord's wife: But the starving!

those who have bad shelter, scanty fire, little food.

God help them, for man can't.

Were we to divide our all with all
we could not ensure their comfort.
For they have none but ruined dwellings,
they have laid in no fuel,
their clothing is but rags,
and provisions are at triple price.
And still the famine progresses:
a frightful reality to be seen in every face.
Idle, improvident, reckless, meanly dependent
on the upper classes whom they so abuse—
call the bulk of the Irish what we will,
and no name is too hard almost for them
(didn't Mr. Disraeli himself say they were
wild, reckless, indolent, uncertain, and superstitious),
[voice shift] but here they are starving round us,
cold, naked, hungry, well-nigh houseless.
To rouse them from their natural apathy
may be the work of future years.
To feed them must be our business in this. . . .
[pleased] I mean to leave a "catalogue raisonné" of our
    population
to leave among our family archives
as a curiosity for future squires and a guide to us now. . . .
True the desolation *is* awful,
but when these bankrupt lands are sold,
will not industry and capital set all to rights?
[weary, hopeless] But God help the people;
the roads are beset with tattered skeletons
that give one a shudder to look at—
for how *can* we feed or clothe so many?

Countryman: Fair play to her, I suppose she felt it.
But 'twas in a different world they were,
and as they say, never the twain could meet.

PAUSE

[fiddle; slow air]

Countryman:	*And were there protests in it?* 'Tis well you might ask.
	Of course there were protests.
	Parish priests, parsons, ordinary people—
	all made an effort.
Schoolteacher:	Committees were formed.
	Letters were written. Petitions were made.
	Some were moderate—
	like this one from a Parish Priest:
Parish priest:	My Lord, these people, my parishioners,
	have come up cheerfully and peaceably
	under the great loss of their former crop of potatoes.
	They have subsisted during this hard summer
	without as yet any government work or food.
	But now, they are totally run out of the old provision
	or money to buy it,
	and they have nothing to feed themselves or their families.
	They have lost their early potatoes by the rot
	and the stalks of the late crop are blighted.
	They are, my Lord Lieutenant, in destitution and despair,
	and most humbly beg for work. They say:
Old Countrywoman:	Even the fowls and swine
	refuse to eat what we must eat now.
	Corn grows not on this gritty soil
	and our barley has been destroyed by black smut.
	And even this poor crop itself
	the landlord claims for the rent.
	So it's starvation we must face now.
Schoolteacher:	Other petitions let their anger be known.
	Some came from the common people themselves.
	A band gathered in Mayo made this proclamation:
County official:	"We beg leave to submit to your notice

that there is a *certain individual* in this town of Ballina
shipping oats at the present time,
when the poor of Ballina are starving for want of food,
and no employment to be had.
We ask you, is it *lawful*
to let the grain out of the country now,
and if so,
you and every one of ye, may look to the consequences.
Furthermore, we do hereby give notice
to all the boys in the parish of
Kilbride, Lackan, Doonfeeny and the mountains,
to attend at Ballycastle,
and to hold there a vestry of our own
on the gentlemen of the country."

Angry farmer: Any man who stops at home,
he will be sawed and quartered.
It is their duty to support us!
If they don't do it,
we will have it by night or by day
out of their houses and gardens.
We are not intending to starve
and they having our earning
and our forefathers' earning.
If they do not relieve us,
we will take it ourselves.
Any man who takes down this notice,
he may as well have his coffin made.
But any man that fails and stops at home,
he may be making his own coffin.

Countryman: *[ironic]* Then, in 1848, there was a rebellion, if you can call
it that.
It fizzled out quick enough, anyway,
in the widow McCormack's cabbage patch in Ballingarry.
But you'd have no trouble seeing why some
took down pike, or the sickle itself, and went out—

heeding the call of Mitchel and Smith O'Brien.
Mad as they were, but no stopping them.
Sure didn't their own parish priest warn them
against herding their cows onto a hilltop
and starting a siege there.
And sure didn't they say to him:

Angry farmer: 'Tisn't the likes of us, yir reverence,
that looks for the right, or the Repale itself,
but the long winter of the famine will be upon us
and we shall die with hunger.
And the blackguard taxes will take all the cattle.
And we took 'em here, please yir riverence,
to ate them and let the soldiers shoot us.
And that will be the quick death for us.
Better than the long hunger, your riverence.
Better than the hunger.

Countryman: And didn't the good English Quaker, Mr. Forster,
say at the time (I read it somewhere):
"This all comes," says he, "of our social system—
that vast numbers of our fellow-countrymen—
of the peasantry
of one of the richest nations the world ever knew—
have not leave to *live*.
Such is the guilt of this fearful *inequality*,
which will be a blot on the history of our country."
And there you have it!

Singer: *There is many a brave heart here, Mother,*
Dying of want and cold,
While only across the Channel, Mother,
Are many that roll in gold;
There are rich and proud men there, Mother,
With wondrous wealth to view,
And the bread they fling to their dogs tonight
Would give life to me and you.

PAUSE

[snatch of music]

Countryman: *And stories?* Oh there's plenty of them . . .
              There's no shortage of stories. Indeed there's not.
              About the priests, about the Protestants.
              There was good and bad in it.
              The good was charitable and kind to all.
              If you were hungry, that was enough.
              They did what they could for you.
              Protestants, Catholics, matter a damn.
              The bad . . . well . . . the less said the better.
              But 'twas a black mark agin'em, for sure.

Old Countrywoman: Some places they'd put a test on you
              before you got a bite or a sup of their soup.
              You might have to deny the Virgin herself,
              or Holy Communion, or go into a Protestant church,
              to their service there.
              Or hear the Bible being read. Things like that.
              "Soupers!" "Jumpers!" "Turners!"
              But sure isn't it hard to blame them,
              and they gone to skin and bone from the hunger,
              and their children howling on them.
              Weren't they only doing it, as one woman said,
              Le grá dom' bholg.
              For the sake of their bellies.
              But the Catholics, and the priests,
              would hammer them anyway.
              But sure the good Protestants,
              and there was plenty of them,
              they'd often get tarred with the same bad brush.

Countryman: *Then* there was the Quakers.
              A lot was saved because of the Quakers.
              All over Ireland they went,

And out in the desolate, godforsaken west.
Feeding the hungry, clothing the naked.
Unswayed, they'd be, by sect or political persuasion.
Just doing their own good, godly human work.
All down the western coast they'd put out the relief.
They wanted nothing in return.
Some came even as far as Mayo, God help us,
to Westport, Castlebar, and on out to Letterfrack.
Didn't the good Mr. Ellis and his wife
come over here from Bradford
and make, 'twas said, "a garden in the wilderness."
And a village as tidy and tasty as any you'd hope to see.
Not long before he came the place was desolate.
And the whole country around there desolate.
Sure the people were in woeful state.
Said one old woman, that time:

Old Woman: There will be nothing for us now,
but to lie down and die.
Aren't the people all like walking skeletons.
Aren't the men all gaunt and haggard from the hunger.
The children all crying with the pain of it,
and the women too weak to stand.
In Clifden, aren't they dying like dogs.
More than once I seen a corpse
carried up the main street there in a wheelbarrow.

Countryman: Mobs of men and women were in it,
and they suffering all the agonies of hunger.
Sure the only medicine they wanted was food.
'Twas a woeful place all right when the Ellises came.
Says Mrs. Ellis herself when they got over here:

Mrs. Ellis: *[polite provincial English]* The appearance of the poor is far
worse than I had conceived.
How they are to meet winter's blast I cannot think.
They seem very careful, though,
to make their rags answer the purpose of decency.

But they are such shreds.
Scarlet is a favourite colour in Connemara.
They weave a coarse flannel and dye with madder.
To see them streaming along the road for their rations,
or sitting (or rather *squatting*) about the house for giving
    out,
have been among the most affecting sights.
Truly it looks so barbarous—
one could fancy it a Polynesian scene.
But so hungry and debased as they are,
the poor creatures look broken down.
It is so hard to know what to do, how to help.

Countryman: But they did know. And they did help, indeed they did.
And then . . . there was an *American* Quaker lady,
from Philadelphia she was.
Went all about the country, she did, bringing relief
and telling what was happening.
In a book. She wrote all about it in a book.
Asenath Nicholson was her name.
I remember in one place she visited,
all the people were sick or dying or dead.

Asenath Nicholson: *[American accent]* And the first thing that called my
    attention
was how empty it all seemed—
no living creature moving about
excepting occasionally a dog.
But these dogs
looked so unlike others I had seen among the poor
I unwittingly said to my companions,
"How can the dogs look so fat and shining here,
where there is no food for the people?"
"Shall I tell her?" asked one of the men of the other,
not thinking I heard. This was enough.
The horrors of the famine were complete, and plain to
    me,

though I had to continue my journey.
And I remember in another country place
one well-off farmer saying to me:

Well-off farmer: This place you see before you now
was once a pretty and a grand spot.
Two years ago, these ruined fields were cultivated.
Content and cheerfulness were in every cabin.
Now, though, from morning to night,
the people wander about in search of a turnip,
or go down to the sea for seaweed to boil.
Indeed, 'tis often I've found a corpse at our door,
so my brother and me "might put a board on'em."
And often we've seen an ass passing our window
carrying a corpse, and it wound about
with some tattered old blanket or a dirty sheet.
And flung across the ass's back like that,
wasn't there some father or mother, wife or husband,
and they being carried to the grave.
And God help us, when the corpse was a little child,
or it might be there was more than one in it,
the pair of them was put into a pair of baskets,
balanced on the two sides of the ass,
and the ass joggin' along like that with its load.
[emotional] And sure God knows, 'twasn't much of a load
   itself.

Asenath Nicholson: Such sights I have seen in my travels,
I can never forget them.
Poor creatures alive and half alive, dead and half dead—
wandering about with nowhere to go.
Their homes destroyed,
whole families out on the road.
Men, women, and children
looking for work—when there was work,
though that didn't last long.
And surely work was impossible anyway:

they hadn't a pick of flesh on their bones.
All hoping for a meal of soup or yellow corn.
Along every green path, every sodden bog road,
spectres with spades in their hands—so thin
a shallow grave would serve them all.
People with hollow cheeks and glazed eyes,
as if they had risen from their coffins
to stare at one another.
Crowds of women and children
scattered over the turnip fields
like a flock of vanishing crows,
and devouring the raw turnips.
The mothers half naked, shivering in the snow and sleet,
and uttering their cries of despair.
Their children screaming with the hunger.
Nothing but sunken frames covered with flesh.
Crawling naked skeletons risen from their graves,
and ready to return, frightened, to that abode.

Countryman: So was it any wonder, asked the same Mrs. Nicholson,
that they wanted to die, the lot of them?
And die indeed is what so many of them did.
But she and the rest of the Quakers—
Americans was in it, and English, and Irish too—
God be good to them, they did what they could.

PAUSE

[slow air; harp; melody of O'Carolan's]

Countrywoman: But mostly 'twas death and dying, dying and death.
Countryman: Though, there was a *poet*, in 1849 it was,
and didn't he *make fun* of the Hunger in a poem.
I suppose only a poet'd be mad enough.
Will ye listen to it:

Countryman & Countrywoman: *[a half stanza apiece]*

A: *To the north of Lough Sheelan in winter, they say,*
The people subsist on a half meal a day;

B: *But when spring comes about, and while summer, too, blesses*
Their fields, they have three meals of—shamrock and cresses.

A: *Ard Uladh, vile sink! has been time out of mind*
But a region for owls; mid its dens you will find

B: *Slaying barnacle snails with a mallet that knavish*
Old hang-dog-faced hangabone hangman, Mac Tavish.

A: *O'Hanlon the Tattered I saw in the Glen*
Getting ready a dinner for Orrery's men;

B: *He was roasting it brown on two bars of a narrow*
Old gridiron there: 'twas the leg of a sparrow.

A: *Poor little Red Robin! the snow hides the ground,*
And a worm or a grub is now scarce to be found.

B: *Still don't visit O'Keefe; rather brave the hard weather;*
He'd soon bring your breast and your backbone together.

A: *Doire Brosnach's bald lands the good God has not blessed;*
They've been wasted and withered by Famine and Pest,

B: *My bed there was thin as the rind of a hen-egg,*
And my fare was a butterball small as a wren-egg.

A: *O'Conor brags much of his cattle; their milk,*
Ne'ertheless, is enough to half-poison that ilk.

B: *They are poor, skinny, hunger-starved stots, the same cattle—*
When they walk you can hear their dry bones creak and rattle.

Countryman: That same poet, Mangan, lived in *Dublin* all his life.
Dublin! The Capital, aye. But it didn't escape.
And when the Hunger struck the city, as it did . . .

Countrywoman: *[Old Dublin shawlie voice]* There'd be a many an' many would creep

out of all them alleys and lanes near the Liffey
in the grey of the evenin'.
an' them makin' mute signs to the passersby.
And you'd see starvin' women and children
and they tryin' their best to sing for alms, beggin' like.
And on every side of you you'd hear
and it'd near break your heart,
all them despairin' and broken voices
and them all chantin' the well-known songs—
like "Where Is the Land Like the Land of the West,"
or "Erin Is my Home," or "Home Sweet Home."

Countryman: Ah, just think of it. *Home, Sweet home!*
'Twould make a stone weep so it would.

Singer: *[Dublin voice] To thee I'll return, overburdened with care;*
The heart's dearest solace will smile on me there;
No more from that cottage again will I roam;
Be it ever so humble, there's no place like home.
Home, home, sweet, sweet, home!
There's no place like home, oh, there's no place like
home!

Countryman: Many's the time the poet heard them, too,
and he wanderin' the streets, hungry and homeless
  himself.
'Twas John Mitchel, wasn't it, who said
"there are two Mangans . . . one well known to the Muses
  . . .
the other to the Police . . ."
Very funny I'm sure.
But the same Mangan—he saw the worst,
and fair dues to him, he didn't flinch.
He only tried to make the poetry out of it.

Mangan: *[a passionate, angry voice] Gaunt Famine rideth in the van,*
And Pestilence with myriad arrows,
Followeth in fiery guise; they spare
Nor Woman, Child, nor Man!

The stricken Dead lie without barrows
By roadsides black and bare.
Down on the burnt-up cottage roofs
The sick sun all the long day flashes . . .
Oh, God! it is a fearful sign,
This fierce, mad, wasting, dragon Hunger!

Countryman: That sorta thing. Powerful poetry, like.
                In another one he said:

Mangan: May that good God ere long
                Redeem from her disasters
                Our sick and groaning country
                And put down her cruel masters!

Countryman: But, poor addict though he was,
                he knew well what was happening:

Mangan: And the Powers abroad
                Will be Panic and BLIGHT,
                And phrenetic sorrow—
                Black pest all the night,
                And death on the morrow!

Countryman: Sure wasn't his last poem itself called "The Famine."

Mangan: [quieter] Despair? Yes! for a blight fell on the land—
                The soil, heaven-blasted, yielded food no more—
                The Irish serf became a Being banned—
                Life-exiled as none ever was before.
                The old man died beside his hovel's hearth,
                The young man stretched himself along the earth,
                And perished, stricken to the core!

Countryman: But he thought he could see the end of it, too,
                and a little light after all that darkness.
                Maybe he was right, too, when you come to think of it.
                History and all that. But, mind now, I'm no expert.
                But this is what he wrote:

                [poetry voice, stiff, by rote]
                Ye True, ye Noble, who unblenching stand

Amid the storms and ills of this dark Day,
Still hold your ground! Yourselves, your Fatherland,
have in the Poets above a surest stay!
Though famine, Pest, Want, Sickness of the Heart,
Be now your lot—all these shall soon depart—
And heaven be yet at your command!
[back to his ordinary voice] Oh aye.
But he heard, too, good luck to him,
the terrible hush that came over the famine fields.
Sure didn't he call the whole of Ireland "Silentland."

Mangan: *[quiet] The gloom . . . in our once bright land, grows deeper . . .*
Through our black harvestless fields . . .
the peasants' faint wail resoundeth . . .
Want, Houselessness, Famine . . .
lastly . . . death in a thousand-corpsed grave . . .

Countryman: His own grave is beyond in Glasnevin.
He had, it is said, a horror of potatoes.

Singer: *[speaking]*
June 20, 1849.
Meath Hospital. Dublin.
James Clarence Mangan.
Cholera. Hunger.
  [Singing]
  The island it is silent now
  But the ghosts still haunt the waves
  And the torch lights up a famished man
  Who fortune could not save.

PAUSE

[slow air ("Róisín Dubh")]

Countryman: And so, the places emptied out.
Especially all over the west, nowhere escaped it.
The hunger, the fever, the evictions, emigration.
The houses knocked, the stones scattered.

Whole townlands cleared. *Cleansed*, aye.
Tá siad go leir imithe anois. True enough.
Gone the lot of them. And *Is mór and trua.* Right.
Once people were as thick in the fields as starlings.
Now there's scarcely a sinner about.
I heard an old woman speak of it once:
The old cottages, says she,
lie like bones over the open fields.

Old Countrywoman: And not the cottages only.
Real bones, human bones, all over the place.
You'd hardly credit the burying ways they had.
They did what they could.
Put the corpses in sacking, in straw mats, they did.
In barrel-staves wrapped in *súgán* ropes, or in baskets.
As close to a churchyard as they could get,
but often just in the open field,
laying them down in a little scrap of earth.
Some coffins they used more than once, they did.
Spilling the corpse out and leaving the coffin lying there
for someone else who'd need it.
And some coffins had a hinge on them on the bottom.
And wouldn't they open
the same as you'd open the bottom of a *bawrthog*
and you spreading dung.
And when you'd take a corpse to the burying ground,
wouldn't you let the corpse out of the coffin
through the floor of it.
And you could use it again, so.

Countryman: Then there'd be big pits dug by the hospital
or by the gable of the work-house itself.
You'd die there, and they'd slide you on a kind of a chute
right down into the grave, and put lime in after you.
All kinds of burial ways they had.
One old woman said to me:

Old Countrywoman:	I once seen a man
	carrying his brother's corpse on his back
	from Bailieboro to Moybologue graveyard.
	He had no one to help him
	and he having to dig the grave and bury the corpse
	himself.
	'Twas the saddest sight I've ever seen.
	And didn't I see poor Tadgh Labhráis
	with a basket on his back
	and the corpse of his dead sister inside of it.
	And, glory be to God, wasn't her head
	droopin' down over the edge of the basket
	and a twist of bright yellow hair
	hangin' down out of it, and it sweepin' the road.
Countryman:	And another woman once told me
	that a famine burial ground *by the sea* is special.
	It lies on the borders of the sea, she said,
	and it has no wall.
	The dead, she said, were put into the earth
	without any coffin at all,
	and so many piles on piles of them
	you could often see the top one
	through the thin cover of earth over the lot of them.
	And they'd lodge loose stones over it, then.
	But sure the dogs, she said, couldn't the dogs
	drag these off, God help us, no bother to them,
	and they tearing away the loose dirt.
Old Countrywoman:	And once I seen a straw rope
	was lying near a fresh dug grave.
	And it belonged to an old man
	I'd seen climbing the cliff two days before,
	and a son of fifteen lashed to his back with that same cord,
	and him bringing a spade in his hand.
	My husband took the corpse from the father's back, he did.
	And with the spade, as well as he could, he made a grave.

And then he put the boy in it.

But so many had been buried in that place,

[slow crescendo] that he couldn't cover him well at all.

PAUSE

[soft music]

Countryman:	So . . . the place is quiet always.
	Quiet as the grave. You can hear it.
	Think of it—
	Eight million or more of us on the island of Ireland!
	Weren't the fields around here full of them.
Countrywoman:	*[ritual voice]* All chattering like magpies.
	Like sparrows.
	Like starlings.
Countryman:	*[ritual voice]* Shouting across ditches and dykes and hedges.
	Calling the news of the world to one another.
	Loud as corncrakes they were, so it is said
	in the old language.
Countrywoman:	And now, listen.
	Not a sound.
	Not a sinner.
	Listen.
Countryman:	Nothing.
	As the man said,
	All the dead voices.
Countrywoman:	They make a noise like wings.
	Like leaves.
	Like wind among the reeds.
Countryman:	Yes. Eight million of us was in it that time,
	and near a half of them went off.
	One way or the other they went and disappeared.
Countrywoman:	Sure the Famine killed everything.

Countryman: And what it didn't kill ended up on ships—
terrible ships some of them, coffin ships—
boatload after boatload of bitter tears.

Countrywoman: Their cargo of shawls and shabby jackets.
Their sods of turf.
Their pocketfuls of Irish clay.

Countryman: Flocks of bewildered men, women, and children—
most speaking Irish . . . all shivering on the docks
in Liverpool or Boston . . . Philadelphia or New York.
Oh yes. Emigration; Emigration . . . *Emigration* . . .
But that's another story, isn't it . . .

Singer: *I am of Ireland,*
And of the holy land of Ireland.
Good sir pray I thee
For of saint charity
Come dance with me
In Ireland.

[Exit]

END

EMIGRATION ROAD

A dramatic recital for two voices

performed by
Tegolin Knowland & Sean Coyne

devised & directed by
Eamon Grennan

" They are going! The Irish are going with a vengeance!!! "

Emigration Road

Introduction

Emigration Road is a play for two voices based on various documents connected to emigration from Ireland over several centuries. Beginning with a historical prologue showing the presence of emigration in Irish life from earliest times, it proceeds to deal with Irish emigration to the United States, concentrating on its history since the Great Famine of the mid-nineteenth century. Since the play wanders about historically and geographically in its references, the various voices brought to life by the two actors can be of the present or the past, can be those of historical emigrants or those contemporary with ourselves. But the main intention of *Emigration Road* is to convey something of the feelings that attach— probably for all of Irish people—to that big word "emigration" in Irish life and psyche.

My intent, so, was to convey something of the *feeling* of it all, the feeling of a society in appalling extremity, exploding in on itself. And what this meant for so many was the destruction of the very notion of "home." (No accident, then, that at the heart of such a tragedy looms the emblematic act of violence we know as "eviction," the literal tearing down of the home.)

In *Emigration Road* I'm trying to represent something of the consequences of that explosion, that catastrophe. For emigration is, in so many ways, simply the enforced search for a new home, while so many of the emotions connected with it concern the nature of, the lamenting for, or even the relief to be away from at last the old home and all it meant for those leaving.

The male's main voice, his principal persona, is that of a sort of country everyman, someone who keeps us in touch with the common sense of the subject. The female voice captures a wider range of characters—Irish, English, and American—all, whether through song or speech, caught and tangled up in it all.

Of books consulted in composing *Emigration Road*, by far the most important and useful to me was *Emigrants and Exiles: Ireland and the Irish Exodus to North America* by Kerby A. Miller (Oxford University Press, 1985). Without Professor Miller's extraordinary gathering of factual material, as well as the illuminating insights he brought to its interpretation, and the purposeful thrust of his endlessly suggestive argument, I couldn't have begun to row my own little boat of impressions over those deep and choppy waters. Anyone who works on (or plays with) this subject cannot avoid being in his debt.

Other works I consulted:

Shelley Barber, ed., *The Prendergast Letters: Correspondence from Famine-Era Ireland, 1840–1850*. University of Massachusetts Press, 2006.

Osborn Bergin, *Irish Bardic Poetry*, with translations. Dublin Institute for Advanced Studies, 1970.

Brian Friel, *Philadelphia, Here I Come!* Faber & Faber, 1965.

Thomas Gallagher, *Paddy's Lament, Ireland, 1846–1847, Prelude to Hatred*. Harcourt Brace Jovanovich, 1982.

J. Matthew Gallman, *Receiving Erin's Children: Philadelphia, Liverpool, and the Irish Famine Migration, 1845–1855*. University of North Carolina Press, 2000.

Arthur Gribben, ed., *The Great Famine and the Irish Diaspora in America*. University of Massachusetts Press, 1999.

J. L. Hatton and J. L. Molloy, *The Songs of Ireland*. Boosey & Co., 1800–1899.

R. Shelton Mackenzie, *Moore's Melodies and American Poems*. International Publishing Co., 1866.

Bryan MacMahon, trans., *Peig: The Autobiography of Peig Sayers of the Great Blasket Island*. Syracuse University Press, 1974.

Louis MacNeice, "Autumn Journal XVI," in *The Collected Poems*. Faber and Faber, 1966.

Lawrence J. McCaffrey, *The Irish Diaspora in America*. Indiana University Press, 1976.

Harriet Martineau, *Letters from Ireland*. J. Chapman, 1852.

Kerby A. Miller, Arnold Schrier, Bruce D. Boling, and David N. Doyle, eds., *Irish Immigrants in the Land of Canaan: Letters and Memoirs from Colonial and Revolutionary America, 1675–1815*. Oxford University Press, 2003.

Gerard Murphy, ed. and trans., *Early Irish Lyrics, Eighth to Twelfth Century*. Clarendon Press, 1956.

Liam O'Flaherty, *The Stories of Liam O'Flaherty*. Devin Adair, 1956.

The Spirit of the Nation: Ballads and Songs by the Writers of "The Nation." Dublin, 1845.

J. M. Synge, *Collected Works*. Vol. 2. Prose. Oxford University Press, 1966.

Emigration Road was first performed by Curlew Theatre Company in Ireland at the Renvyle House Hotel in September 2011 and in the United States at the Dubliner Pub, Poughkeepsie, New York, in October 2011. In the original staging a lectern was used by one or the other of the actors when his or her purpose was to offer official pronouncements, often taken from speeches of the period or newspaper accounts. Many of the songs are set to traditional melodies. However, the following songs were set to music by Arne Richards: "I have heard the curlew crying . . ."; "No food to eat, no drink to sip . . ."; "Though I walked every village and city . . ."; "For that home is replaced by another . . ."; and "It's a hard road that we're walking . . ." (I composed the words to this song). Shona Flaherty composed the music for "The times are looking very hard . . ." and "Far away—oh far away—."

For the original production

PROPS

2 kitchen chairs set midstage a bit back; one stool downstage right; one light wooden lectern downstage left

DRESS

Black polo necks, black pants, black shoes

VOICES

Male Voice: (unless otherwise stated) mostly that of a countryman, a sort of Everyman/ Narrator.

Female Voice: as well as being a female counterpart to the Countryman, various voices, both male and female.

Note: I have given some identifying description to the "characters" as they appear, as well as, occasionally, to their various voices.

Singer: *[song (traditional)—hum first, soft but distinct, three and a*
    half lines, then sing, low, almost to self, the rest.]

    To thee I'll return, overburdened with care.
    The heart's dearest solace will smile on me there.
    No more from that cottage again will I roam—
    Be it ever so humble, there's no place like home.
    Home, home, sweet, sweet, home!
    There's no place like home, oh, there's no place like home!

    [spoken verse]

    They are all gone into a world of light

	And I alone sit lingering here
	Their very memory is dear and bright . . .
Countryman/Narrator:	*Far from Ireland I gaze across the sea*
	Tearful and sad in a strange land.
	This grey eye will gaze backwards to Ireland
	But never see again the men or women of Ireland.

St. Columcille it was said that.

Patron saint of exiles he is.

And homesickness—patron saint of that too.

Near fifteen hundred years ago, imagine.

And him only going as far as Iona.

Countrywoman/Narrator: But sure God knows,

couldn't it be any one of the millions

—five million since 1820, they say—

the millions who've left us, looking back like that.

Always *Ireland, Ireland* for them.

Alive in the eye of the mind.

Countryman: And haven't people been leaving here forever?

Emigration. It didn't begin in the Famine.

Think of all them young fellas in the early days.

Monks like. Speakin' Latin they were. Irish too.

And off with them to faraway places.

Germany, Spain, France, and God knows where.

Exiles for Christ.

Didn't they convert half Europe,

and it swarming at the time with pagans?

Countrywoman: But the mothers. What of all the mothers?

Watching their boys leave home first—

the small cabins in godforsaken places.

Following some saint or other.

Then off with them in small boats.

Sure they'd walk the length and breadth of Europe, then.

Famous they'd get, too, abbots and the like.

	But never much you'd hear of the mothers, or sisters,
	all the lamenting they'd do, and them left behind.
Countryman:	Columcille to Iona. Convertin' half of Britain.
	Then Iona to Europe. Monastery after monastery.
	Like sowin' fields of corn.
	Columbanus to Italy.
	Monasteries all over the place.
	Full of Irishmen, and every manjack of a monk of them
	missin' Ireland.
	Keepin' the lamp of learnin' burnin', they were—
	through the Dark Ages.
Countrywoman:	Oh no. Emigration didn't start yesterday or the day before.
	Nor during the Famine neither.
	Not a bit of it. It was a long story before that.
	In the Seventh Century, indeed, and the Ninth Century.
	Scholars, monks, learned men.
	They knew Greek, Latin, the old philosophers.
	All over Europe they went, as teachers.
Countryman:	All wanderin' about or settled in monasteries—
	out in *la belle France*, frigid Germany, sunny Italy itself.
	Preachin' the word of God.
	singin' their hymns, paintin' their books
	and copyin' over and over the Gospels.
	Lord save us the place was comin' down with Irish monks.
	You couldn't move without bumpin' into one.
	Walkin' all over Europe. Fine men they were.
Countrywoman:	But just think of them: rainy mornings, church bells,
	the smell of fields, the sound of a blackbird,
	and them all dreaming their way back to Ireland.
	The first emigrants, they were,
	leaving the island but keeping it in their hearts.
Countryman:	*[to himself]* Tearful and sad in a strange land.
Countrywoman:	*A grey eye gazing*
	back to Ireland,
	but never to see again

the men or women of Ireland.

Countryman:	Later 'twas nobles and soldiers was quittin' the place.
	Takin' their wives with them, children, the lot.
	A battle lost, off they'd go. Leave Ireland for Europe they would,
	find employment that suited over there.
Countrywoman:	The seventeenth century was full of that sort of thing.
Countryman:	Flight of the Earls at the start of it, after Kinsale.
	Then at the end of it, after Limerick, the Wild Geese.
	Be defeated over here, and off with you then.
	After Kinsale, the O'Neills and that lot cleared off.
	After the Boyne and all that bother whole shiploads headed away.
	After Limerick, 'twas the turn of Sarsfield and his crowd.
	Didn't some Frenchman one time tell the Spanish King:
French courtier *[French accent]*:	Every year Your Highness should order to recruit in Ireland
	plenty Irish soldiers, who are people tough and strong,
	so cold weather or bad food cannot kill them easily
	as they would with the Spanish, hah!
	For in their island, which is much colder than this one,
	they are almost naked, they sleep on the floor and eat oats
	and bread and meat and water, without drinking any wine.
Countryman:	Good to be appreciated for something, I reckon.
	Sure wasn't Dean Swift himself told in 1732
	that in the forty years before that
	120,000 Irishmen—God almighty!—120,000!—
	had been killed and wounded in foreign service.
Countrywoman:	And lord above, don't the history books say
	near two million left Ireland
	in the hundred years after the Boyne.
Countryman:	Sure half a million died for France!
	"Fighters in every clime," 'tis said,
	"For every cause but their own."
Singer:	*I have heard the curlew crying*
	On a lonely moor and mere:

And the seagulls' shriek in the gloaming
Is a lonely sound in the ear:
And I've heard the brown thrush mourning
For her children stolen away;
But it's O for the homeless Wild Geese
That sailed ere the dawn of day—
And 'tis sore in the land of the stranger
They'll pine for the land far away.

Countryman: The Wild Geese, aye. The sky was black with them.
'Twas the end of an era all right.
'Twas all but the end of a race.
After the Earls, after the Wild Geese,
'twas said the soul of the people had gone overseas,
leaving their hearts behind in Ireland.

Exile voice: *When asleep I am in Ireland.*
When awake I am in France.
I have no love for wakefulness,
My goal is ever to be asleep.

Countryman: So you see, plenty of goin's away before the Famine.
All them monks and soldiers, exiles all.
Whatever reason drove them out,
'twas always a sorrow and they going.
They'd stand on foreign shores and sing it.
Sure anyone who left Ireland, they'd say,
was a *deorai*—an exile.
They'd no word for *emigrant*, like.
'Twas always *Deorai*.
'Twas like it sounds, full of sorrow.

Singer: *Erin, my country! An exile forsaken,*
In dreams I revisit thy sea-beaten shore;
But, alas! in a far foreign land I awaken
And sigh for the friends who can meet me no more!

PAUSE

Countryman:	And it went on too, no stoppin' it.
	Right through the eighteenth and nineteenth centuries.
	For most of the eighteenth century
	'twas the Scots-Irish from the North who went.
	Rent increases, famines, fall off in the linen industry,
	all drove them out—men, women, children, whole families goin'.
	Cheap land in the States drew them too.
Countrywoman:	And Quakers, and Presbyterians, they were persecuted and they went off.
	And many made good, they did, up and down the East Coast,
	and on out to the western territories.
	Chopping trees, making fields,
	clearing the wilderness for a place to live.
	One man wrote home:
Sad emigrant:	Dear Mother, I want you to come over here very much
	and live with me. And you can live here
	better than the best man's house in Ireland.
	Any young man or woman could come over
	to be servants, and they'd live happy and respected,
	and have a prospect here not to be met with in Ireland.
Countrywoman:	In the nineteenth century, then, the numbers started growing.
	First they were digging canals, then the railways.
	Indeed there's a lot of Irish blood in the mud
	banking the Erie Canal or the Pennsylvania Railroad.
Countryman:	Workin' in the cities, too, they'd be.
	More than out in the country on farms and the like.
	('Tis funny, they couldn't take to the size of the farms at all
	and them only used to scythe, spade, and hoe.)
	Of course the old sickness came with them.
Countrywoman:	In 1844 weren't there riots in Philadelphia —
	Catholic and Protestant workers, Irish,

	having a go at each other. Mad, it was.

having a go at each other. Mad, it was.
Killing each other. And becoming Americans.
All the old prejudices alive and kicking.

Countryman: But why, you might ask would so many of them
leave home like they did?
'Twas a simple fact. Numbers.
Wasn't the population of the island in 1821
near seven million. Ten years later near eight million.
By the 1840s 'twas way over eight million.
Sure wasn't the whole of the west of Ireland
just one continuous village.

Schoolteacher: There were, you must understand,
Ill-clad people everywhere.
Wretched houses, destructive tillage on the land.
The west coast was worst.
Places that are empty now were *congested districts* then.
Between 1816 and 1842 half the potato crops were failures.
And the people grew old before their time.
Multitudes of them dying from disease and hunger.
Beggars everywhere.
Masses of filth, nakedness, and squalor.
No better, it was said, than vermin.

Countryman: So famine on top of famine, no escapin' it,
and all before the Great Hunger itself.
Not to mention other evils—
all due to Ireland being . . . well . . . Ireland:
and the shockin' state 'twas in then.
The way the country was then 'twas often easy to leave
it—
all the persecution, the plunder, the misrule.
And 'twasn't only the poor what left.
Educated men and women went too.
For none better knew that it was:

Schoolteacher: A tragedy, nothing less—
this wretched degradation of poor unfortunate Ireland:

Where the ignorant, bigoted minion of power
defeats the rights, blasts the hopes
and crushes the energies of her children.

Angry emigrant: So why wouldn't I wish to taste the delights
of freedom and independence beyond the Atlantic?
In Ireland, what drives many of us out—
if we can but go, if we can but find the means—

Schoolteacher: Is the exercise of power—
the undeniable power of the great,
or the petty power of underlings,
all dressed in their little brief authority.

Angry emigrant: So you'd have to be runnin' after
every upstart and hound pup with hat in hand,
and you in danger of a severe reprimand
whenever some Squireen might be passin' you by?
And wasn't it only mean hearts itself and sordid minds
would bear that sorta thing?
Money was a problem too. There wasn't any.

Countrywoman: 'Tis out of people's power to save money in this country.
For there is nothing in Ireland
but failers, bankrupts, and businesses gone to nothing:
flour mills failing, banks all closing.
Times is so bad and wages so little
that all a man can do in this country
will do very little for him.
Cotton weavers, millers, brewers, farmworkers itself—
all famishing for want of employment.

Countryman: And the ambitious left too,
for weren't even the employed themselves
pining in unparalleled misery:

Angry woman: All our clothes are in pawn.
Bed clothes we have scarcely any.
Many of us is obliged to lie on the floor—
expecting daily, God help us, to be turned out on the
street.

Countryman:	'Twas businesses closin' down, shuttin' up shop.
	Pubs too, when the Father Matthew Pledge came in.
	And sure between 1840 and 1844,
	didn't 20,000 bankrupt publicans and shopkeepers
	take the boat? Imagine that!
	Like everyone else, of course,
	they felt they were homeless, heartsick wanderers
	forever separated from the land of their birth.
	Didn't Moore's Melodies and the like get the truth of it?
	Some of it anyway. This sorta thing:
Singer:	*Oh where has the exile his home?*
	Oh where has the exile his home?
	Where the mountain is steep,
	Where the valley is deep,
	Where the waves of the Ohio foam.
	Where no cheering smile
	His woes may beguile,
	Oh! There has the exile his home.
Countryman:	And it just got worse and worse and worse again,
	when the Great Hunger came.
Countrywoman:	One day the potatoes were clean and good.
	Next morning a mist rose up out of the sea
	and you could hear a voice talking
	near a mile across the stillness of the earth.
	'Twas the same for three days or more—
	and then you could see the tops of the stalks
	lying over as if the life was gone out of them.
	And that was the beginning
	of the great trouble and famine that destroyed Ireland.
	The priests, some of them, had their own way of lookin' at it:
Priest:	*[blesses himself]* The angel of death and desolation
	reigns triumphant in Ireland.
	For the Almighty is wishing all men, and women too,
	to be leaving this country.

Emigrate, and you'll be doing God's work.
You will be going from Poverty Island
to streets paved with gold.
From ruined fields to prairie-seas of green.
Dearly beloved, you must leave this place!

Countrywoman: And they went in their thousands, they did.
The blight came, and all was finished.
They headed for the boats.
They melted away, it is said,
like snow on a sunny morning.
Exile before, starvation behind—
It was natural they'd pin their hopes on America.
They believed it was, indeed, an answer to prayer.
There were some, though, who could not get out,
not having the few pounds it took for a ticket.
One poor Mayo man mourned his plight:

Mayo man: It's over there in America I'd be now,
only for the pig the landlord took off me for the rent.
The passage money was in that pig.
Torment and heartbreak this place is to me now,
for it's here I was and here I am.
With no pig to sell, no potatoes to eat,
and no passage money out of the putrid mess.
How am I to get through life at all?

Countrywoman: So, between 1845 and 1855
over two million men, women, and children
took to the ships and sailed away.
More left Ireland in these ten years
than in the previous two hundred and fifty.
Panic and hysteria were everywhere.
I heard it described one time
as a headlong flight of refugees.

Countryman: Marchin' to the sea like lemmings, they were.
Castin' themselves to the mercy of the waves.

Half a million Irish speakers among them.
The Famine broke the back of the language too.
The country was little more than one big funeral.

Young Countrywoman: There are few boys left on our side of the country
and there will be few men soon
for they are pouring out in shoals to America.
Chapels are all empty of a Sunday.

Countryman: Sure the island is nothing but a charnel house, a shambles.

Singer: *No food to eat, no drink to sip.*
The poorhouse bare, the dreadful coffin ship.
In mountain graves they in hundreds lay,
by hunger taken to their beds of clay.

Angry emigrant: And of course *the Saxon foe*, as they said, was the cause of
it all.
There was justice in that, too, no lie.
But there was more reasons, Irish ones, good ones too.
Like the family or the parish or the county itself
couldn't support them at home, so they had to leave.

Angry emigrant woman: Or the agents and jobbers and shopkeepers—
all our own people too—
all cheatin' and chisellin' the unfortunate.

Angry emigrant: But still most of us would whine and wail against England
and be loud and full of sorrow
for our own little stony field, our lovely little
arse-out-of-our-britches life.
Arrah—get over it. Exile's lament—*moryah*.
So we could hug each other and roar in our moonshine
how we were victims, always victims.
Moonshine it was, some of it anyway.
'Twas likely a deal more complicated than that.
Though truth to tell,
our lords and masters across the water
made a terrible bad hash of it.

Schoolteacher: Blame hardly matters now, of course.

The truth is the Famine doubled and redoubled and
    doubled again

the numbers of those fleeing the country.

Countryman: Between people dying and people leaving,

near three million souls disappeared from the place.

The so-called "authorities" weren't entirely sad about it.

English parliamentarian: In conclusion, we feel

it will be gratifying to your Excellency to find

that though the population, between 1841 and 1851,

has been (by famine, disease, and emigration)

diminished in so remarkable a manner—

the results of the Irish census of 1851

are on the whole satisfactory, demonstrating as they do

the general advancement of the country.

Countryman: But the truth behind them "statistics,"

'twas simple enough. And tragic too.

Panic and flight—that was the size of it.

Panic and flight.

And so many speakin' Irish.

Howlin' the word *Deorai, Deorai*

and they stumblin' towards the boats.

Clutching the little bits and pieces

they'd saved from the wreckage.

A wreck all right. The whole country a wreck,

and they desperately seekin' survival.

Countrywoman: Famine, Disease, Emigration.

Our own unholy Trinity!

Changed this place they did anyway.

Changed the world too, you might say.

Sure where would America be today

had we not fled there in our millions that time?

Countryman: Of course there were other reasons too, beyond hunger
    and horror:

Old traditions dying hard.

Farmholdings growin' smaller and smaller,

with never a livin' to be got from the little patch you'd be
    left with,

and it divided between six or seven or maybe eight sons.

If you weren't the oldest you'd have to starve or go off.

'Twasn't a country for young men at all, the way it was,

So in the heel o' the hunt 'twas hard to go marryin' itself.

Which made the girls mighty unhappy too.

Young Countrywoman: There is no fun in Ireland at all.

'Tis all christenings and no marriages.

Dreary discontent has crept over me, and why wouldn't it?

Must I forever oversee the maids,

regulate the wayfarers, visit the sick,

and make butter? Could this be called *living?*

Sure doesn't every servant girl think of the land of
    promise,

where husbands are more procurable than hereabouts.

And sure didn't Mary Brown down the road write to me

and sez she "You would not think

I had any beaux, but I have a good many,

about half a dozen now.

I have become quite the Yankee

and if I was at home

the boys would be all about me."

Countryman: Off they went anyway,

for this reason, that reason, t'other reason.

Some just for the adventure of it,

and the freedom they'd find away from home.

Hoping to start a life they couldn't find in Ireland.

And they found it too, many of them.

But the one upshot is, they left and headed off.

Singer: *The times are looking very hard*

the wages they are small

So now I'm off to America

where there's work and food for all.

Countryman: So off they went, in their hundreds of thousands.

Wild geese, is it? And tame geese too.

Flocks and flocks after flocks of them. Flying off.

PAUSE

Countrywoman: They marked their going in their own way, too.

Countryman: No doubt ye've all heard of the American Wake.

It had different names in different parts of the country.

Countrywoman: *[a litany] The farewell supper.*

The feast of departure.

The night of the bottle drink.

The live wake.

The convoy.

The American bottle night.

Countryman: The occasion would be sad of course,

but sometimes merry enough.

Mostly a mix of the two.

Drink, aye, there was drink—when they could afford it.

And then all sorts of looking forward to America

and what it'd be like over there.

Young Countrywoman: *[harsh voice]* Sure won't it be better to be nicely dressed
over there

than slobberin' barefoot through the mud

with a tub of turnips for the pigs here?

And over there you'll have no more bowin' and scrapin'

and makin' a god of the landlord.

Countryman: And there'd be clay pipes, plenty of tobacco.

And if they could, there'd be a power of poteen, maybe, or
shop whiskey.

And sometimes in some places, strange to say,

this'd be the old days now,

they'd give the one goin' what they called frog bread:

'twas made of flour and a pulverised frog—

to protect against fever on the ship it was.

Superstitions they'd have, and what harm in them.

And the older women would be keenin'

over the virtues of the young one goin' away.

Goin' for good and all of course.

For, as one schoolteacher put it:

Schoolteacher: Money was scarce, travel slow and perilous.

Illiteracy widespread, mail service uncertain,

and destinations only vaguely perceived.

So the departure for North America of a relative or neighbour

represented as final a parting as a descent into the grave.

Countryman: Sometimes there'd be a bit of singin'—dancin' even.

And the fella goin' away, wasn't he like

attendin' his own funeral, and him the remains itself.

Schoolteacher: Going away forever he was,

sailing next day for what they called the Promised Land.

Countryman: And so his old Da would say—late in the night, it'd be,

or early in the mornin', matter a damn—

"Get up here now son," he'd say, "and face me in a step—

for likely 'twill be the last step ever we'll dance."

[to audience] And you would think they were tryin' to see

who could sing the oldest and saddest songs—

and if you were goin' away yourself and heard them

'twould surely break your heart.

Singer: *Gazing back through Barnes Gap on my own dear native hills*

I thought no shame (O who could blame!) 'twas there I cried my fill

My parents kind ran in my mind, my friends and comrades all

My heart did ache, I thought 'twould break, in leaving Donegal.

Countryman: Next mornin', then,

they'd be watchin' the boat or the train go off,

and though they'd be silent, the ones left behind,

their hearts would be wild with grief.

[to Countrywoman] 'Twas just like one big funeral.

Countrywoman:	And the last parting was so sad, 'twas unbearable.
	The parents especially:
	as if the person leaving were really dead.
	You would rather not be there at all
	if you would be any way soft yourself.
Countryman:	And there'd be a keening in it too:
	some old woman would let the wail out of her,
	and others would join in—
	and the young fella looking on, silent, embarrassed like.
Countrywoman:	Then 'twas the fussing over everything—
Countryman:	Have you packed right?
Countrywoman:	Have you your ticket safe?
Countryman:	Have you your Uncle Tommy's address?
Countrywoman:	Have you your rosary beads?
Countryman:	Have you enough grub for the journey?
Countrywoman:	Say anything, anything, till it's all over
	Then the promises, the promises—
	to write letters, to think of them, to send back money.
	Then off he goes, and they see him go.
	And he as good as dead to them forever.
Countryman:	And the tears and the cries,
	and the parents all shouting after them:
	Mind yourself son! Mind yourself a-girleen!
Countrywoman:	And the mothers crying; the fathers staring.
	God in heaven protect ye!—over and over.
Countryman:	Sure you might steal off without a word, and you a young fella,
	to avoid the likes of that, and you a mix of fear
	and looking forward to America, the new life you'd find there.
	At the train station, then, there'd be a great wailing
	when the bell rang, the signal for startin'.
	And sure often when the train moved away at last
	didn't hundreds run along the fields beside the line
	to catch one last glimpse of the friends they'd see no more.

	Of course strangers didn't see this sorta carry-on
	in the same way at all at all.
	Says one Englishwoman, a writer she was:
English writer:	*[very English accent]* What we saw on the road to Cork
	was a procession of two hundred or three hundred
	men and women, boys and girls, between ten and thirty years of age.

Of course strangers didn't see this sorta carry-on
in the same way at all at all.
Says one Englishwoman, a writer she was:

English writer: *[very English accent]* What we saw on the road to Cork
was a procession of two hundred or three hundred
men and women, boys and girls, between ten and thirty
    years of age.
They looked most picturesque, really,
in their gay plaid shawls and straw bonnets.
They were all on their way to Cork,
to go on board the emigrant ship, you see.
When we arrived at Cork, we glimpsed them again.
The last embraces, then, were terrible to see.
But worse were the kissings and claspings of the hands
during the long minutes that remained.
When we saw the wringings of the hands
and heard the wailings,
we became aware, for the first time perhaps,
of the full dignity of a civilisation such as England,
which induces control over the emotions.
All the while, that *lamentation* was giving me a headache.
Still, there it was, the pain and the passion—
and the shrill united cry that still rings in our ears,
and long will ring when we hear of emigration.

Countryman: True for her, the wail of emigration.
But you'd hear a different class of story about going away,
    now,
from that good island lady, Peig Sayers.

Peig Sayers: *[Kerry accent]* When a person leaves for America it's like
    death—
for only one out of a thousand ever again returns to
    Ireland.
I remember one time I went with my friends to the station,
and you'd think 'twas a funeral procession,
the lot of us walking the road like that.

	Then when we got there, before I had time to wipe my eyes,
	they were all swept out of my sight.
Countryman:	And in the years after that, didn't her own family
	all up and away to America, one followin' the other,
	the way it often happened.
Peig Sayers:	Well, my son Tomás was killed, and six months after that
	my son Pádraig headed off to America.
	And soon as he had earned the passage money,
	he sent for his sister Cáit, and she went to him.
	Then my husband died, and my son Muiris
	decided he had to take to the road like the others,
	and his heart laden with sorrow.
	The morning he left he was standing with his luggage
	and his papers on the table beside him.
	And unknown to him I was watching.
	He stood there stiff as a poker
	with his two lips clamped together as if he was thinking.
	Then he rounded on me.
Son Muiris:	Here!
Peig Sayers:	Says he, handing me something wrapped in paper.
	I opened it and it was the Irish flag.
Son Muiris:	Put that away now to keep in a place
	where neither moths not flies can harm it!
	I have no business of it from this out.
Peig Sayers:	Son dear, says I, this will do me more harm than good,
	for 'twill only make me lonely.
	I followed him down to the slip, then,
	and what with all the people making their way to the haven
	'twas like a funeral that day.
	And says he:
Son Muiris:	Promise me when I go you won't be lonely.
Peig Sayers:	If I promised you that son, says I,
	I'd promise you a lie.

	But I'll do my best not to be troubled. And says he,
Son Muiris:	I hope mother we'll be together again.
Peig Sayers:	Then off he went
	and I was desolate when he was gone.
	Then Eibhlin my daughter went,
	and then my youngest, Micheál, went off too.
	So the upshot of all that was that one by one
	the children left me and I was left alone.
	Without a cow or a sheep or a penny in my pocket
Countryman:	There you have it.
	And the emigration didn't only hurt the people.
	It hurt the *place*, too.
	A place'd never be the same after.
Schoolteacher:	It took the language. It took the music.
	"In the old times," said a Connemara man to me:
Connemara man:	It's many a piper would be moving around
	through those houses for a whole quarter together,
	playing his pipes and drinking poteen
	and the people dancing round him;
	but now there is no dancing or singing in this place at all,
	and most of the young people is growing up
	and going to America. Even the lace-making girls—
	there isn't a young one among them
	that isn't saving up, and saving up
	till she's enough gathered to take her to America
	and then away she will go, and why wouldn't she?
	God knows, it's soon to America we'll all be going,
	leaving all these wakes behind us.
Countrywoman:	Wakes and goings away. We had our fill of them.
	Sure wasn't the whole of Ireland
	one big American wake for a while there—
	during the Famine, and well after it too?
	And listen to me now, to what I'm telling you:
	what was dying was a bit of Ireland itself, wasn't it?

	A whole way of life, that's what was dying.
Countryman:	And then the harbours crammed with all those going.
	All ended up one way or the other at the edge of the western sea.
	Ready or not for the crossing, it had to happen.
	You had to cross the Atlantic
Singer:	*Far away—oh far away—*
	We seek a world o'er the ocean spray!
	We seek a land across the sea,
	Where bread is plenty and men are free,
	The sails are set, the breezes swell—
	Our own dear country, farewell, farewell.

PAUSE

Countryman:	But many were afraid to go, too.
	They'd hang back, hungry and needy as they were.
	Sure the sea frightened the life out of many.
Frightened woman:	If 'twas any place I could travel by land,
	I would not mind it so much . . .
	but I feel a kind of terror of the sea.
Countryman:	But 'twas hard not to go, with people all sayin'
	only fools were stayin' in Ireland.
	From near every parish in the island they came—
	shoals of them swarming away overseas
	without a penny in their threadbare pockets.
Countrywoman:	Forty or fifty miles they'd be walking
	to get to the nearest port.
	And there they'd shiver in fear and excitement,
	waiting till they'd be aboard
	and off over the Atlantic with them.
	Homespun jackets, red petticoats and black.
	The roads were thick with them.
	The lucky ones fleeing the hunger.
Countryman:	They'd head off so—

hordes of them huddled onto boats.

'Twas all strange to them.

Hadn't their whole world been a townland or two?

Not the port, not the sea, not the weird wonders of
America.

Masses of them.

The *Times* of London had its own comment:

London journalist: They are going!

The Irish are going with a vengeance!

Soon a Celt will be as rare on the banks of the Liffey

as a red man on the banks of the Hudson.

Ireland will be rescued so

from its slovenly old barbarism—

and so we may plant there at last

the institutions of a more civilised land.

Countryman: Going they were, right enough,

and their ears ringin' with all the advice they were gettin'.

Countrywoman: Bring herrings plenty with you

for that is the mainstay onboard ship.

Be wise and take care of yourselves,

for board of ship is an awful place

and make no freedom with any person

and no one will enterfere with yous.

You will want a tin pan, tin plates too,

and some tin cups and a boiler.

But you need not at all get any new clothes

as 'tis not the fashins in America that they has at home.

Countryman: All aboard!, then.

And sure most had never been on a ship before.

And half of them near dead with hunger and exhaustion.

All crowded together with the ducks and geese and pigs.

Schoolteacher: The steerage was a dark and smelly maze of passages.

The poor were hemmed in there day and night, unable to
go fore or aft—

and only up into a little space of open air.

	And of course not mingle with the other passengers.
	For food they had gruel, daily bread, bone-hard biscuits.
Countryman:	And all piled on each other in lines of bunks.
	And the lost children bawlin' like calves for their mothers.
	And the air all smelly with damp homespun,
	with frieze, sweat, and worse than sweat.
	A dungeon woulda been more comfort.
	No better than horse stalls, or pens for cattle or sheep.
	You'd have no more space than in your coffin.
Countrywoman:	'Twould take a month at least, back then, to cross.
	But sure they'd try to make the most of their bad lot.
	Someone might have a flute or a fiddle, or a bodhrán, maybe,
	and they'd contrive a set dance, when the sea allowed.
Countryman:	Or they'd be out at the rails
	staring at the sight of some strange fish or other unlikely creatures—
	dolphins, like, or sharks, or whales maybe,
	or flying fish at dusk, and they glitterin'.
	Or someone'd be singin' a song in Irish maybe, or in English itself.
Singer:	*Ye lovers all both great and small who dwell in Ireland*
	Oh I pray you pay attention whilst I my pen command.
	It was my father's anger that drove my love away
	But I still have hopes we'll meet again in North Amerikay.
Countryman:	And such goings on they'd have onboard.
	The rumours flyin' about.
Scared woman:	The captain's lost his reckoning.
	He's taking us the Lord knows where.
	Oh God in heaven, the ship's sprung a leak!
	This boat, bad cess to it, 'tis a leaky tub.
	Sure we'll all have to eat our shoes
	before ever we'll see land again!
Countryman:	All kinds of horror and sufferin' they'd have them days,

whether under sail or steam. Said one woman from
    Cork city—
she'd a bad enough crossing:

Distressed Cork woman: Nothing was now to be heard aboard our ship,
but the cries of distressed children,
and of their distressed mothers unable to relieve them,
until our ship became a Spectacle of Horror!
Many kill'd themselves by drinking salt water.
Their own urine was a common drink.

Calm emigrant: And storms, is it? Plenty of them.
And the devil's own wrecking storms they'd be.
One night we were wakened out of our beds
by a huge wave crashing over the bows
and lashing along the decks and down the hatchways.

Distressed Cork woman: Lord, the shaking of the ship:
creaking of boards, banging of casks, smashing of glass.

Calm emigrant: The pitching and heaving and roaring—
the creak of masts, the rippin' and tearin' of shrouds and
    rigging,

Distressed Cork woman: The jangle of chains, the pitching and weaving in torrents
    of water,
the wind screaming so you couldn't shout over it.

Calm emigrant: Beddin', luggage, passengers, all tumbled together.
Containers smashed, provisions ruined, valuables lost
    forever.
And the sailors among the sails and they wailin' and
    shoutin'—
everyone thinkin' they were for a watery grave.

Distressed Cork woman: We'd be praying then, holding onto one another
in the terror of it all, in the suffocating darkness.
Nothing but storm sounds, and people getting sick.
We thought we were in a watery cold hell.

Calm emigrant: Not one of us but was quaking with fear:
some crying, some cursin' and singin',

	Or people flockin' like sheep,
	cryin' out on the captain to save them.
Distressed Cork woman:	*[calmer]* And then the calm when the storm passed,
	and the wreckage after—
	like a hurricane swept through the place.
	Everybody came out on deck for a breath of fresh air.
	And you could hear them, then,
	laughing, and talking, all excited, among themselves.
Countryman:	Of course on ships like that, overcrowded and all,
	there was no place to be easy in yourself.
	Weren't the men and the women all in a heap together.
	And wouldn't some women, young girls too,
	sit up all night upon boxes in the steerage,
	because they couldn't think of goin' to bed
	near the strange man that'd be lyin' next to them.
Countrywoman:	*[slightly censorious]* But let me tell you, there was the devil's own amount
	of caressin' going on, and the girls going hysterical
	or giving strange looks to the young men
	they were cheek by jowl with.
	And for six weeks or eight they'd be like that.
	And if the crossing made men of many a young fellow,
	'twas mothers it made of some of the young women.
	And God above don't mention
	what they called the privy or water closet.
	Disaster pure and simple. Don't mention it. Don't!
	Two of them for three hundred and fifty passengers.
	Coffin ships. They earned that name, they did,
	with deaths in plenty on every voyage.
	[to audience] Said one poor man from the Roscommon:
Roscommon man:	*[matter-of-fact]* Sure you'd get used to the deaths, you would.
	'Twas nothing but splash splash splash all day long—
	first one then another. There was one man,
	his name was Martin, I remember,

onboard with a wife and nine children.

Well first his wife died, and they threw her into the sea.

And then he died and they threw *him* into the sea.

And then the children one after the other,

till only two were left alive. The eldest,

a girl about thirteen who had nursed them all, and seen
    them die.

Well, she died, and then there was only the little fellow
    left,

and didn't he go back, as I heard, to Ireland

in the same ship with the Captain.

Countrywoman: But in the end, the ocean would be crossed.

One day—it might be

a day of rain or shine—you'd hear a cry

from someone somewhere on the ship.

And next thing there'd be a rush aloft to the rails

and they'd all be gawking up at a pair of seagulls maybe

and they floating about above the boat.

Or they'd all be pointing down at something in the
    water—

a bit of wood maybe, or a barrel, or even

a load of floating seaweed. Or they'd be saying

the smells they'd smell, they'd be different,

earth smells, like, and sure maybe they were.

And then the word would spread like wildfire. "Land!"

Countryman: And next thing there'd be people down on their knees

thankin' God for bringin' them safe to America,

though 'twas miles away yet. And there'd be others

rushin' back down to tell the good news

to their sick mother or father or children.

And it'd be a tonic so 'twould

that'd take them through the rest of the journey.

Countrywoman: *[excited]* And lord above when land itself would be seen

wouldn't they all be pointing and saying "Can you see?
    Can you?"

And running to get a better look. And there, sure enough,
rising out of the distance, after weeks and weeks
of nothing but a world of salt water and stormy seas,
there, getting clearer by the minute, the risen shapes
of land, dry land, hills, and soon, lord above, trees,
and an end to their trials and tribulations.

Countryman: Such excitement, then! The New World, their own new
world,
rising up out of the sea before them,
and all their hopes coming out in the one word,
"America!"
The nightmare was over: starvin' Ireland well behind
them,
and the dream of America near enough to touch.

PAUSE

Schoolteacher: Of course the dream was indeed a dream.
And soon, very soon, for many,
there'd be a rude awakening.
For after such a nightmare crossing,
where would they end up?

Countryman: Down the plank they'd come and wait by their bundle.
Dumped in a land of strangers and strange customs.
Innocents they were. Ignorant of everything.
They could be fleeced, too, by their own,
by the Irish who were there before them!
No one to trust at all.
Nothing but beggars and swindlers, misery and
wretchedness.

Countrywoman: Alleys and cellars clogged with children and grownups,
Or they'd end up in some desperate shanty slum,
living in shacks they'd put together, poor creatures,
out of discarded boards and bits of rubbish.
No streets, only narrow mud-paths,
all turning to ditches whenever it rained.

Countryman:	Congested districts they were, infected too.
	Sure the official reports were full of them.
	None too sympathetic either, by the sound of them.
American official:	*[harsh voice]* In one almost isolated neighbourhood
	we find a vagrant population half fed and half clothed—
	all crowded together in open and humid cellars,
	in narrow streets and narrower alleys.
	So many ripe causes for disease.
	Here . . . we have a depraved and mixed population,
	their constitutions undermined
	through the ravages of intemperance and exposure.
Countryman:	Not to mention, the hunger, and the crossing.
	Oh aye—'twasn't a paradise they found at all.
	Though God knows they'd set off
	with high hopes for the rosy future ahead of them.
Countrywoman:	Letters and the like they'd be getting
	telling them the grand place they'd be coming to.
Satisfied emigrant:	This is a splendid country—I can sit at a table
	as good as the best man in Belmullet.
	Thank God I left miserable Ireland.
	So come on over, why don't ye!
	America is a sort of Paradise, don't you see,
	after the Hell of hunger and poverty at home.
Singer:	*Where the rents are high, and taxes great, and victuals*
	growing dear,
	and riches hurdled up in store by those who persevere.
	In adding to oppression's weight such laws as curb the
	poor.
	Which makes me leave my heart's delight and the sweet
	Shamrock shore.
Satisfied emigrant:	But here in America you'll find
	hazels, wild roses, and grapevines in abundance.
	No house without its apple, peach, and cherry orchard.
	There's freedom here too,
	so you can speak as man to man.

No need to uncover your head or bend your knee.
We're our own masters over here.
So I would advise all my friends to quit Ireland—
though it be the country most dear to me—
for as long as they remain in it
they will be in bondage and misery.

Satisfied woman emigrant: I shudder when I think starvation
prevails in poor Ireland.
Here the meanest labourer has beef and mutton,
with bread, bacon, tea, coffee, sugar
the whole year round. Sure every day here
is as good as Christmas day in Ireland!

Countrywoman: Of course that wasn't the whole story, was it?
You might find more horror
and you after landing safe ashore.

Countryman: Right you are!
What many found here wasn't streets of gold
but shanty towns and lice-ridden rooms.
Not peace and plenty but sorrow and starvation.
Cold nights, cold days.
And hunger, nothing but hunger.
Instead of fruitful fields
wouldn't they find only woods and trees
and wild rough places with no people in them.
High mountains, empty valleys, misty regions.
Wild animals, poisonous snakes even.
And the heavens rumblin' with wicked wild weather.
Thunderbolts splittin' trees, wreckin' roads, knockin' to
    bits
all those wooden houses on the lonesome prairie.

Countrywoman: At first, though, for many there was work in plenty.
Sure the Irish built the Erie Canal, they did.
In the 1820s that was: hordes of immigrants
working from sunup to sundown
for fifty cents a day, and a few jiggers of whiskey.

'Twas said in the paper:

American journalist: There are several kinds of power working
at the fabric of the republic:
water-power, steam-power, and Irish-power.
The last works hardest of all.

Schoolteacher: But the dark side of all that was just that—*dark*:
Their lives could be nasty, brutish, short.

American journalist: Irishman drowned! Irishman crushed by a beam!
Irishman suffocated in a pit!
Irishman blown to bits by a steam engine!
Ten or twenty Irishmen buried alive!
Priests very busy among the Irish!

Priest: We see so many die there is hardly any time
to give Extreme Unction to everybody.
We run night and day anointing the sick.

American journalist: There are "Paddy Towns" and "Little Dublins" all over the
place.
Nothing but disease-ridden slums.
And then laws are broken, and don't they end up in jail.

Censorious American lawmaker: The Irish fill our prisons and our poorhouses.
Scratch a convict or a pauper woman, and the chances are
you'll tickle the skin of an Irish Catholic.
Putting them on a boat and sending them all home
would put an end to crime in this country.

Countryman: Many, don't you see, would keep up the old ways:
wakes and sports, faction fights, secret societies.

Countrywoman: And weren't the shanties along the banks of the canals
just like Irish villages—
each shanty with its cow and pig and praty garden.
They'd not forget, you see,
but would hang on to what was behind them
even if they'd never be seeing it again.
They had a hard life of it, that's for sure.

Countryman: But in spite of all the bad that happened—
and they surely suffered their share of it—

	didn't a power of them make good out there too.
	Said one American, a famous one too:
Sympathetic American:	Out of these narrow lanes and dirty streets,
	out of these damp cellars, and suffocating garrets,
	will come forth some of the noblest sons of our country,
	whom she will delight to own and honour.
Countryman:	And didn't loads of them fight in the Civil War.

Sympathetic American: Out of these narrow lanes and dirty streets,
out of these damp cellars, and suffocating garrets,
will come forth some of the noblest sons of our country,
whom she will delight to own and honour.

Countryman: And didn't loads of them fight in the Civil War.
On both sides, they'd be,
though many threw in with Lincoln and the North.
But there they'd be, Irishmen in blue or grey uniforms,
and they shootin' at each other and shoutin' at each other
over the stone walls and ditches
of Maryland, Virginia, or Kentucky.
And then lyin' dead—boys from all over Ireland—
in the muddy battlefields of a dozen campaigns.
The honourable dead, indeed, and them real Americans at last.
Early and late, so, they had their successes.
Taming the wilderness, bossing the cities, rising to the top.
And sure haven't there been near a dozen presidents
who had Irish ancestors somewhere.

Countrywoman: And not presidents only, but writers too—Irish Americans!
Poets, playwrights, story-writers, actors even.
Not to mention rich men, church men, nuns too.
Army generals and politicians.
Police chiefs, oh big gangsters too. Ship's engineers, the lot.
You'd never get through the roll call of them.
[to Countryman] True for the man who said
Ireland's best export was her people.

Countryman: Land was cheap and good, work was plenty,
in what they'd call
the free and blissful regions of the United States of America.

Countrywoman: And in a very few years, they'd say, people could become independent.

Countryman:	Independence, that was it.
	And they found it so they did.
	Said a young Dublin seamstress, in the 1890s it was:
Young Dublin woman:	I'm gettin' along splendid and likes me work.
	It seems a new life
	for I'll soon have a trade and be independent.
	And though I wouldn't write home to me family about it,
	I do think of the foreign men here too.
	Handsome, they are, with lovely dark eyes.
	And sure there's the clothes to buy you'd never find
	in any draper's shop, on Grafton Street even.
	And someday soon I'll surely have a house with three rooms,
	and lace curtains in the windows.
	And meat near every day o' the week.
Countryman:	Many found their independence, they did.
	They'd left home looking for adventure, and found that too.
	And many would say America
	was "the best place aside from heaven."
	The first ones over might suffer, d'you know.
	But by degrees they'd make good.
	And then their children would make better.
Countrywoman:	Sure 'tis said that in a couple of generations,
	what with education and the like,
	weren't they universally respected.
	"Irish Americans" they were,
	getting to be mayors, lawyers, journalists, nurses, firemen,
	secretaries and schoolteachers, and running trade unions.
	Not only respected, but, God help us, *respectable*!

PAUSE

Countryman:	Still and all, in the early days, and long after, God knows, things could be bad too.
	Like they'd be slighted and despised by Americans—

"No Irish need apply! . . . Paddies go home!" . . . that sorta thing.

Second-class citizens, like.

So they'd feel all this yearnin' for what they'd left behind.

And even if they got to be well off, some of them,

they might still curse the day they first saw America

and look back with regret across the Atlantic.

Homesickness: that was part of it. Isn't it always?

Emigrant woman: Every night since I left Ireland I do go home in dreams.

But when I wake and see 'tis only a worthless vision

I am sad and despondent and wish for sleep.

Over there I could go to a fair, or a wake, or a dance,

or I could spend the winter nights

in a neighbour's house cracking jokes by the turf fire.

If I had there but a sore head

I'd have a neighbour within every hundred yards of me

that would run to see me.

But here everyone can get so much land,

that they calls them neighbours that lives two or three miles off.

Often I do sit down and cry

and curse him that made me leave home.

Countryman: And even a rich farmer's wife could moan

about the frightful restless life she had:

Rich farmer's wife: It has made a mush of my mind.

And a day never dawned on me

that I thought more sorrowful than the day I left Seanachoill.

Even if we owned America

there's no place I know of under the sun

I'd rather die in than Ireland.

Countryman: 'Twas a common sentiment.

This pining for home, for Ireland.

Singer: *I long for those whom I shall see*

In this fair earth no more,

> *And wish in vain for winds to flee*
> *Back to my native shore.*
> *Back to the friends I left behind*
> *When first I went away*
> *And my sweetheart dear I'd hold her near*
> *And never more will stray.*

Countryman: But after singin' a sad song like that, in a tavern somewhere,

wouldn't the singers go happy enough back to their jobs in office or shop or building site.

But homesick? Well, they were that, most of them.

No matter what they'd left behind

they'd remember all the good things.

The gatherings of an evening:

songs, dances, cards, the chat, oh the endless chat, the craic.

The kitchens you'd visit: the fire of turf,

the steam off a pot of tea, the smell of somethin' baking.

The sense of . . . what was it at all?

A sort of *togetherness* I reckon . . .

The *safety* of that, like . . . the not being alone.

Countrywoman: You'd never be alone. People on top of people.

Community we say now. You might be ploughing

or planting spuds, cutting whins or footing turf,

talking across hedges or ridges, or over the backs of donkeys.

Just like flocks of birds they'd be.

And the townlands with all their known names

The map of your own small world. Every inch of it,

You'd know it by heart, *Home* . . .

And whatever beats, like a heart, in that one little word.

Countryman: Little tribes of them, full of gossip and goings on.

No wonder many went with no love for the going,

and all them rituals at parting.

Wouldn't they take a burnin' sod of turf itself

from the fireplace of the ones goin' away—
from the last fire lit in that cottage.
And wouldn't they put it in their neighbour's fire,
a fire that'd be always going, never out.

Countrywoman: So when the ones who'd gone away would return,
wouldn't they be able to start their own fire again
from their neighbour's fire.
And so 'twould be as if their own fire never went out.
Of course few came back in the end.
But still they'd be writing home, sending the remittances.
Yet sick at heart and nothing would cure them—
like this Kilkenny man, to his wife left behind:

Sad emigrant: Oh Nora, it makes my very heart break
when I do think of home.
I hate to think of it, Nora,
because I do be that homesick and lonely.

Countrywoman: *[a bit satirical]* Others were homesick too but in a different
way.
Sick of home, they were:
scrawny fields, famished cattle, swamps of rotten potatoes.
No work. And always the rent, the rent, the rent.

Countryman: *[angry]* And the hand-to-mouth of it all.
And the children coughing in smokey corners.
And the landlords and bailiffs and agents
all lookin' down on them.
And fear always, like a mad dog at the door.
No wonder they'd be sick of it, want to get away.
And never look back neither.
Shake the dust of it off, they would.
For 'twasn't an easy place to live in at all,
the Ireland of those times. Maybe it never is.
"Dark Rosaleen," said one man,
"has nothing to offer me but a spade!"

Countrywoman: *[angry]* And it could be a blind and bitter land, God
knows.

	Parents against children. Brothers and sisters
	fighting all hours of the day
	over who'd get the little biteen of land
	the family owned for themselves.
	Slander, gossip, the vicious talk
	in all them villages with their squinting windows.
Countryman:	Weren't the lucky ones
	only too pleased to be thousands of miles
	away from all the slander and all the talk.
	All the worry for what the neighbours'd think.
Angry emigrant woman:	Sure we can breathe in freedom now—
	far from all the smothering smoke
	of small minds and small streets.
	And be free of the priests, too, and them tellin' us
	to keep our heads down and our knees bent
	and our prayers ready at every minute.
	All that hypocrisy and all.
Angry emigrant:	So why wouldn't we clear out of the place,
	with the priest and the politician and the schoolmaster
	not to mention the policeman and the publican—
	all the big people, and they lording it over
	the poor lot of us? Trying to keep us the slaves
	we'd always been. Not the English at all
	but our own kind did that—our own kind, aye.
Angry emigrant woman:	Bullies they were! But of course, much better than us!
Angry emigrant:	Poverty and piety playin' off one another,
	and the whole place just a *leaba an caca*—
	a shite bed of gossip and pretend godliness.
	Wouldn't you only thank God and you to be shut of it.
	Mother Ireland indeed!
	God keep us far from your apron strings!
Angry emigrant woman:	We had to go, no way we could stay.
	No way Cathleen Ni Houlihan could give us a living
	with the priests and politicians and big farmers

and whatnot all grinding us down.

What was there for us? How could we stay?

Countryman: *[ironic]* Indeed, didn't one man hate his oul' bully of a
    father so much,

that not only did he wish him dead,

but hoped he would spend the afterlife in a place

where he'd have no problem lighting his pipe.

Countrywoman: Not much homesickness in that fella, I'd warrant,

sick of home as he was.

But many was homesick the other way.

Some because 'twasn't the promised land they found at all.

Emigrant: Even the weather was a problem for us.

The summer is hot as hell here,

and the winter cold as the north of the world.

Indeed 'twould be better to stay in Ireland—

where there is neither cold nor heat,

only now and again a soft bit of rain.

Weather, aye, and the lonesomeness too.

Young emigrant woman: Indeed I'm very lonesome here,

for the ways of this place is so different from home.

There is not one here known to me.

And if I went out in the morning and walked all day

I would not meet one face I know.

[sings]

> *Though I walked every village and city*
> *From Boston to Provincetown Bay,*
> *I never saw a place like the village*
> *That I left at the break of day.*

Countryman: True. Most of them—successful or not—

kept a warm spot for the old country,

suffering the homesickness, and no right cure for it.

'Twas a whole world they were grieving for,

and they'd cling tight to it.

Said one woman, writing home—

from Lisburn in County Antrim she was:

Emigrant woman:	*[Northern accent]* I can picture everything so vividly as I	

Emigrant woman: *[Northern accent]* I can picture everything so vividly as I
write:

the hills and the fields, the bogs and the turf,

and all that simplicity and hospitality

which is not to be equalled any place in the world.

I miss it very much and pray to God

to hasten the day when I may go back once more.

For however fine and splendid this world here is

it is not home, it has no associations.

Countryman: It's not home. It has no associations.

I suppose that sort of sums it up.

And then, just think of all those towns with Irish names

scattered across the face of America.

Just to keep the home places alive out there.

[Countryman and Countrywoman chant, alternating, a litany of names]

Woman: Dublin Ohio

Man: Dublin New Hampshire

Woman: Killarney Florida

Man: Kilkenny Minnesota

Woman: Avoca Indiana

Man: Strabane North Dakota

Woman: Belfast Maine

Man: Derry Pennsylvania

Woman: Londonderry Vermont.

Countryman: And hundreds more like them.

Homesickness. Say what you like, few escape it.

It's like you're leadin' one life

but there's another one goin' along with it,

pressin' on you at odd moments, like a face,

or a smell, or somethin' else brings it up.

Countrywoman: A sort of presence it is, a kind of sixth sense,

so you feel you're living two lives at once,

being in two places at once, never just the one.

Maybe it means once you've left your own place,

you'd never be at home again in the world.

You'd be there but not there, if you know what I mean.

Countryman: But we're islanders, sure we have to leave sometime or
    other.

And we go back, and leave again, and go back once more.

But whether we go back or just stay away

there's no escaping it, the homesickness.

It seems we all have it, every one of us.

As one man said to me, in the Blarney Stone, it was,

on Third Avenue in New York City.

"Homesickness is something that's natural," says he.

"I often do get a relapse of it.

But somehow there seems to be no cure only to stand it."

Schoolteacher: And so they went away.

In their thousands. Millions in the end.

Clutching their scant belongings.

Speaking the last of their language. Keeping their faith.

Protestants, Catholics, hanging onto what they'd known.

Countryman: And to be fair to the Catholics, mind, 'twas the parishes

and the good priests in the cities they'd settle in

that kept them together a long while after.

Irish Catholics they were,

and Irish Catholics they stayed for generations.

'Twas the parishes, don't you see,

replaced the villages they'd come from.

The parish would give them an identity, like.

Schoolteacher: Quite right. The parish, you see,

prevented them disappearing

into the great melting pot of America.

It was the largest, the most important

of all those bits and pieces they kept to comfort them.

When they went *Slouching round the world* as the poet
    says,

with a gesture and a brogue

and a faggot of useless memories.

Countryman: Maybe so. Whatever about all that, they'd left Ireland.
               And, in the old days, few ever came back.
               Going away, they said, 'twas like death itself.
               Now of course there's busloads of them coming back.
               Descendants, like. Irish Americans.
               Busload on busload, and them staring at everything.
               Stoppin' in small villages in the back of beyond.
               Then they'd be rootin' about in graveyards
               that'd be all overgrown with grass and weeds—
               tryin' to read the names on the gravestones.
               Or lookin' about at the faces of the locals.

Countrywoman: Gazing at heaps of fallen stones
               where the cottage of the great-grandparents stood, maybe,
               till it was emptied out and the weather made bits of it,
               or someone used it as a cattle pen, maybe.

Countryman: *[almost to himself]* Stones only. And they themselves
                                  strangers.

Singer: *For that home is replaced by another,*
               Beside which the Shannon rolls on.
               And if I should revisit that island,
               That cottage which once I called home,
               There is none who would now recognize me,
               A stranger around there I'd roam.

                        PAUSE

Countryman: Leaving. We've always been leaving.
               Never look back, they'd say.
               But sure of course they did. They always did.
               Dreaming back, like.
               But what's wrong with dreaming?

Countrywoman: Aren't we all dreaming our way back.
               And after this our exile, like the prayer says,
               we'll find a way home.

Countryman: As the sean-fhochail says

Away's OK. But home is best.
Our home here. This little corner of the earth.

Countrywoman: As for dreaming back:
Isn't that what Columcille himself was at?
A grey eye open, always looking back.
First the going away. Then the looking back.

Countryman: *[angry]* It's happening yet, of course it is. Listen to me.
Plenty of reasons for leaving, and plenty going—
from the country, the cities, the towns and villages.
With the bankers, the builders, the gangster politicians
and all kinds of cowboys,
all singin' from the same hymn sheet.
Spend and expand! Borrow, build, and buy!
And our own breath helpin' to blow up that bubble
till it burst all over us.
And we're left, so, with only a one-way ticket
to the door marked *Exit,*
and the hard road ahead of us.

Countrywoman: Fair play to you.
But whenever or whyever you go off, back you'll look, true
   as God,
At the disappearing hills and spires
of Dun Laoghaire, Rosslare, or Cobh—
and the big boat slowly turning, heading into the wind.

Countryman: Or down you'll be lookin' from the airplane window,
down on the cloudy day over Shannon.

Countrywoman: On the trees, the neat green fields, the toy houses.
On all the cows, the sheep, the horses.
On the tiny figures of people
still getting on with their own lives down there. *At home.*

Countryman: Then it's out to sea or up and away with you,
and everything growing dimmer by the minute—
the fields, the rooftops shiny with rain,
the floating white shapes of seagulls.

Countrywoman: Till there's nothing there at all.

	Nothing except memory. Looking back.
Countryman:	The way Columcille's grey eye itself looked back.
	And all them lonesome soldiers looked back,
	And all the hungry ones, hopin' to start over.
	Dreaming back. Back indeed to a place
	that might be a dream itself. But what harm?
Countrywoman:	In the old times—and sure it happens still —
	wouldn't you take a pocketful of Irish clay
	from your own place and you going.
	Or a seashell maybe, picked up off the strand
	that'd be your daily walk all weathers.
	Or the leaf off a tree. Or a bit of loose whitewash
	off a cottage wall. Or a stone you'd kick out of your way
	on any town or village or city street.
	Anything at all you could hold on to.
Countryman:	Exiles, emigrants, All wanderers over the earth.
	Dreamers all. Always some dream of home
	comes knocking at your sleep.
Countrywoman:	So many dreams. Enough, you might say,
	to build a bridge across the broad Atlantic itself.
	And so over you'd go, you would, walking home.
Countryman:	Walkin', sailin', flyin' back—in dreams or not.
	In the old days 'twas the coffin ships.
	Now it's the liners, or the airplanes.
	Off they go, back they come.
Countrywoman:	And just think of the fine sight that is:
	at airports, train stations, harbours—
	all the people waiting for the travellers to come out.
Countryman:	Then the huggin' and kissin'!
	The Grannies scoopin' up the grandchildren.
	Brothers, sisters, mothers, fathers,
	all gettin' in on the act. *Laughin'.*
Countrywoman:	*Grief melts away*
	Like snow in May,

As if there were no such cold thing.

Countryman: Going away. Coming back. Goin' away again.
Sure that's the way of it.

Singer: *It's a hard road that we're walking,*
Many thousands have walked it before—
We follow it over the ocean
To knock on Uncle Sam's door.
Our uncles and cousins have walked it,
Our grandparents walked over and back,
We find our own way by their footprints—
It's a well-trodden, beaten-down track.
We know it's the road we must travel—
There's nothing for us here at home—
So we'll kiss our goodbyes, hold our heads high,
And step out on the same hard road.

Countryman: It's a way of life, isn't it?
And many has known no other.
All gone into a world of light, is it?
Hard to know, now, which world we're talking about.
Or where the light is. Home is it? or away?
But when you're away, hard to deny,
it's home you'd be thinkin' of right enough.

Countrywoman: *[speedy voice, play against the Yeatsian lyricism]*
I will arise and go now, for always night and day
I hear lakewater lapping with low sounds by the shore;

Countryman: *[abrupt]While I stand on the roadway, or on the pavements*
grey,
I hear it in the deep heart's core.

Singer: *[make "home" overlap with "core"]*
Home, home, sweet sweet home—
There's no place like home,
oh there's no place like home.

Countryman: Home, aye. But then we're off again, aren't we? Leaving
home.
Like swallows, comin', then goin'.

Havin' to go, right. But with hope in our hearts.

For the new life, and the home we're buildin' over there.

We need to go, and we love to come back.

Then we go again—because we have to,

and sometimes isn't it it's just for the love of going?

Countrywoman: Bad reasons. Good reasons.

But *we need to go, and we love to come back.*

True. And maybe we leave for the lift it gives us.

Bad reasons there are, no question. Just look around you.

But there are good ones too:

ambition, love, a better life. All the different hungers.

Countryman: For the simple joy of flight, maybe; turning our face to the future.

Home is behind us and all belonging to it.

So we turn for where we're headed. And on we go!

Singer: *So we'll kiss our goodbyes, keep our hopes high,*

And dance along that same hard road.

[spoken] And *dance* along that same hard road.

[Exit]

END

Curlew Theatre Company
Presents

HIST⊙RY!

Reading the
Easter Rising

Performed by
Tegolin Knowland
and Seán Coyne

Written and Directed by
Eamon Grennan

History! Reading the Easter Rising

*I care not if my life has only the span of a night and a day
if my deeds be spoken of by the men of Ireland.*
—CUCHULLAIN'S MOTTO, ON A WALL
IN PEARSE'S SCHOOL, ST. ENDA'S

*We revolt simply because, for many reasons, we cannot
breathe.*
—FRANTZ FANON

Darling Nancy . . . It was a good fight anyhow. . . .
—THE O'RAHILLY'S DYING NOTE TO HIS WIFE

*We had fed the heart on fantasies,
The heart's grown brutal from the fare;
More substance in our enmities
Than in our love . . .*
—W. B. YEATS

Introduction

On Easter 1916 a group of Irish nationalists rose up against British rule, in an armed struggle centered in the General Post Office in the middle of Dublin. This was the beginning of a protracted struggle that led first to the Irish Free State and eventually to the establishment of the Republic of Ireland. This play for voices was inspired by commemorations of these events that took place in Ireland on the one hundredth anniversary of the uprising in 2016.

The play *History! Reading the Easter Rising* takes a multifaceted look, through documents, poems, songs, and eyewitness accounts, at not only the Rising itself but its violent aftermaths: the Anglo-Irish War and the Civil War. It brings the tangled history of this period to life, through the simple but directly affecting medium of human voices, voices of both major and minor figures caught up in the events. Neither celebration nor critique, this "play for voices" offers a particular "reading" of the complicated events leading up to and then away from Easter 1916 by seeing the Rising from a number of different perspectives. It is a brief, intentionally balanced, commemorative account of those still-crucial foundational events. An Englishman, Haines, says to Stephen Dedalus in *Ulysses* in a conversation about the vexed relations between Ireland and England, "It seems history is to blame." That might be the play's epigraph.

In addition to contemporary documents, I have relied for information about some of the events narrated in the play on the following works by scholars and others:

Max Caulfield, *The Easter Rebellion*. F. Muller, 1964.
Darrell Figgis, *Recollections of the Irish War*. E. Benn Limited, 1937.
Roy Foster, *Vivid Faces: The Revolutionary Generation in Ireland, 1890–1923*. W. W. Norton, 2015.
Maud Gonne, *The Gonne-Yeats Letters, 1893–1938: Always Your Friend*, ed. Anna MacBride White and A. Norman Jeffares. Norton, 1993.
Fearghall McGarry, *The Rising: Ireland: Easter 1916*. Oxford University Press, 2010.
Fearghall McGarry, *Rebels: Voices from the Easter Rising*. Penguin Group, 2011.
Margaret Skinnider, *Doing My Bit for Ireland*. Century Company, 1917.
James Stephens, *The Insurrection in Dublin*. Macmillan, 1916.
William Irwin Thompson, *The Imagination of an Insurrection, Dublin, Easter, 1916: A Study of an Ideological Movement*. Oxford University Press, 1967.
Charles Townshend, *Easter 1916: The Irish Rebellion*. Ivan R. Dee, 2006
Clair Willis, *Dublin 1916: The Siege of the GPO*. Harvard University Press, 2009.

The first production of the play by Curlew Theatre Company took place in the Clifden Arts Festival in September 2016. In the original production, the set had two parts: on each side of the stage was a lectern. When a performer stood at either one of the lecterns he or she acted as a commentator on the event from the perspective of a time contemporary with the theater audience. The other part of the set, in the middle of the stage, was a wooden structure with railings representing something like a witness box. When an actor stood behind these railings, he or she became a "witness" contemporary with the events: either someone who participated in the Rising or experienced the effects of these events and their aftermath.

For the original production

SET
   2 music stands, at opposite sides of the stage, though not too far apart
   2 high stools, so speakers can sit if they need to
   Black dress

VOICES
   Voice 1: female (usually a Teacher)
   Voice 2: male (usually a Commentator)

Notes: Beyond these two main voices, Voice 1 shifts voices a fair amount to register speeches of other characters drawn from events in Dublin and beyond. Besides Commentator, Voice 2 alternates between rougher country voice and a plainer voice. For both Voice 1 and Voice 2, these various voices are indicated where necessary. The notations "Dublin" and "Country" mark the accents needed.

There are also a number of overvoice passages. Where an overvoice is described as a "WBY voice," the speaker may attempt a Yeats-voice imitation—deep, rhetorical, resonant. The rhythm of the piece alternates between quick-fire exchanges and longer statements, observations, descriptions, and so forth. But a certain momentum is crucial throughout.

[Music—"The Rising of the Moon"—instrumental (fiddle), soft]
   Voice 1:   [Shan-van-vocht (Poor Old Woman)—country voice: low, musical, a sort
                  of spirit-whisper, ritualistic. She wears a red shawl.]
               Some call me the Poor Old Woman,
               and there are some that call me
               Cathleen, the daughter of Houlihan—
               there have been many songs made for me.

I heard one on the wind this morning.

[sings, chants]

> *Do not make a great keening*
> *When the graves have been dug to-morrow.*
> *Do not call the white-scarfed riders*
> *To the burying that shall be to-morrow.*
> *Do not spread food to call strangers*
> *To the wakes that shall be to-morrow;*
> *Do not give money for prayers*
> *For the dead that shall die to-morrow . . .*

[plainer speech]

they will have no need of prayers,
they will have no need of prayers.
It is a hard service they take that help me.
Many that are red-cheeked now will be pale-cheeked;
many that have been free to walk
the hills and the bogs and the rushes
will be sent to walk hard streets in far countries;
many that have gathered money
will not stay to spend it;
many a child will be born,
and there will be no father at its christening.
They that had red cheeks
will have pale cheeks for my sake;
and for all that, they will think they are well paid.

[chanting, deep and strong]

> *They shall be remembered for ever,*
> *They shall be alive for ever,*
> *They shall be speaking for ever,*
> *The people shall hear them for ever.*

[Exit]

PAUSE

Overvoice: *[hard] Did that play of mine send out*
                Certain men the English shot?

PAUSE

[Enter dressed in black, Voice 1 (female; Teacher) & Voice 2 (male; Commentator) speaking to each other, or to audience]

Voice 2:   Maybe it did. Maybe not. *Certain men,* eh?

Voice 1:   They were shot anyway.

Voice 2:   At dawn in the Stonebreakers Yard of Kilmainham Jail.

Voice 1:   One dawn after another. Fourteen of them.

Voice 2:   Between the 3rd and the 12th of May, 1916. *History* that is.

Voice 1:   May 3:

Voice 2:   Pearse MacDonagh Clarke

Voice 1:   May 4:

Voice 2:   Plunkett Daly O'Hanrahan Willie Pearse

Voice 1:   May 5:

Voice 2:   Major John MacBride

Voice 1:   May 8:

Voice 2:   Ceannt Mallin Heuston Con Colbert

Voice 1:   May 12:

Voice 2:   Sean MacDermott.

Voice 1:   And James Connolly—

Voice 2:   Wounded, dying, strapped to a chair.

Voice 1:   *It is a hard service they take that help me.*

Voice 2:   Isn't it just! But brave men the lot of them. In their own way. No question.

Voice 1:   *[reciting]*
                "O words are lightly spoken,"
                Said Pearse to Connolly,
                "Maybe a breath of politic words
                Has withered our Rose Tree;
                Or maybe but a wind that blows
                Across the bitter sea."

Voice 2:	*[reciting]* *"It needs to be but watered,"* *James Connolly replied,* *"To make the green come out again* *And spread on every side,* *And shake the blossom from the bud* *To be the garden's pride."*
Voice 1:	*"But where can we draw water,"* *Said Pearse to Connolly,* *"When all the wells are parched away?*
Voices 2 & 1:	*O plain as plain can be* *There's nothing but our own red blood* *Can make a right Rose Tree."*
Voice 1:	But beyond those deaths . . . many others. . . . Rebels, soldiers, police, civilians . . . *children!*
Voice 2:	*[clipped official voice: statistics]* *485 men, women, and children were killed during or as a direct result of the 1916 rebellion.* *Over half of the dead were civilians.* *Over a fifth of those civilians were children under sixteen.* *A quarter of those killed were British Army soldiers, some of them Irishmen.* *13 policemen killed. All Irishmen.* *In the rebel forces 58 killed, including one woman.*
Voice 1:	Numbers. Yes. *Statistics.*
Voice 2:	But every one with a name, an address, a family. A *history.*
Voice 1:	The greatest number civilians and children.
Voice 2:	The republic was born from their sacrifice too, wasn't it? What is it they call it nowadays?
Voice 1:	"Collateral damage."
Voice 2:	"Collateral damage." Isn't language lovely, sugarcoating things like that! But no sugarcoating the reality. Listen.
Voice 1:	*[flat Dublin accent] A man had his brains blown into the roadway. I seen a young girl run into the road an' pick up his cap and scrape the brains into it. Then didn't she cover this with a little straw, and carry the hat—pious like—to the hospital so the brains might be buried with the body.*

Voice 2: Kids too. Boys, girls, babies. Little Sean Foster was killed on Easter Monday. He was two years old.

Voice 1: *Christopher Andrews was fourteen. I knew his sister. He was shot dead on Mount Street Bridge an' him givin' a drink of water to a wounded soldier.*

Voice 2: Animals too. From ordinary pets to the lancers' horses rotting in front of the GPO for days.

Voice 1: *There isn't a cat or a dog left alive in Camden Street. Lyin' stiff out in the road they are, and up on the roofs. There's a lot of women'll be sorry for this war, and their pets killed on them.*

Voice 2: So much for all that then.

PAUSE

Voice 1: *[teacher]* But we should go back, shouldn't we? Back to the start. Back to . . . *[a litany]*

Voice 2: *[commentator] History!*

Voice 1: Yes. History.

Voice 2: Home Rule.

Voice 1: Yes. Home Rule.

Voice 2: To govern ourselves.

Voice 1: Yes.

Voice 2: Wanted. Denied. Wanted again.

Voice 1: All those revolutions.

Voice 2: Too many to go into now.

Voice 1: One a generation, they said.

Voice 2: For a few hundred years. Yes.

Voice 1: 1641

Voice 2: 1689

Voice 1: 1798

Voice 2: 1803

Voice 1: 1848

Voice 2: 1867.

Voice 1: All failed.

Voice 2: Goes without saying.

Voice 1: Home Rule . . . Always that hope.

Voice 2: That hunger, that thirst. Says Parnell, 1893 it was:

Voice 1:   *[upper-class Irish] Home Rule would be the introduction of a system which would remove the rankling sting of suppressed but not extinct enmity between our two islands. Give back to Ireland her nationality, her individual existence, and soothe thereby her wounded pride.*

Voice 2:   Poets and writers were involved too, of course they were. Sure didn't Lady Gregory

say of all the plays and books and poems they were writing:

Voice 1:   *[upper-class Irish with country element; quiet] We are not working for Home Rule. We are preparing for it.*

Voice 2:   *[commentator]* And late, after it all happened, didn't Maud Gonne herself say:

Voice 1:   *[more dramatic, "Maud" (upper-class Irish) voice] Without the inspiration of the Literary Revival and the glorification of beauty and heroic virtue I doubt there would have been an Easter Week. . . . They were poets and writers who led Irish youth to die, that Ireland might live.*

Voice 2:   *Dreams* these were. Dreams and dreamers.

Voice 1:   But, as the poet says . . . *In dreams begin responsibilities . . .*

Voice 2:   Well anyway, in 1911, at last the English Government, helped by John Redmond's Irish Party, introduced a Home Rule Bill. Says Redmond:

Voice 1:   *[educated Irish country voice] I pray earnestly that this Bill may pass and that the result of all our counsels may be the maintenance of true religion and justice, the safety, honour, and happiness of the King, and the public health, peace, and tranquillity of the realm . . .*

Voice 2:   Nice . . . if a bit . . . *old-fashioned.* But then . . . The North . . .

Voice 1:   The North. . . . Oh yes.

Voice 2:   Aye, the North. . . . Ulster. . . . Unionists mostly. . . .

Voice 1:   Who, for the most part, didn't feel the same way. They wished to keep the Union intact.

Voice 2:   Understandable, I suppose, some of it. History, you see. Settler people from, oh, way back.

Voice 1:   A different tribe, I suppose.

Voice 2:   Some of them.

Voice 1:   Different religion too, of course.

Voice 2:   Some of them.

Voice 1:   And certainly not for turning.

Voice 2:   *[ironic]* Not exactly.

Voice 1:   September 1912: the Ulster Covenant and Declaration.

Voice 2:   Half a million men and women signed.

Voice 1:   *[Northern accent] We vow to use all means which may be found necessary to defeat the present conspiracy to set up a Home Rule Parliament in Ireland. Let all nine counties of Ulster be excluded.*

Voice 2:   The English Conservative Opposition was on their side.

Voice 1:   *[English voice] We have given a pledge that if Ulster resists we will support her in her resistance. We intend to keep that pledge.*

Voice 2:   By 1913, so, Volunteer Armies were all the rage:

Voice 1:   Ulster Volunteer Force in the North, the UVF. Irish Volunteer Force in the South, the IVF.

Voice 2:   The island ripe for civil war.

Voice 1:   Yes, 1913 was a bad year. Strikes, lockouts, police brutality, general disorder. The poet Yeats had his say—Irish values were corrupt, he said. The heroic past was dead.

Overvoice: *["WBY voice"] What need you, being come to sense,*

      But fumble in a greasy till
      And add the halfpence to the pence
      And prayer to shivering prayer, until
      You have dried the marrow from the bone?
      For men were born to pray and save:
      Romantic Ireland's dead and gone,
      It's with O'Leary in the grave. . . .

      Was it for this the wild geese spread
      The grey wing upon every tide;
      For this that all that blood was shed,
      For this Edward Fitzgerald died,
      And Robert Emmet and Wolfe Tone,
      All that delirium of the brave?
      Romantic Ireland's dead and gone,
      It's with O'Leary in the grave.

Voice 2:   *All that delirium of the brave.* Oh aye.

      Little did he know what was in Ireland's near future.

Voice 1:   Or in England's, Europe's, the world's.

Voice 2: With the great clock of History sounding the hours. Driving everything on.

Voice 1: On to August 1914, and the "Great War to End War"!

Voice 2: Bit of a laugh, that! "To end war!" But didn't Home Rule get put on the back burner.

Voice 1: Yes. And John Redmond—right or wrong, who can say?—went along with that.

Voice 2: And thinking 'twould help the cause of Home Rule, didn't he encourage the Irish Volunteers to join the British army for the duration of the war.

Voice 1: *[well-bred Irish country voice] The interests of Ireland—of the whole of Ireland—are at stake in this war. . . .*

Voice 2: Redmond named those who stayed with him the *National* Volunteers.

Voice 1: Of the 80,000 that enlisted in the first 12 months of the war, half were from Ulster, half from the south. By war's end over 200,000 Irish people had joined.

Voice 2: The poet Francis Ledwidge enlisted because, as he said, *I cannot stand aside while others seek to defend Ireland's freedom.* Others had other reasons.

Voice 1: *[Dublin accent] I joined the* British Army *because she stood between Ireland and an enemy of civilization.*

Voice 2: And Northerners sympathetic to the Home Rule cause thought joining up would help.

Voice 1: *[Northern voice] I wanted it. That's the why I joined the Inniskillings. Aren't we all Irishmen?*

Voice 2: But Eoin MacNeill, Patrick Pearse, and others held on to the Irish Volunteers. No joining up there.

Voice 1: And Connolly, of course, feared conscription. The horrors of the trenches for the Irish who would be forced to join up. As he said in early 1916 itself:

Voice 2: *[stricken and strong] All those mountains of Irish dead, all those corpses mangled beyond recognition—all those horrors buried in Flanders or the Gallipoli Peninsula—This is what Ireland pays for being part of the British Empire. . . .*

Voice 1: He and his comrades were thinking now, you see, beyond Home Rule.

Voice 2: Thinking, they'd say, of a real *Republic.* And of course they went on drilling.

Voice 1: *[Dublin lady voice, posh] Scarcely a Sunday passed through the summer* and autumn of *1915* that there was not a muster of Volunteers—to spread the gospel of physical force as the only way to win back our country from England. The rebel poems and songs of those gatherings helped foster a rebel spirit. Thomas Davis's poem "A Nation Once Again" was very popular:

Voice 2: *[country voice, poetic, assertive]*
"For freedom comes from God's right hand,
And needs a godly train;
And righteous men must make our land
A Nation once again."

Voice 1: *[Dublin lady] Poems in Irish there were too. This one by Mr. Pearse was very popular:*

Overvoice: *[female] Mise Éire*
Sine mé ná an Chailleach Bhéarra.
Mór mo ghlóir:
Mé a rug Cú Chulainn cróga.
Mór mo náire:
Mo chlann féin a dhíol a máthair.
Mór mo phian:
Bithnaimhde do mo shíorchiapadh.
Mór mo bhrón:
D'éag an dream inar chuireas dóchas.
Mise Éire:
Uaigní mé ná an Chailleach Bhéarra.
I am Ireland:
I am older than the old woman of Beare.
Great my glory:
I who bore Cuchulainn, the brave.
Great my shame:
My own children who sold their mother.
Great my pain:
My bitter enemy who harasses me always. . . .
Great my sorrow
Those, in whom I placed my trust, all died.

I am Ireland:

I am lonelier than the old woman of Beare.

Voice 1: *[Dublin lady]* And so many songs. I loved this one:

[sings a bit of "Down by the Glenside," *traditional song]*

Voice 2: *[commentator]* And 'twasn't only poems and songs. Speeches too. Here's Pearse in August 1915, at the funeral of the old Fenian, O'Donovan Rossa.

Voice 1: *[quiet] Our foes are strong, and wise, and wary; but they cannot undo the miracles of God. . . . Life springs from death and from the graves of patriot men and women spring live nations. The defenders of this realm think that they have foreseen everything. But the fools, the fools, the fools! They have left us our Fenian dead. And while Ireland holds these graves, Ireland unfree shall never be at peace.*

Voice 2: Oh I know: it all sounds very . . . . masculine. And it was. But the women played their part. Sure didn't Connolly himself praise them? *Let us not forget the women,* says he, *who have everywhere stood by us and cheered us on. . . .* Indeed they did. And did more than cheer them on. *Joined them.* With the suffragettes behind them, they insisted, you might say, on their equal rights.

Voice 1: *[Dublin lady; voice well-bred, slightly breathless] It is a curious thing that many men seem unable to believe that any woman can embrace an ideal . . . accept it intellectually, feel it as a profound emotion, and then calmly work for its realisation. Men give themselves endless pains to prove that everything a woman does (outside nursing babies or washing pots) is the result of being in love with some* man, *or disappointed in love of some* man, *or looking for excitement, or limelight, or indulging their vanity. . . . Ridiculous! . . . Our aim is to advance the cause of Irish liberty, and to teach our members First Aid, Drill, Signalling, and Rifle Practice in order to aid the men of Ireland.*

Voice 2: Indeed and more power to them! And weren't there over a hundred women in the Rising itself? And on Easter Monday wouldn't forty of them be in the GPO with the Volunteers, the Citizen Army, and the IRB. Fighting. Said one of them, Min Ryan:

Voice 1: *[breathy, enthusiastic] If the men were to die, we would too; that is the way we felt.*

Voice 2: And didn't Hanna Sheehy-Skeffington herself say:

Voice 1: *[calm Dublin middle-class, slightly high-pitched] It is the only instance I know of in history when men fighting for freedom voluntarily included women. . . .*

Voice 2: That was her opinion, yes. Anyway, by nightfall that Easter Monday, women insurgents would be established in all of the major rebel strongholds throughout the city—

Voice 1: *Except for one. In Boland's Mill, defying the orders of Pearse and Connolly, DeValera refused to let women fighters in. But our women in the other rebel garrisons fought alongside the men, or were dispatch carriers between garrisons, and were not confined only to nursing duties or other "feminine" pursuits, such as making tea and sandwiches for the fighting men.*

Voice 2: However and wherever they served, they would be indispensable.

[a litany]

Voice 1: Helena Molony,

Voice 2: Madeleine ffrench-Mullen,

Voice 1: Dr. Kathleen Lynn,

Voice 2: Rose McNamara,

Voice 1: Nurse Elizabeth O'Farrell,

Voice 2: Winnie Carney,

Voice 1: Julia Grenan,

Voice 2: Rose McNamara,

Voice 1: Margaret Skinnider,

Voice 2: Linda Kearns MacWhinney,

Voice 1: Margaretta Keogh . . . and others, many others.

Voice 2: Men and women of all sorts, so, drawn from all the ordinary trades and professions:

Voice 1: Poets, teachers, lecturers,

Voice 2: Shopkeepers, secretaries, journalists,

Voice 1: Doctors, actors, writers,

Voice 2: Labourers, nurses, trade unionists,

Voice 1: Barmen, tram conductors, dockers,

Voice 2: Printers, corporation clerks, farmers,

Voice 1: Bookkeepers, chemist's clerks, and newspapermen.

Voice 2: They were all part of it, you see. Romantics. Socialists. Tried or untried Revolutionaries. And ordinary people. All dreaming their own dreams of that *Nation once again.*

Overvoice: *[quiet, "WBY voice"] I have met them at close of day*
    Coming with vivid faces
    From counter or desk among grey

Eighteenth-century houses.
I have passed with a nod of the head
Or polite meaningless words,
Or have lingered awhile and said
Polite meaningless words,
And thought before I had done
Of a mocking tale or a gibe
To please a companion
Around the fire at the club,
Being certain that they and I
But lived where motley is worn:
All changed, changed utterly. . . .

[strains of slow "Rising of the Moon" *under next speeches*]

Voice 1:   [*Wexford lady, mild country*] For little more than a week before the Rising there was tremendous excitement. Holy Saturday evening came. The air was electric. All volunteer officers suspected the Easter manoeuvres arranged for the next day were really "the day." But on Easter Sunday morning, the newspapers carried Eoin MacNeill's notice:

Voice 2:   [*loud announcement*] *Volunteers completely deceived! All orders for tomorrow Sunday are completely cancelled!*

Voice 1:   [*teacher*] Some wondered if he was a coward. But events in the previous days between those for and against an immediate rising had become quite intense. And very confused.

Voice 2:   And said one Volunteer, a Scotswoman, Margaret Skinnider:

Voice 1:   [*Scots*] *No one who knew MacNeill could doubt his loyalty to Ireland. . . . It was his love for the Volunteers, the love of a man instinctively pacifist, that made him give that order. He feared a very grave catastrophe.*

Voice 2:   But that same Easter night, Connolly, Pearse, and other leaders decided to carry on.

Voice 1:   Connolly said to Maeve Cavanagh of the Citizen Army (he called her "the poetess of the revolution"):

Voice 2:   [*plain, gruff*] *We fight at noon tomorrow. And MacNeill's lot can do as they like.*

Voice 1:   [*ordinary Dublin*] *What time will I come down in the morning so?*

Voice 2:   *Come down at 8 o'clock.*

Voice 1:   *As early as that?*

Voice 2: *[ironic, humorous] Do you think that too early for a revolution?*

Voice 1: *[teacher]* Of course they knew what faced them: as The O'Rahilly said to Countess Markievicz:

Voice 2: *[enthusiastic] It's madness, but it's glorious madness!*

Voice 1: More realistic was the remark of one volunteer officer:

Voice 2: *[country, resigned] We're going out to be slaughtered.*

Voice 1: But Pearse was ready. He knew what he was doing. Had always known it.

Voice 2: *[commentator] Sacrifice,* you see. That was it. *Sacrifice.*

Voice 1: *[quiet, recites] I blinded my eyes*
And my ears I shut,
I hardened my heart
And my love I quenched.

Voice 2: *[quiet recites] I turned my back*
On the dream I had shaped,
And to this road before me
My face I turned.

Voice 1: *[quiet recites] I set my face*
To the road here before me,
To the work that I see,
To the death I shall meet.

Voice 1: *[teacher]* And so, while the big clock of History kept ticking, Easter Sunday turned into Monday, April the 24th. Easter Monday 1916.

Voice 2: *[commentator]* That morning, as Pearse bade his mother goodbye and headed from St. Enda's into the city, she says to him:

Voice 1: *[mother—strict, concerned, middle-class Dublin] "Now Pat, above all do nothing rash."*

Voice 2: *[blandly reassuring] "No, Mother, I won't."*

Overvoice: *["WBY voice"] Hearts with one purpose alone*
Through summer and winter seem
Enchanted to a stone
To trouble the living stream. . . .
A shadow of cloud on the stream
Changes minute by minute. . . .
The long-legged moor-hens dive,

And hens to moor-cocks call;
Minute to minute they live;
The stone's in the midst of all.

Too long a sacrifice
Can make a stone of the heart. . . .

Voice 1:   *[teacher]* And maybe that's true too. Though it would be hard to say the Rebels were stony-hearted. They responded in any case, and out they went.

Voice 2:   *[quiet, young, eager voice] I was in bed when told. I dressed while my father and mother got out my rifle and some sandwiches. I will always remember my father as I saw him that morning. He worked the bolt of the rifle, sighted it, and fired imaginary shots. As he handed me the rifle he remarked, "If I was a few years younger I would go with you." Mother and Father wished God's blessing on me as I hurried away.*

Voice 1:   *[Dublin] We formed up in a procession and moved along the quays, and me feeling as if I were walking on air. An old working man cheers as we go by:*

Voice 2:   *[loud] "Hurrah for the Volunteers! Hammer the shite outa them!"*

Voice 1:   *[teacher] Walking on air.* I suppose it was a sort of *enchanted rapture* they were in the grip of, wasn't it? Some felt they were taking part in a great Romantic Drama.

Voice 2:   *[commentator]* Like we said: Dreams and dreamers. But one way or another, for one reason or another, here they were. Doing their bit for Ireland.

Voice 1:   Youngsters so many of them. Most between nineteen and twenty-five. Even the leaders were young.

Voice 2:   Tom Clarke was fifty-eight, and he the old man of them.

Voice 1:   On they marched, so, with the big unstoppable clock of History beating out time for them.

        [a litany of names]

Voice 2:   Pearse!

Voice 1:   Over six feet tall. Upright, stern . . . eager-eyed . . . visionary . . .

Voice 2:   Connolly!

Voice 1:   A squat figure: impeccable uniform: polished leggings . . .

Voice 2:   Joseph Mary Plunkett!

Voice 1:   Emaciated. Throat enveloped in bandages: hands glittering with rings . . .

Voice 2:	Old Tom Clarke!
Voice 1:	A spare, grey man.
Voice 2:	Sean MacDermott!
Voice 1:	Leaning on his cane.
Voice 2:	Major John MacBride!
Voice 1:	Dapper in a blue suit; carrying a cane, smoking a cigar.
Voice 2:	And all the volunteers—Citizen Army and others—with their rifles, shotguns, picks and spades, homemade pikes.
Voice 1:	In marching order, so, they *walked on air*—till they got to Sackville Street at noon and heard the command.
Voice 2:	*[loud] Left turn! Charge! Take the GPO!*
Voice 1:	*[Dublin accent] I remember there was a pause. Then one volunteer gave a whoop of delight.*
Voice 2:	*[country] Jesus! Something was actually going to happen!*
Voice 1:	*[teacher]* Some, indeed, thought it was a joke.
Voice 2:	*[commentator]* But it was no joke. The Rising was on! History was being made.
Voice 1:	*[participant] Other units arrived. They dashed in a beeline across the emptiness of Sackville Street . . .*
Voice 2:	*[excited country] The windows of the GPO loom suddenly before us.*
Voice 1:	*[Dublin] I hear someone shouting:*
Voice 2:	*[loud] "Break the windows, you bloody fools!"*
Voice 1:	*Someone's rifle splinters wood and glass. Cut and bleeding, we scramble in.*
Voice 2:	*[country] Glass crashes, locks are blown in, undefended windows are barricaded with sacks, sandbags, boards, books, typewriters.*
Voice 1:	*Things speed up . . . it's all a bit of a blur. But we're in, God knows.*
Voice 2:	*There's a lull. We catch our breath. Then Commander Pearse goes out and stands in front of the GPO—while our flag, the tricolour, is raised above the building.*
Voice 1:	*[teacher]* Pearse then read, and pinned up, the Proclamation. You all know it.
	[all this next bit rather brisk recitation]
Voice 2:	*[country] IRISHMEN AND IRISHWOMEN* *In the name of God and of the dead generations . . .*
Voice 1:	*[Dublin] . . . Ireland, through us, summons her children to her flag*
Voice 2:	*. . . and strikes for her freedom . . .*

Voice 1:   *. . . religious and civil liberty, equal rights . . . equal opportunities . . .*

Voice 2:   *. . . cherish all the children of the nation equally, . . .*

Voice 1:   *. . . under the protection of the Most High God . . .*

Voice 2:   *. . . and the readiness of its children to sacrifice themselves . . .*

Voice 1:   *. . . for the common good . . .*

Voice 2:   and so on . . . and so on . . .

Voice 1:   *[Dublin lady, middle-class] Very pale, Pearse was, I remember. Cold of face, he scanned the small almost indifferent-seeming crowd that had gathered . . . who warmed only to show positive hostility; a few thin perfunctory cheers; no enthusiasm whatever.*

Voice 2:   *[commentator]* The English authorities responded with a proclamation of their own:

Voice 1:   *[very English, reciting report] An attempt, instigated and designed by the foreign enemies of our King and Country to incite rebellion in Ireland, and thus endanger the safety of the United Kingdom, has been made by a reckless though small body of men, who have been guilty of insurrectionary acts. . . . Therefore the CITY OF DUBLIN and COUNTY OF DUBLIN are under and subject to MARTIAL LAW. And I do hereby call on all Loyal Subjects of the Crown to aid in upholding and maintaining the peace of the Crown and the supremacy and authority of the Crown. . . . GOD SAVE THE KING.*

Voice 2:   So there we are. History in action. On Tuesday the *Irish Times* took notice:

Voice 1:   *[brisk, posh Dublin, report] Yesterday morning an insurrectionary rising took place in the City of Dublin. The authorities have taken active and energetic measures to cope with the situation. These measures are proceeding favourably. In according with this official statement, early and prompt action is anticipated.*

Voice 2:   And ordinary Dubliners, what did *they* think?

Voice 1:   *[Dublin middle-class] This has taken everyone by surprise . . . today, our peaceful city is no longer peaceful.*

Voice 2:   *[a citizen from the country] Guns are rolling and crackling from different directions, And the rattle of machine guns can be heard. . . .*

Voice 1:   *I spoke to a man with a revolver near Stephen's Green. He was no more than a boy, not more than twenty years of age, short in stature, with close-curling red hair and blue eyes—a kindly looking lad. His face was sunburnt and grimy with dust and sweat. I asked him what had happened?*

Voice 2:   *[hurried, young country voice] We have taken the City! We are expecting an attack from the military at any moment, and those people won't go home for me. . . . We have all the City. We have everything. This morning the police rushed us. One ran at me to take my revolver. I fired but I missed him, and hit a . . .*

Voice 1:   *He trailed off and I walked away. Glancing back I saw he was staring after me, but I know that he did not see me—he was looking at turmoil, and blood, and at figures that ran towards him and ran away—a world in motion and he in the centre of it, astonished.*

Voice 2:   *[commentator]* The Countess Markievicz was by Stephen's Green, too, observed by one of her lieutenants—the Scot, Margaret Skinnider:

Voice 1:   *[Scots accent] I saw the British soldiers coming up Harcourt Street. The countess stood motionless, waiting . . . in her officer's uniform and black hat with its great plumes. At length she raised her gun to her shoulder. The shots rang out and I saw the two officers leading the column drop to the street. As the countess was taking aim again, the soldiers, without firing a shot, turned and ran in great confusion—from a woman! Of course, later, she shot a policeman.*

Voice 2:   *[commentator]* A little later, Margaret Skinnider herself was in the thick of the action.

Voice 1:   *As I rode along on my bicycle, I had my first taste of street-fighting. Soldiers on top of the Shelbourne aimed their machine gun directly at me. Bullets struck the wooden rim of my bicycle wheels, puncturing it. I rode as fast as I could. My speed saved my life, and I was soon out of range around a corner. . . . Whenever I was called down to carry a despatch, I took off my uniform, put on my grey dress and hat, and went out the side door of the college of surgeons with my message. As soon as I returned, I slipped back into my uniform and joined the firing squad.*

Voice 2:   Ye know, of course, Monday was the Bank Holiday. Not too many about. Off at the Fairyhouse Races. Soldiers too. But as the week wore on 'twas different. Crowds gathered. Like a play it was.

Voice 1:   *[posh Dublin] An ever-inquisitive crowd stands in Dolier Street and on O'Connell Bridge. Right between the two firing parties. They appear quite unconcerned. One would think from their appearance that the whole thing was merely a sham battle got up for their amusement. . . .*

Voice 2:   *[plain country voice] I saw boys in the middle of the road playing with cricket bats and balls. . . . There was no use in warning of danger. Bullets were whining but they didn't seem to mind. . . .*

Voice 1:   *A group of old women sitting on chairs on the street near Stephen's Green said they had "come out to see the battle." As if it was all a play.*

Voice 2:   *[commentator]* But maybe in its way 'twas just that. A play. A deadly serious play. Didn't Michael Collins himself say 'twas like a Greek tragedy. Though, mind you, as a military man himself, he didn't mean it as a compliment. And lord, didn't some of the young volunteers make a raid on the waxworks museum and came back wearing things like the dress of Queen Elizabeth the first. Swear to God! Young lads! And one of them an American!

Voice 1:   *[teacher]* A play so, packed with . . . well . . . *symbols.* Easter, you see: sacrifice, death, and resurrection. Pearse's idea.

Voice 2:   But in truth, real life, too, and real death—whatever about resurrection.

Voice 1:   And don't forget real *hostility.* At what the rebels were doing to the city. The rebels and the British Army. People didn't like it.

Voice 2:   Pure foolishness, they'd say.

Voice 1:   Toy soldiers with pikes and rifles on one side, big guns on the other.

Voice 2:   And riots? Of course there were riots, riots and lootings. No stopping them once they started.

Voice 1:   The *separation women,* as they were called, made the most indelible impression.

Voice 2:   Wives and mothers, they were, of Irishmen off fighting in Europe. Very poor they were, living in terrible slum conditions.

Voice 1:   Their pensions were held up, you see. It was a disaster for them. They knew they'd go hungry. So naturally they hated the rebels.

Voice 2:   *[rebel country voice, excited] Jesus! they attacked us. We were on bicycles. They pulled us off. We had to use the butts of our rifles on them. A big fat woman in white apron and flapping shawl leapt in front of us, beating her huge bosom with clenched fists and near grabbing my bayonet.*

Voice 1:   *[woman, flat Dublin accent] Put it through me now for me son who's out in France!*

Voice 2:   *[rebel country voice] Booing and jeering and shouting at us. . . . And the kids looting the sweetshops, setting off fireworks. Chaos. The women around the Coombe were like the furies of the French Revolution . . . shoeless, hatless, filthy faces, shouting, shrieking, yelling at us.*

Voice 1:   *[woman, flat Dublin accent, harsh, at audience] Indeed an' there they were: Breakin into th shops! Smashin the windas, batherring in th doors an whippin away ever' thin! An the Volunteers is firin on them. I seen two men an a lassie pushin a piano down th street, an the sweat rollin off*

them thryin to get it up onto the pavement; an' an oul wan that musta
been seventy lookin as if she'd dhrop every minit with the dint of heart
beatin', tryin to pull a big double bed out of a shop winda'. An' out there in
France there's th' men like me own son marchin out into th' dread dimness
o' danger, while th lice is crawlin' around feedin' on th fat o the land. . . .
[sings a bar or two]

    It's a long way to Tipperary . . . oh it's a long way to go. . . .

Voice 2:   *[commentator]* Indeed, most of the women—well-dressed or in shawls and rags—seemed hostile.

Voice 1:   *[upper-class Dublin] I hope every man of them will be shot.*

        [lower-class] They ought to be all shot. They'll be done for soon.

Voice 2:   But—whatever about being shot—they lasted, so they did, longer than most people, even themselves, expected.

Voice 1:   *[teacher]* Lasting was the point, wasn't it? Putting up a good fight. Not toy soldiers.

Voice 2:   Dead and wounded all round the place—outside the Post Office and inside too.

Voice 1:   Soldiers, civilians, Volunteers, . . . children. *Sacrifice,* you see.

Voice 2:   As Pearse had said, and the old Fenian Tom Clarke himself had said:

Voice 1:   *[English accent: south coast, Hampshire] At all periods in the history of*
Ireland the shedding of blood has always succeeded in raising the spirit
and morale of the people . . . our only chance is to make ourselves felt by an
armed rebellion. . . . Of course we shall all be wiped out.

Voice 2:   *Sacrifice.* That was it. No avoiding it. Oh the little black rose, the *róisin*
dubh, was red at last—just as Joseph Mary Plunkett said it would be. And bloody right he was too!

Voice 1:   *[quiet] We shall not fear the trumpets and the noise*
Of battle, for we know our dreams divine,
And when at last the blood
O'erleaps the final barriers . . . ,
Praise God if this my blood fulfils the doom
When you, red rose, shall redden into bloom.

Voice 2:   *[resigned]* Fair enough, I suppose. But History's clock kept ticking . . . and though they lasted longer than most thought possible, the end came soon enough.

Voice 1:   *[teacher]* Though not before they'd seen a great deal: Woundings. Dyings. Shattered bodies. Corpses.

Voice 2:   *[country] I seen Paddy Doyle and Dick Murphy lying dead. Murphy was still holding his rifle. Poor Reynolds was on the floor in a pool of blood. The place was swimming in blood, Decomposing corpses lay scattered throughout the city by week's end. I seen several dead bodies lying in the street in the broiling sun. Two had sacks over them.*

Voice 1:   And it wasn't just their own either. They had reminders, too, of the Great War raging out in the big world.

Voice 2:   *In one press in the GPO we found the blood-stained British Army uniform of the post office secretary's son.*

Voice 1:   He'd been killed a little before in France, you see. In an envelope they found a lock of his fair hair, marked by the boy's mother . . .

Voice 2:   And maybe reminding them that among the English soldiers firing at them were many Irishmen, killing and being killed by their own countrymen.

Voice 1:   Yes. Like Bill Mulraney—Kildare-man and GAA man in the King's Hussars—shot dead outside the GPO. And many others.

Voice 2:   Such a tangle when you look at it. And as for those inside the GPO itself—they knew hunger, so they did.

Voice 1:   Indeed they did. Bitter hunger. Thirst too.

Voice 2:   *[country] By Tuesday the food had run out. We had nice strong tea but in a bucket used for Jeyes Fluid. By Friday I was exhausted and the only thing I could get to eat was a raw egg and a square of Chivers jelly.*

Voice 1:   Fear too—how could they not feel it?

Voice 2:   *Some of our lads began to cry when they heard shots . . . because they were a long time from confession. But hearing Pearse praise us, and knowing my name would live in history . . . I felt elated. Pearse stood very solemn, then, and we looking at him, his right hand on his breast.*

Voice 1:   *[Dublin] And there was rumours all over the place: common as rosary beads round the necks of the volunteers.*

Voice 2:   *[loud country] Volunteers marching in from the country! Two German warships docked in Dublin Bay!*

Voice 1:   *Plenty of priests were part of it all, you know. Oh lord yes. A priest in the Pro-Cathedral tried to stop me from going to the GPO . . .*

Voice 2:   *[country priest] You're not going! Let those people be burned to death! They're murderers!*

Voice 1:   *[Dublin] But there was different kinds of priests too. In the middle of the fightin', with bullets flyin' and the road strewn with the dead and the dyin', didn't Father Wall of Haddington Road come along on his bicycle. I could see he was frightened, but he left his bike against a railin' and went from one body to another givin' them the last sacrament.*

Voice 2: *[commentator]* By Friday, the GPO was on fire. Nothing to be done. The noise of the incendiary bombs exploding was terrific, along with the bursting glass of the big windows and falling walls.

Voice 1: *The heat was wicked awful. In my simplicity I picked up the phone to call the fire brigade. They said they intended to let us burn out.*

Voice 2: *[country accent] I could see the whole place was a mass of flames. . . . An inferno. . . . Not a soul was now to be seen, only a huge wall of flames . . .*

Voice 1: *By Friday morning we were well ablaze. The noise of bursting shells and tumbling walls and roofs was indescribable.*

Voice 2: *When the roof finally collapsed . . . pieces of burning timber began to fall from the ceiling over us . . . I thought we were going to stay in the building till we died. . . .*

Voice 1: *Evacuation began at 8 in the evening. Pearse praised us before we left.*

Voice 2: *Though we had lost the fight, he said, "Be assured you will find victory, even though that victory may be found in death. . . ."*

Voice 1: *"I'm glad we fought," he said. "We seem to have lost. We haven't lost. To refuse to fight would have been to lose; to fight is to win." He said that.*

Voice 2: *"We have kept faith with the past," he said, "and handed on a tradition to the future. . . ."*

Voice 1: *"I'm satisfied we have saved Ireland's honour." He said that.*

Voice 2: *[commentator]* Honour! Oh, fair enough. Honour. But it was Desmond Ryan, wasn't it, who saw Pearse in a different mood altogether?

Voice 1: *[as Ryan: quiet, plain] Sitting on a barrel. Staring at the flames. His slightly flushed face crowned with his turned-up hat. Suddenly, he turned to me with a question.*

Voice 2: *[deep, plain, sober] It was the right thing to do, wasn't it?*

Voice 1: *[intense] Yes!*

Voice 2: *If we fail it means the end of everything, Volunteers and all.*

Voice 1: *Yes.*

Voice 2: *When we are all wiped out, people will blame us for everything*

Voice 1: *I suppose so.*

Voice 2: *[thoughtful, protesting] But . . . , but for this, the war would have ended and nothing would have been done. After a few years they will see the meaning of what we tried to do.*

Voice 1:   *[conclusive] They can never despise us again.*

Voice 2:   *[commentator]* Well . . . that's true too, no doubt about it. Very . . . *human.* Still . . . fair name or not . . . Dublin city by now was in tatters.

Voice 1:   *[teacher]* Yes. It was devastated. The centre was in ruins.

Voice 2:   By now the *dream* was a nightmare.

Voice 1:   *[Dublin, working-class] The finest part of our city has been blown to smithereens and burned to ashes. The English soldiers say the ruins o' this quarter is more complete than anythin' they've seen at Ypres, or in France or Flanders. And it's a gruesome sight, so it is, to see the dead all piled on top of each other in the morgues, an' not enough marble slabs to put the bodies on.*

Voice 2:   The doctors were operating day and night. Neither gas nor electricity so they had to operate by the light of candles . . . no sterilization of instruments or dressings: no boiling water . . . sad stuff. . . . Said one nurse:

Voice 1:   *[country nurse] A badly wounded woman died here on Thursday, as did also James Kelly—a schoolboy who was shot through the skull. Another schoolboy, John Healy aged fourteen—whose brain was hanging all over his forehead when he was brought in—died on the Saturday.*

Voice 2:   *[volunteer] But God, the evacuation was pure hell. Leaving the GPO I never felt closer to death. The place became a bedlam Hell of flame and noise . . .*

Voice 1:   *[plain Dublin] Clarke said he'd go down with the building. . . . He wanted a glorious last stand. . . . We sang "the soldier's song" to keep our spirits up . . .*

Voice 2:   *[commentator]* And so the garrison poured out into Henry Street with no semblance of order. . . . No one seemed to have any idea what to do. . . . Nobody seemed to be in charge . . .

Voice 1:   *[Dublin] We crossed the lane by rushes—three at a time—between bursts of heavy fire. . . .*

Voice 2:   *[country] Bullets like hailstones were hopping off the street . . .*

Voice 1:   *With head down as if I was runnin' in heavy rain I ran as I never ran before, and got over Henry Street without a scratch.*

Voice 2:   *I was passed by a young Volunteer named Macken . . . as he moved past me he shouted Oh my God! and fell in my path, I caught him in my arms but he was dead in a minute, shot in the centre of the forehead. I laid him on the path and said a short prayer.*

Voice 1:   *Rebels lay where they had fallen—I saw one lying on his back, his arms outstretched, blood oozing from his body in a pool under him and flies buzzing about his head. Two or three others lay dead near him.*

Voice 2: *[commentator]* With the wounded Connolly, then, Pearse got safe to a house in Henry Place off Moore Street. There he saw two dead civilians—a father and a daughter. And three dead bodies on the path outside. One poor man with a white flag grasped in his hand lying dead on the doorstep of his house.

Voice 1: *I felt sorry I did for the people livin' in those houses on Moore Street an' Henry place. When Pearse came in and saw what had happened to that family, and saw the bodies outside, he was, like, stricken. I could see that.*

Voice 2: *[country] But what in God's name did he expect? Says he to the mother, trying to comfort her, "My God, I'm sorry this happened. What can we do?" He said that.*

Voice 1: *[teacher]* In that moment, I suppose, the true horrors of the Rising were at last brought home to him. And he said to someone:

Voice 2: *[sober] They're shooting women and children in the streets. I saw them myself.*

Voice 1: Beyond all the heroics of the takeover, so . . . beyond all the fighting. . . beyond all the *delirium of the brave,* he knew . . . what he had to do.

Voice 2: *[official] In order to prevent the further slaughter of Dublin citizens, and in the hope of saving the lives of our followers, now hopelessly outnumbered, the members of the provisional Government present at Headquarters have agreed to an unconditional surrender, and the Commandants of the various districts in the City and Country will order their commands to lay down arms.*

Voice 1: *[Dublin] When I heard of negotiations, the relief I felt was like an answer to prayer . . . to say I was glad and thankful to God would be putting it mildly. . . . It was a friend of mine, Nurse Elizabeth O'Farrell, who at risk of her life carried the surrender to General Maxwell, and the* "no conditions" *back to Pearse. Terrified she was. But brave.*

Voice 2: *[commentator]* And so to surrender. Unconditional Surrender. And the defeated Rebels laying down arms.

Voice 1: *[teacher]* At all outposts men and women were weeping freely, some breaking their rifles against the walls.

Voice 2: Then, after the laying down of arms, the long walk to the surrender points.

Voice 1: *[Dublin, posh] Good Lord, it's a sight I shall never forget. That thin line, some in the green uniform of the volunteers, others in the plainer equipment of the Citizen Army, some looking like ordinary civilians, the others looking mere lads of fifteen, not a few bandaged and wounded, and the whole melancholy procession wending its way through long lines of khaki soldiers, and some jeering onlookers.*

Voice 2: *[solid country citizen] But downhearted, No! Dockers, labourers, shop assistants, all conditions of men; all have the same look of defiance which will haunt me to my dying day. Whatever else they were they were not cowards. . . .*

Voice 1: *[teacher]* And then the big clock of History simply goes on ticking. On to trials, imprisonment, executions.

Voice 2: *[commentator]* Over ninety were at first condemned by the hastily formed military court, you know. Countess Markievicz among them.

Voice 1: But most, including the Countess, were commuted to life imprisonment.

Voice 2: You've heard of the leaders' deaths already.

Voice 1: They prepared in their own ways. John MacBride gave this advice to his fellow prisoners:

Voice 2: *[soldier, clipped] Some of you may live to fight again. If you do, take to the open country for it. Avoid a death trap like this.*

Voice 1: Pearse wrote a letter to his mother:

Voice 2: *[dignified] We are ready to die and shall die cheerfully and proudly. . . . You must not grieve for all this. We have preserved Ireland's honour and our own. . . . I will call to you in my heart at the last moment.*

Voice 1: He also wrote a poem, imagining her thoughts. Curious, but that's what he did.

Voice 2: *[commentator]* Like Yeats's *Shan Van Vocht*, she is—the Poor Old Woman. Like Kathleen Ni Houlihan herself, I suppose:

Overvoice: *[female] I do not grudge them; Lord, I do not grudge*
    My two strong sons that I have seen go out
    To break their strength and die, they and a few,
    In bloody protest for a glorious thing.
    They shall be spoken of among their people,
    The generations shall remember them,
    And call them blessed;
    But I will speak their names to my own heart
    In the long nights;
    The little names that were familiar once
    Round my dead hearth.

> *Lord, thou art hard on mothers:*
> *We suffer in their coming and their going;*
> *And tho' I grudge them not, I weary, weary*
> *Of the long sorrow—And yet I have my joy:*
> *My sons were faithful, and they fought.*

Voice 2:   Thomas MacDonagh wrote to his family: *"The one bitterness that death has for me,"* he said, *"is the separation it brings from my beloved wife and children. But I have not wept or murmured,"* he said. *"I counted the cost of this and am ready to pay it."*

Voice 1:   *[teacher]* Plunkett wrote to his fiancée: *"Darling Grace,"* he wrote, *"This is just a little note to say I love you. . . . My actions have been as right as I could see and make them and I cannot wish them undone . . ."*

Voice 2:   They got married, you know, in his cell—just before his execution.

Voice 1:   While James Connolly said to his weeping wife, Lily, and his daughter Nora:

Voice 2:   *[gruff, content] Wasn't it a full life, Lily, and isn't this a good end?*

Voice 1:   You've heard of the executions already. Even on the enemy they made a lasting impression. One soldier witness said MacDonagh *died like a prince.* MacBride was offered a blindfold.

Voice 2:   *"I have looked down the muzzles of too many guns in the South African war to fear death,"* he said. *"Now please carry out your sentence."* And said one of the soldiers in the firing party:

Voice 1:   *[English, Cockney] Ain't it sad to think that these three brave men, who met their death so bravely, should be fighting for a cause which proved so useless, and has been the means of so much bloodshed.*

Voice 2:   *[commentator]* Like Pearse, Yeats in his poem had mothers on his mind.

Overvoice: *["WBY voice"] Too long a sacrifice*
> *Can make a stone of the heart.*
> *O when may it suffice?*
> *That is heaven's part, our part*
> *To murmur name upon name,*
> *As a mother names her child*
> *When sleep at last has come*
> *On limbs that had run wild.*
> *What is it but nightfall?*
> *No, no, not night but death. . . . .*

Voice 2:   *[commentator] Not night but death.* Aye. Of course voices were raised against the executions. How could there not be? In Westminster itself, Redmond and Dillon spoke out.

Voice 1:   *[teacher]* They'd been against the Rising, yes, calling it:

Voice 2:   "This insane and wicked attempt to destroy all Ireland's hopes just when they were about to be realized."

Voice 1:   Yes. They knew it would destroy all hopes of the Home Rule they'd worked for all their lives. But . . .

Voice 2:   But still they made their opposition—as Irishmen—known.

Voice 1:   *[stolid, well-off country Irish] You are letting loose a river of blood between two races who, after three hundred years of hatred and strife, we had nearly succeeded in bringing together.*

Voice 2:   *[same] It is not murderers who are being executed; it is insurgents who have fought a good clean fight, a brave fight, however misguided. . . .*

Voice 1:   *The Irish people will regard these executions with helpless rage, the rage with which you'd watch a stream of blood dripping from under a closed door.*

Voice 2:   *[commentator]* And so the clock of History ticks on—past trials, past swift and brutal executions. But then:

Overvoice: *["WBY voice"] I write it out in a verse—*
  MacDonagh and MacBride
  And Connolly and Pearse
  Now and in time to be,
  Wherever green is worn,
  Are changed, changed utterly:
  A terrible beauty is born.

Voice 1:   *[teacher]* That was it. For as if by magic, these same executions and the spreading stories of how the condemned men had faced into them . . .

Voice 2:   . . . transformed, and utterly, both the Rising and the rebels. As one Dublin lady put it:

Voice 1:   *[well-off Dublin accent] Requiem masses gathered huge exultant crowds. . . . The leaders in death had a greater power over the hearts and minds of any stripe of nationalist opinion than they ever had in their lives.*

Voice 2:   *[commentator]* More was achieved, people said, by six days of fighting and their aftermath, than in twenty-five years of constitutional politics. *All changed, changed utterly . . .*

Voice 1:   *[teacher]* Indeed! And indeed *A terrible beauty was born . . .*

Voice 2:   Weren't grown men standing in Sackville Street crying their eyes out? And didn't the poet Ledwidge, before he went back to the trenches where he'd die, write an elegy for the poets among the executed men:

Overvoices: *[male & female, soft] I heard the Poor Old Woman say:*
"
    At break of day the fowler came,
    And took my blackbirds from their songs
    Who loved me well thro' shame and blame.

    No more from lovely distances
    Their songs shall bless me mile by mile . . .

    And when the first surprise of flight
    Sweet songs excite, from the far dawn
    Shall there come blackbirds loud with love,
    Sweet echoes of the singers gone.

    But in the lovely hush of eve
    Weeping I grieve the silent bills"
    I heard the Poor Old Woman say
    In Derry of the little hills.

Voice 1:   *[teacher]* And no doubt you know that the executed men—even the few Protestants among them, some of whom converted at the end—became Catholic martyrs.

Voice 2:   The logic of *sacrifice*, you see, overwhelmed everything.

Voice 1:   Yes. But . . . *Catholic* martyrs. . . . Remember the rebels' rosary beads. I suppose the church was laying its claim. Which of course might in time become a problem.

Voice 2:   But that's another story, isn't it? Back in 1916, though, when the leaders were executed:

Voice 1:   *[Dublin; posh] It was difficult to believe the change we saw—everywhere except in Ulster. . . . A new Ireland had been born. . . . After the orgy of blood, we said, Ireland cannot be the same . . . a once familiar world is overwhelmed. . . . As yet one knows nothing of the future except that it must be very unlike the past.*

Voice 2:   True enough, as we now know. Sure, on hearing the news, didn't Maud Gonne herself—who years before had played Kathleen Ni Houlihan in

Yeats's play—didn't she write to him from France:

Voice 1: *["Maud" voice] I am overwhelmed by the tragedy and the greatness of the sacrifice our countrymen and women have made. . . . I am ill with sorrow—so many of my best and noblest friends gone. . . . They have raised the Irish cause to a position of tragic dignity. . . . Those who die for Ireland are sacred. . . . The deaths of those leaders are full of beauty and romance. "They will be speaking forever, the people shall hear them forever."* The poet himself was stricken by it all:

Voice 2: *I had no idea,* he said, *that any public event could so deeply move me. I am trying to write a poem on the men executed—"terrible beauty has been born." I am very despondent about the future. The leaders shall live while Ireland lives. People we have known with familiarity and regarded with contempt have joined at a stroke the mythic company of Emmet Fitzgerald and Tone. . . .* It was in that mood, of course, that he wrote his poem, wasn't it?

Voice 1: Quite so. "Easter 1916." With all its ambivalences and shifts of mind and heart—with its *"too long a sacrifice / can make a stone of the heart,"* and its *"for England may keep faith / For all that is done and said . . ."*

Voice 2: 'Twas a risky poem, indeed. People shy from complexity and ambiguity, don't they? It's simplicity they want, isn't it? The simplicity, maybe, of Pearse's vision of sacrifice.

Voice 1: I suppose that's it, yes. Maud Gonne, for example—now the widow of the martyred MacBride—was on the side of sacrifice.

Voice 2: No surprise in that. Of course, Yeats sent her the poem. She wrote back to him right away. From France:

Voice 1: *["Maud's" voice]*

My dear Willie—

> *No I don't like your poem. It isn't worthy of you, and above all it isn't worthy of the subject. . . . You know quite well that sacrifice has never yet turned a heart to stone. . . . You could never say that MacDonagh and Pearse and Conally were sterile fixed minds: Each served Ireland . . . which was their share of the world . . . with varied faculties and vivid energy! . . . As for my husband he has entered eternity by the great door of sacrifice which Christ opened. . . . There are beautiful lines in your poem . . . but it is not a great WHOLE, a living thing which our race will treasure and repeat.*

Voice 2: That was telling him! But wasn't she his Kathleen Ni Houlihan, after all, so what could he expect?

Voice 1:   And then . . . the aftermath.

PAUSE

Voice 2:   Yeats sensed what was to come.

Voice 1:   He saw that the rational politics of the Home Rule Party might, just might, have restored some trust in the constitutional effort to bring about Home Rule.

Voice 2:   But he knew it could not compete with the great emotional wave rising to support the rebels' cause.

Overvoice: *["WBY voice"] O but we talked at large before*
The sixteen men were shot,
But who can talk of give and take,
What should be and what not
While those dead men are loitering there
To stir the boiling pot?

You say that we should still the land
Till Germany's overcome;
But who is there to argue that
Now Pearse is deaf and dumb?
And is their logic to outweigh
MacDonagh's bony thumb?

How could you dream they'd listen
That have an ear alone
For those new comrades they have found,
Lord Edward and Wolfe Tone,
Or meddle with our give and take
That converse bone to bone?

Voice 1:   *[teacher]* True. And we know what happened then to the party of Redmond and Dillon.

Voice 2:   Indeed we do. For the clock of History kept ticking, and in time it brought the party to its knees. People, you see, knew they'd been—like many another indeed—against the Rising. . . .

Voice 1:   . . . so their protests at the executions didn't matter. . . .

Voice 2:   Not a whit! And when *conscription* in Ireland was announced, even though they opposed it, it sealed their fate.

Voice 1:   It was the last straw. Yeats, ever vigilant, knew the score: *"It seems to me a strangely wanton thing,"* he said . . .

Voice 2:   *"that for the sake of 50,000 Irish soldiers, England is prepared to hollow another trench between our countries and fill it with blood . . ."*

Voice 1:   And then John Redmond himself (whose own brother was killed fighting in France) died soon after.

Voice 2:   Died, it was said, *a broken-hearted man.* His life's work buried in the rubble of Dublin. Washed away by the blood of martyrs.

Voice 1:   True. That was sad. And sad to write him out of History, too, was it not?

Voice 2:   Of course History's clock didn't stop its ticking even then, did it? No indeed. How could it? Its hands, blood-soaked as they were, kept moving as they have to move: forward. And forward now in a changed Ireland.

           [quick bit: a litany]

Voice 1:   *[teacher]* Forward to December 1918 . . . United Kingdom elections.

Voice 2:   Sinn Fein wins by a landslide in Ireland.

Voice 1:   Many of those elected are in jail or on the run.

Voice 2:   They form a breakaway legislative body. The *Dáil.*

Voice 1:   They *ratify*—as monument to the *glorious martyrs*—

Voice 2:   the Rising's declaration of a Republic . . .

Voice 1:   *[slower]* And on the 21st of January 1919, they sit as Dáil Eireann in Dublin . . .

Voice 2:   Nationalists, then, and not only nationalists, ask each other:

Voice 1:   *[country lady] Did you ever think you'd live to see this day? Was the past ever so near, the present so brave, the future so . . . full of hope . . . ?*

Voice 2:   *[commentator]* Hope, aye. But 'twasn't long—with the Great War ended in Europe—that History brings along another one.

Voice 1:   *[teacher]* Yes. The Anglo-Irish War.

Voice 2:   The War of Independence.

Voice 1:   The Black and Tan War.

Voice 2:   Take your pick. A guerrilla war, anyway.

Voice 1:   Assassinations. Reprisals. IRA. Flying Columns.

Voice 2:   Auxiliaries. Martial law. Black and Tans. Croke Park. Bloody Sunday.

Voice 1:	Sectarian murders north and south.
Voice 2:	Killings. More killings. Shootings. Hangings.
Voice 1:	Over 1,400 dead: Irish Police, British soldiers, IRA Volunteers.
Voice 2:	Statistics. Again.
Voice 1:	And of course . . . again . . . as always . . . civilians . . . children.
Overvoice:	*["WBY voice"] Violence upon the roads . . . violence of horses . . .*
	Now days are dragon-ridden, the nightmare
	Rides upon sleep: a drunken soldiery
	Can leave the mother, murdered at her door,
	To crawl in her own blood, and go scot-free;
	The night can sweat with terror as before
	We pieced our thoughts into philosophy,
	And planned to bring the world under a rule,
	Who are but weasels fighting in a hole.
Voice 2:	On and on, so—on at last to stalemate, ceasefire, talks, a truce.
Voice 1:	July to December, 1921. You can imagine the relief! The whole country drawing breath.
Voice 2:	And still on marches history—tick tock, tick tock . . . to a treaty.
Voice 1:	Oh the Treaty! The Treaty! The vexatious Treaty!
Voice 2:	Offers, counteroffers, drafts, agreements, disputes.
	[quickening, teacher and commentator]
Voice 1:	The North.
Voice 2:	Enough said.
Voice 1:	Partition had to stay on the table.
Voice 2:	No surprise. Remember 1912! *History!*
Voice 1:	*[English] We have given a pledge that if Ulster resists we will support her in her resistance. We intend to keep that pledge.*
Voice 2:	Same again. Still intact. No treaty would shift it.
Voice 1:	*[teacher]* So there's DeValera in Dublin waiting results . . .
Voice 2:	Collins and his advisors in London making offers . . . .
Voice 1:	Offers, counteroffers. Back and forth . . .
Voice 2:	Back and forth. . . . Until canny Lloyd George forced the issue:
Voice 1:	*[Welsh accent] Sign the Treaty as is or it'll mean the renewal of immediate and terrible war.*
Voice 2:	No mistaking that.

Voice 1:	*[teacher]* Michael Collins said it was the best they could get from Britain at that time:
Voice 2:	*[country voice] It's a useful first step. From here further freedom can be achieved. It gives us freedom.*
	Not the ultimate freedom that all nations desire. But the freedom to achieve it.
Voice 1:	It sounds reasonable enough, I suppose, yes. But—according to *his* lights—which opposed such terms—Liam Mellowes answered:
Voice 2:	*[plain country] The delegates . . . have no power to sign away the rights of Ireland and the Irish Republic.*
Voice 1:	Fast forward so to the 7th of January, 1922.
Voice 2:	Oh these dates! These chimings—big and little—of History!
Voice 1:	The 2nd Dáil—with a hundred and twenty-one members—ratifies the Treaty by a margin of seven votes.
Voice 2:	Close. Two opposing traditions facing off, so.
Voice 1:	Constitutional on one side;
Voice 2:	Physical Force on the other.
Voice 1:	Going back to long before 1916.
Voice 2:	But here and now it's not just in debates . . .
Voice 1:	or councils, or rational discussions.
Voice 2:	The stakes are higher than ever. It could be war! Bloody War! Between . . .
Voice 1:	. . . those who'd been allies in 1916 and through the War of Independence . . .
	[another quick exchange]
Voice 2:	Republicans stand firm.
Voice 1:	Free Staters won't budge.
Voice 2:	Militarists versus Politicians, you might say.
Voice 1:	Lines harden. Confusion in plenty. But lines harden.
Voice 2:	Positions fixed.
Voice 1:	Unbending Rhetoric.
Voice 2:	No way out.
Voice 1:	Resignations.
Voice 2:	Walkouts.
Voice 1:	Repudiations.
Voice 2:	'Til it's the 28th of June, 1922.

Voice 1: History just won't call a halt.

Voice 2: Will it ever?

Voice 1: The Republicans take over the Four Courts.

Voice 2: So Collins bombards it.

Voice 1: And here's another war indeed!

Voice 2: But Merciful God! . . .

Voice 1: Now it's *Civil War*!

Voice 2: *[country]* Free Staters. Irregulars.

Voice 1: *[country]* Republicans. Diehards.

Voice 2: Ambushes, shootouts, killings.

Voice 1: Retaliations. Reprisals. Executions.

Voice 2: The country split.

Voice 1: Heart's blood leaking out.

Voice 2: Suffering Jesus! Near a year of it.

Voice 1: Eleven blood-drenched months!

Voice 2: Pacts. Broken pacts.

Voice 1: Old laws. New laws.

Voice 2: After killings by Republicans . . .

Voice 1: the Free State government . . .

Voice 2: executes Republican prisoners.

Voice 1: Seventy-seven of them. Merciful God!

Voice 2: The whole country running blood.

Voice 1: Families divided. Friends killing each other.

Voice 2: Our own countrymen and women.

Voice 1: And so many of the dead . . . innocent civilians . . . children. As usual.

Voice 2: No reliable numbers of killed and wounded. Maybe three thousand.

Voice 1: Carnage!

Voice 2: Far from the sacrificial dream of Pearse, the socialist dream of Connolly, the Romantic dream of MacDonagh, isn't it?

Voice 1: Not the watering of a little rose tree with blood, no.

Voice 2: But *the whole country* drenched in it.

Voice 1: It was nothing but a "blood-saturated ground."

Voice 2: You'd ask yourself, who the hell is who? What's been fought for?

Voice 1: *Not Pearse's simple blood sacrifice, was it?*

Voice 2: *No! For what would Pearse have done in all this . . . this tangle?*

Voice 1:	*Our own internecine bloodletting.*
Voice 2:	Mellowes. Collins, O'Connor, O'Higgins, Cathal Brugha.
Voice 1:	*And hundreds maybe thousands of others.*
Voice 2:	*The mound of dead growing higher by the day.*
Voice 1:	Atrocities.
Voice 2:	No shortage.
Voice 1:	Ambushes aplenty.
Voice 2:	House burnings. Abductions. Maimings.
Voice 1:	Sectarian murders.
Voice 2:	And in the midst of it all what could you do but pray,
Voice 1:	As the poet Yeats in his Tower prayed.
Overvoice:	*["WBY voice"] The bees build in the crevices*

> *Of loosening masonry, and there*
> *The mother birds bring grubs and flies.*
> *My wall is loosening; honey-bees,*
> *Come build in the empty house of the stare.*
>
> *We are closed in, and the key is turned*
> *On our uncertainty; somewhere*
> *A man is killed, or a house burned.*
> *Yet no clear fact to be discerned:*
> *Come build in the empty house of the stare.*
>
> *A barricade of stone or of wood;*
> *Some fourteen days of civil war:*
> *Last night they trundled down the road*
> *That dead young soldier in his blood:*
> *Come build in the empty house of the stare.*
>
> *We had fed the heart on fantasies,*
> *The heart's grown brutal from the fare,*
> *More substance in our enmities*
> *Than in our love; O honey-bees,*
> *Come build in the empty house of the stare.*

Voice 1:	And so on . . . and on. Another sweep of History's bloody hand . . .
Voice 2:	. . . ticking on to the 23rd of May, 1923.
Voice 1:	And the order coming down from DeValera to his Republican forces:
Voice 2:	*[slow, nasal voice] Further sacrifice on your part would now be in vain, and the continuance of the struggle in arms unwise in the national interest. Military victory must be allowed to rest for the moment with those who have destroyed the Republic.*
Voice 1:	*Sacrifice!* There's that word again.
Voice 2:	As if it could put the blood back in all those bodies.
Voice 1:	*History.* It happens. It happened. Has happened.
Voice 2:	Mingled yarn, to say the least. And still argued over.
Voice 1:	Often in a clamorous dialogue of the deaf.
Voice 2:	What if? What if? What if?
Voice 1:	*[recites] And what if excess of love /*
Voice 2:	*[recites] Bewildered them till they died?*
Voice 1:	How History teases us with its *what ifs.*
Voice 2:	What would Pearse have done had he survived?
Voice 1:	Or MacDonagh, or Connolly, or any of them?
Voice 2:	Visionaries the lot, I suppose. Dreamers and others. Poets. (Though wasn't it Pearse himself who said during the planning for the Rising, *Well, if we do nothing else we will rid Ireland of three bad poets . . .*)
Voice 1:	Yes. And it's good to know he had a sense of humour.
Voice 2:	But, God knows, were they all as pure and innocent as MacDonagh's poem makes it sound?
Voice 1:	*[recites] His songs were a little phrase* *Of eternal song. . . .* *His deed was a single word* *Called out alone* *In a night when no echo stirred* *To laughter or moan.*
Voice 2:	*[ironic]* Poems! But what if the executions hadn't happened? Would any of this have been averted?
Voice 1:	Still no end to the *what ifs* of history.
Voice 2:	And we'll never—no matter all our hindsights—we'll never know, will we?

Voice 1:   And who's to blame? Or is it any use asking?

Voice 2:   Blame is it? Don't make me laugh. Remember what I said once, taking words out of that wise man's mouth? *History, it seems, is to blame.*

Voice 1:   Yes. But I suppose we must say it all started—for better, for worse—

Voice 2:   In the GPO and Kilmainhain Yard at Easter 1916, and went on—year by tumultuous year.

Voice 1:   Through 1922 and 1923 . . . and the Irish Free State.

Voice 2:   Near seven years, so, seven bloody years to the end of it. And in truth of course, no true end to it.

Voice 1:   A country's long-enduring birth pangs.

Voice 2:   *It is a hard service they take that help me,* said Kathleen Ni Houlihan.
          Oh you could sing that, no lie. And history didn't give her the lie either.

Voice 1:   For of course it didn't stop there. We all know that.

Voice 2:   Through the Twenties, and after.

Voice 1:   Shootings and killings by diehard Republicans.

Voice 2:   Executions by the Free State Government.

Voice 1:   All our yesterdays. And some of our todays too, in a different yet same key, if truth be told . . .

Voice 2:   *[commentator] Brave delirium,* is it? Noble sacrifice? Or "glorious madness"? Or what?
          [to audience]

Voice 1:   *[teacher] We had fed the heart on fantasies,*

Voice 2:   *[commentator] The heart's grown brutal from the fare,*

Voice 1:   *More substance in our enmities*
          Than in our love;

Voices 2 & 1:   *O honey-bees,*
          Come build in the empty house of the stare.

Voice 1:   But can there be any end to it at all? To all that History?

Voice 2:   I suppose not. Still . . . we're here aren't we?

Voice 1:   True. And now we have our 32nd Dáil. Democratically elected. A bit of a mess, but no matter.

Voice 2:   Full of arguments and fiery words and silly words and this party and that party and God knows what party. But what matter, it's there.

Voice 1:   And isn't that History too?

Voice 2:   No question. The winding rocky road of it.

Voice 1: True. But do you remember those little copy-books we had at school— years ago?

Voice 2: Oh indeed I do! The ones with the little bit of history, dates and the like, on the back cover. 1798, 1829, 1916, and 1919, and 1922, and 1923, and so on. All there.

Voice 1: And I always remember feeling, as a child, . . . *good* . . . when I saw the date 1949, and next to it a simple phrase: *The Republic of Ireland*.

Voice 2: God yes! There it was. No fanfare. Just a little penny copy-book. *The Republic of Ireland!* That was it. That was *us*! *History* indeed!

Voice 1: Coming all the crooked way down from that Easter, I suppose.

Voice 2: True for you. Though of course we're still a divided *island* aren't we?

Voice 1: We are, oh we are. And that's surely a pity. But oh, isn't it so deeply . . . *complicated*.

Voice 2: Right you are. . . . But . . . well . . . that's it so. . . .
And . . . I suppose . . . we may as well . . . end here, so.

Voice 1: True. . . . In . . . the present moment.

Voice 2: Fair enough, God knows. *The present moment!*

[Pause, then Voice 2 walks, unbent, slowly off. Snatch of "The Rising of the Moon," *slow air, as he goes.]*

PAUSE

[Voice 1 gathers and wraps the old shawl loosely as she walks slowly—but not stiff-and-bent old-woman—off, music continuing]

Overvoice: *[repeating the opening lines of the play] Some call me the Poor Old Woman . . . , and there are some that call me . . .*
Kathleen, the daughter of Houlihan. . . .
There have been many songs made for me. . . . .
I heard one on the wind this morning. . . .
[fading] I heard one . . . on the wind this morning . . .

END

Part Two

The Muse
&
Mister Yeats

A Play for Voices

Presented by Curlew Theatre Company

Performed by
Tegolin Knowland & Seán Coyne

Written and Directed by
Eamon Grennan

"Man is in love and loves what vanishes"
W. B. Yeats.

The Muse and Mr. Yeats

Man is in love, and loves what vanishes.

—W. B. YEATS

Introduction

The Muse and Mr. Yeats is a play for voices in which the women loved by the poet in his life, his "muses," talk about their life with him. In the play an "interviewer" questions each woman in turn and elicits a brief account of her relationship with Yeats that reveals much about her in her own right and paints a richly complex portrait of the poet himself.

The list includes Maud Gonne, his lifetime preoccupation, as well as Maud's own daughter, Iseult, a complex young woman for whom he later developed a passion that was surely part fantasy. This "Muse gallery" also contains George Hyde Lees—of crucial importance—who became Yeats's wife and the mother of their two children and was also his collaborator on many of the poems, influenced by their mutual interest in and commitment to the occult as subject and belief. The fictional "Crazy Jane"—based on an old garrulous Sligo woman Yeats had encountered—also figures among the "muses," as well as seven others who were important to the poet at various points in his life. It all adds up to quite a varied picture of interesting women and their views of the poet and each other. Each in her own way and in her own voice reveals herself and her reality, as well as sketching an element in the poet's life. It is the immediacy of each of their voiced accounts that brings the audience into close contact with the richness of their lives and Yeats's life as lover and poet. An overvoice reciting several of Yeats's poems makes connections between the presence of these women in Yeats's life and the poems he composed.

The interviewer is imagined to be a contemporary of the theater audience, interviewing women who lived at the beginning of the twentieth century. While the play therefore situates the audience in the present day, the attitudes of the women reflect their own time. The disparity in attitudes toward women's lives then and now is particularly apparent in the way some of the women are called "mad." While that description in some instances is spoken in a tone of voice that suggests flippancy or irony, it is also true that at the time women like Ruddock, Iseult, and others were often labeled "mad" as a way of explaining their unusual attitudes, choices, and ways of living.

In preparing this play for voices I was prompted by and especially indebted to the book *WB Yeats and the Muses* (Oxford University Press, 2010) by Joseph Hassett for its very fine, suggestive treatment of the subject.

I also found helpful:

R. F. Foster, *WB Yeats, A Life*. Oxford University Press, 2008.
Brenda Maddox, *George's Ghosts: A New Life of WB Yeats*. Picador, 1999.
Ann Saddlemyer, *Becoming George: The Life of Mrs. WB. Yeats*. Oxford University Press, 2002.

The Muse and Mr. Yeats was first performed by Curlew Theatre Company in October 2013 at University College Dublin. In the original production Tegolin Knowland played all the women. She wore a different kind of scarf or wrap and altered her physical gestures and stance to distinguish her interpretation of each of the women.

For the original production

SET

One chair upstage; two chairs downstage left and right

Silk scarves of different colours: one for each of the women. When the parts are played by a single actor, the putting on of a different scarf occurs just before her entrance as that particular character.

A red shawl for Crazy Jane

A single-coloured kerchief for Singer to hold at the start and finish

Voice 1's costume: contemporary, casual

CHARACTERS

Voice 1: A guide/interviewer/commentator. Sceptic and admirer in his attitudes regarding Yeats.

The Muses: Maud Gonne, Olivia Shakespeare, Florence Farr, Iseult Gonne, George Yeats, Margot Ruddock, Dorothy Wellesley, Edith Shackleton, Ethel Mannin, Mabel Dickinson, Crazy Jane.

Notes: Each character speaks both to the other character and to the audience. This change of direction is constant.

Where an overvoice is described as a "WBY voice," the speaker may attempt a Yeats-like voice: deep, rhetorical, resonant.

[For this play I've left the stage directions from the original production, to give a suggestion of the fluency of the piece and as a rough guide to any stage production. But naturally they are not binding.]

[Dark stage. Overvoice: Recording of WBY himself, reciting "Lake Isle of Innisfree," fading out. Lights up.]

Singer: *[holding kerchief, seated, chair upstage. alternating humming and*
            singing "The Salley Gardens"]
            Down by the Salley Gardens my love and I did meet;
            She bid me take life easy, as the grass grows on the weirs;
            But I was young and foolish, and now am full of tears.

[Actor who has sung "The Salley Gardens" now becomes in sequence the different women, each
distinguished by a different scarf]

Voice 1: *[sitting on chair right] Young and foolish . . . full of tears.* Isn't it the truth?
            [rise, walks about, to audience:]
            William Butler Yeats. *Mister* William Butler Yeats.
            Oh a strange man, a strange man.
            Poet. Oh a great poet by all accounts. But strange.
            Believed, you know, in magic. The occult.
            Oh that's all right. Many do. But with him
            'twas the most important pursuit of his life.
            "The centre of all that I do," he said,
            "and all that I think and all that I write."
            The occult. Oh aye. Other stuff too.
            Being a poet, like, he believed, fair play to him,
            in *Inspiration.* That's right.
            And what was it inspired him?
            The *Muse.* Right. The *Muse.* In fact,
            to be perfectly honest, many Muses. True.
            And swear to God wasn't near every one of them
            a *devotee,* as they said, of the occult too.
            And who might "The Muse" be?
            Well, of course 'twas a *woman.* That's natural.
            And in his case—as things turned out—
            'twas a few, well. . . more than a handful . . . of women.
            He'd be stricken by a *particular* woman.
            And it'd take over his whole life—
            or at least the part where the poetry came from.
            His Muse. Never lost it. Kept it going to the end.
            And God knows, it could be a *fleeting* thing. . . .

or last a lifetime . . . or anything in between.
When he was only a young lad, now,
wasn't he taken with a young cousin of his:
red-haired, a bit wild, Laura Armstrong. *Laura*—
that's right, same name as Petrarch's lady.
Interesting that, given that Mister Yeats was, you might say,
in the *Petrarch* line. In the *Dante* and Beatrice line too.
Not to mention the troubadours. Unrequited love and all that.
Understandable about Laura Armstrong of course:
he was a young lad.
Sure when I was a young lad myself
I had a crush on my own cousin, I had.
Red hair too, though her name wasn't Laura.
No. Maura she was. But that's another story.
Right so . . . where was I? The Muse. . . . Right.
Of course ye all know about Maud Gonne.
Love of his life, I suppose you'd have to call her.
Though divil a bit they did about it as far as . . . well, you know . . .
Aside from a wee while in nineteen o' eight or nine.
Otherwise 'twas what they called a *spiritual marriage*.
Or a few encounters on what they called *the astral plane*.
Oh don't be talkin'. Strange stuff. Years of it.
But like I say it could be a fleeting thing too.
Like the girl he glimpsed from a window once—
oh he was an old man that time, *[sit chair right]*
and he sittin' there, musing about this and that,
the world and its wars and all—
and doesn't he catch sight of this young one out on the street—
and doesn't he make a poem of it.
I have it here. I'll play it for ye now.

Overvoice: *[a "WBY voice"]*
             How can I, that girl standing there,
             My attention fix
             On Roman or on Russian

Or on Spanish politics?
Yet here's a travelled man that knows
What he talks about,
And there's a politician
That has read and thought,
And maybe what they say is true
Of war and war's alarms,
But O that I were young again
And held her in my arms!

Voice 1:   *[rising]* He's a long road there from the Salley Gardens.

But the Muse flame . . . 'twas burning yet.

But the first was Miss Maud Gonne. Miss . . . Gonne. *["Maud" puts on scarf]*

Well now, there's a name for you.

That's a pair of words now that might sum it all up.

Miss . . . Gone. Gone missing, you might say. And *missed.*

But there were others

No shortage of muses for Mister Yeats. . . . *[sit chair right]*

Maud: *[English voice, a touch haughty, steely, and a bit ironic. She is tall, rather iconic in demeanour. Rises and comes forward.]*

But of *course* there were others! He was a *poet,* for God's sake!

But *I* was first. Yes. 1889.

What a checkered time we had of it.

Fifty years, Willy and I. Myself and my poet.

We were in so many ways so *different.*

But all for Ireland, for poetry, for love.

Well, *he* was all for *poetry* first, and *I* was all for *Ireland.*

But *of course* there were others.

Olivia, certainly. Olivia Shakespeare.

I liked Olivia. Very *English* . . . but nice.

I was English myself, true. But different. Irish inside.

By . . . passionate attachment, belief, all that.

I was a servant of the *Queen,* you see, of *Cathleen Ni Houlihan.* *[sit chair left]*

But Olivia had culture. A good *writer.* And she was *gentle.*

And a beauty. Yes I admit she was beautiful. . .

And of course George. His wife. I liked George too.

She was in so many ways *good* for him.

Young of course, half his age when they married.

But much better as a wife than I could ever have been.

And of course there was *Iseult.*

Yes. I know. My *daughter.* Sad isn't it?

Half French. Wholly wilful.

A beauty though. Too young for him of course.

But Willy proposed anyway.

After proposing for the . . . oh . . . *umpteenth* time to myself.

I'm glad she said *No.* It would have been a disaster.

(Well *I* would *probably* have been a disaster too . . .

No, I'm *sure* I would.)

Then he went—same month I think, Summer . . . Autumn . . .

Nineteen seventeen, yes, . . . a terrible time for him really—

and proposed to George. George Hyde-Lees. Georgie.

Same age as Iseult. But somehow . . . *older.*

She was English too. But she fitted in, in Ireland.

People liked George. Interesting mixture, you see.

Mystic one minute, practical *wife* the next.

Most *sensible* thing he ever did, I'd say.

And she accepted. Lucky for him.

Voice 1:   Others too, weren't there?

[to audience] As I said no shortage.

Florence Farr, for example. The actress.

Maud: Well yes, of course. English. Actress. Lovely *voice.*

Willy fell in love with her voice, I suppose.

Yes, Florence *was* his Muse, for a time.

A beauty too. And, well, very *Bohemian.*

And like me, she believed in women's rights.

Of course she was Shaw's mistress.

[to audience] George Bernard Shaw, you know.

Oh, there was a lot of *that sort of thing* going on then.

	Even, God forgive me (and He will), in my own life.

Even, God forgive me (and He will), in my own life.
Though not with *Willie.* . . . Well not really, except . . .
except for that brief interlude in—well, let it go.
Then later on, he was getting on, there were the . . .
what shall I call them? . . . the *liaisons.*

Voice 1:   Dorothy Wellesley was one, wasn't it?
And Ethel Mannin. Gorgeous she was. And a writer.
Didn't *they* inspire a few poems too?

Maud: Well yes. Rather different, of course,
from those he wrote to me, or for Olivia.
But of course *they* were rather different *kinds* of muses.
Dorothy, after all, was a Lesbian, wasn't she . . .
while Ethel was, well, Ethel. She *had* a rather *risqué* reputation.

Voice 1:   And what about Margot Ruddock?

Maud: Oh yes of course. *[ironic]* How could I forget poor Margot?
Mad. Not always but . . . yes . . . some of the time.
They had, it's been said, *many romantic assignations.*
After my time of course. An actress too.
Very touching how she latched onto Willy.
Endearing, really, how he encouraged her.
He loved her, in his own *Muse* way, I suppose.
And he wrote some lovely little poems for her.
Well that seems to complete the list.
Except for Edith of course. Edith Shackleton Heald.
Edith was the last. Yes. English too, and a journalist. Very *intellectual.*

Voice 1:   But, Mabel Dickinson now . . . what about her?

Maud: Oh yes, Mabel Dickinson. . . . But that, I believe,
was mostly . . . just *sex?* Purely *amorous.*
She was a gymnastics trainer, you see, and a masseuse.
Perfectly decent person I suppose.
Protestant Dublin. Father a vicar, I believe.
Willy was *carrying on* with her—I believe that's the expression—
while he and I were, well, sorting ourselves out.
In nineteen-o-eight, that was.

He and Mabel *carried on* until . . . oh . . . nineteen thirteen . . .

But there *was* true *affection* between them.

Then there was a pregnancy scare you see,

and Willy panicked. And that sort of finished that.

[slower] But Mabel never rose to the ranks of *Muse*. No.

Voice 1: Still, Muse-wise, as you might say,

Mister Yeats had what you might call a busy life?

Stressful too, I'd reckon.

Maud: Oh indeed yes. But it *did* result in so many wonderful poems.

Not *all* to *my* liking, mind you.

In some he was . . well, quite harsh about *me*.

In one he said I had a *heart of stone*, and in another

I was *an old bellows full of angry wind*.

But yes, he *was* a great poet. And I like to think—

without taking any of the credit from *him* of course—

that I was part of all that.

Wouldn't you say? *[rise, walk back to chair centre]*

Voice 1: *[rise, turn to audience, pacing]* Of course she's right, she is. Without Miss Gonne

William Butler Yeats wouldn't have become, well . . .

William Butler Yeats.

Sure didn't she tell him once

that where a lot of his poems were concerned

she was their *father*. So he was their *mother*, I suppose.

Oh they were a strange lot they were.

Extraordinary the goings-on.

If you seen it in an *opera* now, you wouldn't believe it.

Tragedy, comedy, tragicomedy, farce, the lot.

Sure wasn't Miss Gonne herself a beauty, they said,

in the Valkyrie mode—Wagner you know, and all that class of thing.

And then the poems. Like *Arias* they are. *Arias*.

Such words, such feelings!

But an opera, true enough: Magic. Spirits. Table-rapping.

Astral plane visions and visitations, the lot.

Ghosts too—oh don't get me started. *[sit chair right]*

The Muse and Mr. Yeats 135

But that was the ground the poems grew in.

Little and big, they all sprung up out of that soil.

Sure didn't they all start, as he said himself,

in *the foul rag and bone shop of the heart.*

That's a good one now.

The foul rag and bone shop of the heart.

He wasn't one to mince his words, our William Butler Yeats.

But here's a wee poem now, a little one from early on. *[rise, walk]*

'Twas for Olivia Shakespeare.

She was a writer, by the way. And married.

The first woman he ever went to bed with.

But a *Muse* she was, no doubt about it—

with the poems to prove it. This one's called

"He Gives His Beloved Certain Rhymes."

Fasten your hair with a golden pin,

And bind up every wandering tress. . . . [sit chair left]

Olivia: *[changes scarf, rises, comes forward: soft, gentle English voice]*

Oh yes indeed. He said it for me once.

In his dreamy voice. Not long after we'd become lovers.

And indeed we'd chosen a bed together, for his flat.

He was quite embarrassed. It was his first time.

Every inch increased the expense, you see. Of the bed.

I was his first *real* lover.

Maud? Well, Maud was the lover of his *imagination.*

But this was *my* poem.

He's telling me to fasten my hair with a golden pin.

And to *bind up every wandering tress.* Oh . . . yes . . .

[lost in memory, sit chair right; eyes closed]

You need but lift a pearl-pale hand,

And bind up your long hair and sigh;

And all men's hearts must burn and beat;

And candle-like foam on the dim sand,

And stars climbing the dew-dropping sky,

[open eyes] Live but to light your passing feet.

Voice 1:   Old high style that, sure enough. Very *romantic*.
            And I know 'twas about you he said:
            When my arms wrap you round I press
            My heart upon the loveliness
            That has long faded from the world.
            But didn't he write poems in the same vein for Maud Gonne?
            Hard to tell apart they are: yours, hers.

Olivia: Quite so. They were in *The Wind Among the Reeds*.
            Lovely book. I liked it very much. It came out in 1899.
            The very last gasp of the nineteenth century, imagine.
            Fin de siècle, yes.
            I liked this one . . . though I don't really recall
            if it was for Maud or for myself.
            That was the kind of poems they were, you see.
            [eyes closed, smiling] Had I the heaven's embroidered cloths,
            Enwrought with golden and silver light,
            The blue and the dim and the dark cloths
            Of night and light and the half-light,
            I would spread the cloths under your feet:
            But I, being poor, have only my dreams;
            I have spread my dreams under your feet;
            [eyes open] Tread softly because you tread on my dreams.
            Lovely, isn't it. A love poem of course.
            Though Willy did say, eventually,
            that this kind of thing *was the way to* lose *a lady*.
            Perhaps it was. Still . . .

Voice 1:   And wasn't there the one where you had to break up with him?
            You knew you couldn't compete with Maud's image.
            He just couldn't forget Maud.

Olivia: It's true. We had met as usual in his flat.
            But things did not *go* as usual.
            Instead of reading much love poetry—
            as was his way, to bring the *right mood* around—
            he wrote letters. And as he says himself somewhere,

My friend found my mood did not answer hers
and burst into tears. And so indeed I did.
And I said, "There is someone else in your heart."
And he admitted it was so. And, sadly, that was it.
Though we remained *such* close friends. For life.
I always treasured that. And he did too.
But that poem, oh yes . . . I remember it very well. *[slow back to chair centre]*

Voice 1: *[to audience]* Of course she does. How could she forget it.
Simple it was. Simple and sad.
Pale brows, still hands and dim hair,
I had a beautiful friend
And dreamed that the old despair
Would end in love in the end:
She looked in my heart one day
And saw your image was there;
She has gone weeping away.

Maud: *[coming forward to stool right; standing]* Yes. Poor Olivia. She *was* brokenhearted.
But I believe *my* favourite among those poems
was "The Song of Wandering Aengus."
About his pursuit of me. I love Irish myth, you see.
Aengus the God of love.
And you'll notice the apple blossom, that was me too.
When we met first, he said I was as luminous
as apple blossom through which light falls.
He recalled me standing beside a vase of apple blossom.
Though I *believe* it was actually *almond* blossom.
You see I remember too. Could you say a bit? *[sit chair right]*

Voice 1: *I went out to the hazel wood*
Because a fire was in my head
And cut and peeled a hazel wand
And hooked a berry to a thread
And when white moths were on the wing
And moth-like stars were flickering out

I dropped the berry in a stream
And caught a little silver trout

When I had laid it on the floor,
I went to blow the fire a-flame
But something rustled on the floor,
And someone called me by my name:
It had become a glimmering girl
With apple blossom in her hair
Who called me by my name and ran
[to Maud] And faded through the brightening air . . .

Maud: *[seated, chanting] Yes! . . . Though I am old with wandering*
Through hollow lands and hilly lands
I will find out where she has gone
And kiss her lips and take her hands
And walk among long dappled grass
And pluck 'til time and times are done
The silver apples of the moon,
The golden apples of the sun.

Voice 1:   *The silver apples of the moon.*
The golden apples of the sun.

Very striking. Always in pursuit, he was.

Unrequited love, that was it.

Maud: Yes. And he loved what he called *the pilgrim soul* in me.

Well. I *was* a pilgrim of sorts.

He even wrote a poem about my being dead.

Can you imagine!

Beautiful I suppose, in its own rather *morbid* way.

I was amused.

Reports of my death, as they say, were greatly exaggerated.

But God love him, our first real *kiss*

was a full nine years after we'd met.

Not for a lack of wanting.

And it was *ten years* after *that*

before we *graduated* . . . to the *next* stage.

For a little bit.

Voice 1: And of course that got into a poem too, didn't it?

Maud: *[embarrassed, evasive]* Well . . . yes it did. And well, yes, . . . I *do* remember it. Although . . .

Voice 1: Oh he covers it up a bit—Helen of Troy and all that—
but sure a blind man could tell what he was at:

[Maud closes eyes]

The first of all the tribe lay there

And did such pleasure take—

She who had brought great Hector down

And put all Troy to wreck—

That she cried into this ear,

Strike me . . .

Maud: *[interrupting] Strike me if I shriek!*

Voice 1: *[to audience]* Well, that's telling us, it is, I'd say.

Maud: Yes. *[coming out of trance]* Quite. . . .

Thank you . . .

[more matter of fact] But then I decided

I could only give him *spiritual love and union.*

And that was that.

Of course he did keep asking me to marry him.

No . . . Thank you, Willy, but no.

Then he asked Iseult. *No* again.

And then he asked George, who of course said *yes.*

Voice 1: But he was tethered to *you*, he was.

One poem, a lovely one he wrote then, was "Adam's Curse."

About meeting you along with your sister Kathleen.

[to audience] I suppose ye all remember it?

We sat together at one summer's end, and talked of poetry.

And he goes on to say something about love—

the old style of it going back to Dante himself,

and to Petrarch and the troubadours and the like.

Here's the end of the poem anyway: *[rises and walks to back of chair left, standing]*

We sat grown quiet at the name of love;
We saw the last embers of daylight die,
And in the trembling blue green of the sky
A moon, worn as if it had been a shell
Washed by time's waters as they rose and fell
About the stars and broke in days and years.
I had a thought . . .

Maud: *[rising, to centre]* Oh, may I go on? Even if it *does* praise myself?

[chanting, standing, eyes open]
I had a thought for no one's but your ears:
That you were beautiful and that I strove
To love you in the old high way of love;
That it had all seemed happy, and yet we'd grown
As weary-hearted as that hollow moon.

Voice 1: *[walking out to her]* Alive that is, as you are yourself in them words. *The old high way of love.* The very thing. *[sit chair centre]*

Maud: *[to audience]* Of course the *actual event* wasn't quite as . . .
. . . *poetical.* Willie came to visit, you see.
Kathleen and I were sitting together on the big sofa. *[sit chair left, close eyes, remembering]*
I saw Willie looking critically at me.
Then he told Kathleen he liked her dress
and that she was looking younger than ever.
Next day, then, when he called to take me out, he said to me:

Voice 1: *[eyes closed, quiet, serious "ghosted" voice, not "with" Maud; she is hearing Yeats in her mind]*
"You don't take care of yourself as Kathleen does,
so she looks younger than you. Your face is worn and thin.
But you will always be beautiful,
more beautiful than anyone I have known.
Oh Maud, why don't you marry me—
and give up this tragic struggle and live a peaceful life?"

Maud: *[eyes closed, remembering, straight out to audience; quiet and sincere]*
Willie, are you not tired of asking that question?
How often have I told you to thank the gods

	that I will *not* marry you. You would not be happy with me.
Voice 1:	I am not happy without you.
Maud:	Oh yes you are, because you make beautiful poetry
	out of what you call your unhappiness
	and you are happy in that.
	[eyes open, still quiet] Marriage would be such a dull affair.
	Poets should never marry.
	The world should thank me for *not* marrying you.
Voice 1:	"Are you happy or unhappy?" *[coming forward towards chair right]*
Maud:	*[straight out; quietly serious]* I have been happier and unhappier than
	most. . . .
	But . . .
	I don't think about it. . . . *[rise, stately walk to chair centre; sit]*
Voice 1:	And there you have it. The voice of the Muse herself.
	Quite down to earth, I'd say,
	for all the poet's talk
	of moon and stars and embroidered cloths and the like . . .
	His own poems changed in time though, they did.
	After his Muse married John MacBride
	a bit of iron entered his heart, and it hardened his words too.
	But she was still his beloved, complicated as it might be.
	His Helen of Troy, and he couldn't blame her for anything.
	You can hear how he is, full of questions and all,
	in this poem he called "No Second Troy." *[sit chair right]*
Overvoice:	*Why should I blame her that she filled my days*
	With misery, or that she would of late
	Have taught to ignorant men most violent ways,
	Or hurled the little streets upon the great,
	Had they but courage equal to desire?
	What could have made her peaceful with a mind
	That nobleness made simple as a fire,
	With beauty like a tightened bow, a kind
	That is not natural in an age like this,
	Being high and solitary and most stern?
	Why, what could she have done being what she is?

Was there another Troy for her to burn?

Voice 1:   Tough stuff that. Honest too.

[rising] And there was that one he called "Words":

He wondered what would have happened

if Maud *had* understood

What I have done, or what would do

In this blind bitter land.

And doesn't he go on to say:

[But] had she done so who can say

What would have shaken from the sieve?

I might have thrown poor words away

And been content to live.

But he wanted to hold on to the *poor words*, he did,

and the *life* too, *content* or not. And in the heel of the hunt

I suppose he got them both. Though 'twas a life

not of *content*, you'd say, but of tangles and complications.

And the richer for it, I reckon, given what came of it.

But beyond Miss Gonne, as I've said, there were other Muses.

Let me see now. . . .

Well, take Florence Farr. The actress with the *beautiful voice*.

He thought of her, he did, as a priestess of the White Goddess.

A *priestess*, mind. Oh don't ask—

'twas all part of the *Order of the Golden Dawn*.

Mystical stuff. The '90s were full of that sort of thing.

Seances. Madame Blavatsky. Secret Wisdom and the like.

But as for Florence:

magical studies and a beautiful voice—plus the *Bohemian* thing,

and a fine intelligence to go along with it—

well that was the right cocktail for a poet, wasn't it?

So he was enchanted by Florence, he was.

And there *she* was—ready, willing, and able . . . to be his Muse.

Able, as he said, with her lovely voice

to re-kindle the sensitivity of the soul. [sit chair right]

Florence Farr: *[putting on scarf, coming forward; crisp actorly musical voice, quite gestured]*

Yes. He wanted to hear me speak, he'd say,
in a sort of speech
that was *delighted with its own music.*
I liked that.
Although that awful man, the writer, David Lawrence
did describe my performance as *ping-wanging*!
Chacun à son goût, I say.
And (as the Christians say) "May he roast in Hell."
But Yeats, oh all sorts of high thoughts and mythologies
he connected with me.
Of course it would have been nice to be of *this* world too—
[to chair left; sit] and for a little while that did happen.
But very *discreet* we were,
even when he suggested we take a *bicycle trip* together!
To Canterbury (for Chaucer's sake, you know).
And he said we'd take some *harmless person* along with us
to keep up appearances. Oh lord! *[eyebrows raised]*
But we had lovely talks, yes. That was so . . . satisfying.
In the end, though, I called it a day with my friend.
We remained close. But as for, well, the other . . . *[eyebrows raised]*
it was just after Maud married that dreadful MacBride . . .
it was short for Yeats and me, and I suppose, yes, it *was* sweet.
He decided he'd read *sensual literature* to me—
to see what would happen. Well . . . it *did* happen.
But in time I ended it. It just wasn't . . . oh . . . you know . . .
and so I told him, *I can do that for myself.*
Eventually of course, as you may be aware,
I left that world—the theatre and so on—for Ceylon.
I was—strange occupation for a *Muse*—
headmistress of a girls' school there.
Indeed I spent the rest of my not very long life there—
in the society of *the wise,* as the wise books say we should.
And death *[tone shifts]* when it came . . . well . . for me it was no great
    shakes.
And then there was that poem in which I appear.

"All Souls' Night." When the spirits of the dead revisit.
How does it go?
On Florence Emery I call the next . . .
Oh how discreet, he calls me by my married name. Sweet.
Although I had been divorced for some time by then.
But he makes out I left London out of vanity—
when *finding the first wrinkles on a face*
Admired and beautiful. Oh, I don't know.
I don't *really* believe that was the cause.
Poetic license you see. It allows a little libel.
The rest, he got roughly right. You know it, I suppose

Voice 1:   Oh yes, I've heard it. In fact, I have it here.

Overvoice: *["WBY voice"]*
On Florence Emery I call the next,
Who finding the first wrinkles on a face
Admired and beautiful,
[Florence touches face, smiles]
And by foreknowledge of the future vexed;
Diminished beauty, multiplied commonplace,
Preferred to teach school
Away from neighbour or friend,
Among dark skins, and there
Permit foul years to wear
Hidden from eyesight to the unnoticed end.

Florence: Dear Man.
You know what follows?

Voice 1:   *Before that end much had she ravelled out*
From a discourse in figurative speech
By some learned Indian
On the soul's journey . . . .

Florence: *[breaking in, rising, to centre stage]* Yes, yes. I know . . .
[she chants the rest, quite elaborately voiced]
How it is whirled about
Wherever the orbit of the moon can reach,

Until it plunge into the sun;
And there, free and yet fast,
Being both Chance and Choice,
Forget its broken toys
And sink into its own delight at last. . . .
[ordinary voice] And sink into its own delight at last.
Yes. That is so. He . . . he *understood. [sit chair centre]*

Voice 1:   *[rising]* She's right.

Knew a thing or two about the *soul,* our Mister Yeats did.
But Florence Farr, God rest her, Muse as she was,
she took him a distance along the poet road:
she gave his poetry its own sort of *musical speech.*
And for that he loved her.
After that . . . ?
Well, in time, 'twas the turn of Iseult.
As Maud's daughter grew from child into a woman
he turned to her. Another *muse.*
Half-French, she was. Her father was *Lucien Millevoye.*
Very political and radical, he was.
Lovers he and Maud were. Oh for years.
Had a son that died. And wasn't Iseult *conceived*—
I'm serious—on the grave of her dead brother.
Strange stuff, you couldn't keep up with it.
Yeats was driven near demented when he found out.
Odd name, odd mother, odder bringing-up,
that was Iseult. Bright of course. Very.
Wilful, independent, a beauty. Like her mother.
Hard to resist I'd say . . . and while *she* thought of *him*
like a sort of *uncle,* well *he* had a few *other* feelings too.
No wonder. Flirting one minute, she'd be,
childlike pupil the next, coquette the next,
sad and frustrated the next. *[sit chair left]*
Quicksilver, that was about the size of it.

Iseult: *[putting on scarf, rising, coming forward; slightly French-inflected precise*
English, quick voice]

	Quicksilver, yes, that is true.
	Always I wanted to be moving, moving.
	Whatever I was doing, I would make it a dancing.
Voice 1:	Right. Sure wasn't his first poem for you called
	"To a Child Dancing in the Wind."
Iseult:	Exactly so. I loved that poem. I was only . . . eighteen.
	Shall I say it for you?
Voice 1:	Please do. Isn't it yours?
Iseult:	*[standing centre] Dance there upon the shore;*

What need have you to care
For wind or water's roar?
And tumble out your hair
That the salt drops have wet;
Being young you have not known
The fool's triumph, nor yet
Love lost as soon as won . . .
What need have you to dread
The monstrous crying of the wind.

Of course it is a sad poem too, is it not? *[sit chair right]*
He feels old and he feels hurt, a bit weary.
He saw me, yes, I was alone and with bare feet.
With *so much* of a young girl's . . . *vitality.*
Of course I was pert too.
When I was sixteen, imagine, I suggested that he *marry* me.
We had such good talks about things. Books and everything.
But he said no. But he *was* watching me very closely.
And when I was twenty, he decided he felt *much more* for me.

Voice 1: And didn't he give the game away by writing another poem.
"Two Years Later" he called it.
Very strong it was in praise of you. And full of advice.

Has no one said those daring
Kind eyes should be more learn'd?
Or warned you how despairing
The moths are when they are burned?

Iseult: Yes, he could not hide anything.
            Was it not his wife, Georgie, who called him *William Tell*?
            But he wanted to save me from unhappiness, yes.
            O you will take whatever's offered
            And dream that all the world's a friend,
            Suffer as your mother suffered,
            Be as broken in the end.
            It was a touching poem, and kind. But sad too.
            He saw my destiny, I suppose. Yet he loved what he saw.

Voice 1:   And wasn't it you he was thinking of
            when he said he longed for a woman
            who would make it possible
            for *our minds and bodies to find rest?*
            I know you two had powerful talks. Letters too and all.
            Body was another thing of course.
            That poem "On Woman" says it all.
            Maybe 'twas yourself he had in mind:
            Harshness of their desire
            That made them stretch and yawn . . .

Iseult: Yes, I remember.
            It made my eyes grow wide when I read it.
            Very strong it was. Strong drink.
            Pleasure that comes with sleep,
            Shudder that made them one.
            Of course it was not *only* about *me.*
            But I was part of it, so I think.

Voice 1:   And didn't he ask you to marry him?
            And what was it you said back to him?

Iseult: Oh sad to say I could only tell him—
            Ah, if only you were a young boy.
            I suppose that may have hurt him.
            And so he made a poem. It said,
            O would that we had met
            When I had my burning youth.

Age bothered him very much, you see—
and thinking of his loss of . . . *strength*.
But he was always after the unattainable *[rise, to centre]*
I suppose that is what poets do.
[Voice 1 crosses behind her, to chair right; Iseult sits chair left]
Hungering always, as he said,
for the apple on the bough most out of reach.
(Just like *Sappho*, do you believe it!)
In fact, to be quite honest, I had thought
of *keeping him about*, just like my mother did.
But I woke up then, and I saw that being a Muse
was a . . . *strangely useless thing.*
Of course I also did not want to hurt Mother by accepting him.
He wrote a great poem about it all.

Voice 1:	*[sits]* True for you. "The Wild Swans at Coole." I know it well.
Overvoice:	*["WBY voice"]*

The trees are in their autumn beauty,
The woodland paths are dry,
Under the October twilight the water
Mirrors a still sky;
Upon the brimming water among the stones
Are nine-and-fifty swans.
The nineteenth autumn has come upon me
Since I first made my count;
I saw, before I had well finished,
All suddenly mount
And scatter wheeling in great broken rings
Upon their clamorous wings.

Iseult: Yes—lovely isn't it.
I have looked upon those brilliant creatures,
And now my heart is sore.
All's changed since I, hearing at twilight,
The first time on this shore,
The bell-beat of their wings above my head,

	Trod with a lighter tread.
Voice 1:	*Unwearied still, lover by lover,*
	They paddle in the cold
	Companionable streams or climb the air;
	Their hearts have not grown old;
	Passion or conquest, wander where they will,
	Attend upon them still.
Iseult:	*But now they drift on the still water,*
	Mysterious, beautiful;
	Among what rushes will they build,
	By what lake's edge or pool
	Delight men's eyes when I awake some day
	[to Voice 1] To find they have flown away?
Voice 1:	*[to audience]* Of course—you can hear it—the poet was downcast.
	'Twas crisis time. How could it not be?
	Rejected by the mother, then by the daughter.
	Near a nervous breakdown, I'd reckon.
	Life, says he, *is a good deal at white heat.*
	Oh you could sing that, you could.
	But lord, didn't he up then and head for London,
	and ask Georgie Hyde-Lees to marry him.
Iseult:	*[to Voice 1]* But he was right to do that. Georgie was young too,
	as young I was, but so much steadier, *deeper,* no?
	And not at all just the *friendly serviceable woman*
	he thought he would find.
	[rising, to centre]
	But he said he was *tired of romance,* and ready for a *normal life.*
	[to audience] How could *he* find the *normal* life?
	Of course not! *[quick turn, back to chair]*
Voice 1:	*[rising, pacing]* Well to cut a long story short, Georgie said yes.
	And wasn't our poet embarking, though he hardly knew it,
	on another Muse journey. Very different this one.
	At first he thought he was just searching for a sort of *refuge* in marriage.
	Sure wasn't the poor man's psyche in shreds.

And marrying a fine intelligent sympathetic young woman
seemed the sensible thing to do. Though *"sensible"* is not a word
you'd likely use much of Mister Yeats.

'Twas understandable her mother was against it, and Georgie only
twenty-four.

Of course her young friends were against it too. *[sit chair right]*

George: *[putting on scarf, coming forward; English voice, cultured, lower in pitch
than Iseult; seems older; quite humorous, sane, ironic, self-aware]*

Oh indeed yes, I can hear them yet.

[puts on their shrill voices] For God's sake Georgie are you *mad*! Don't do
it! He must be *dead*!

[ordinary voice] But I went ahead with it.

And as a *choice*—for him at least—it *was* sensible.

I was young. I was capable.

And we shared a good deal—

being devoted to occult matters, things of the spirit. *[sit chair left]*

Voice 1:   *[to audience]* Right enough. Sure in his letters to her, love letters, like,
wouldn't he be saying things like:

"Did you notice that Venus conjoins Mars and trines Saturn . . .
and Venus is in mutual reception with Jupiter."

That sorta thing. Some love letter. Each to his own.

At least he had enough lover in him to add

"your body and your strong bones fill me with desire."

Strong bones indeed! Strong will too, she had, that young woman.

Not even twenty-five, but she knew her own mind.

George: And so we married. Twentieth of October 1917.

In a London registry office.

A nasty frowsy pokey little place. I hated it.

Not a very promising start, given everything.

And of course all this was happening in London
in the middle of the war.

Air raids and the like shaking the place. *Air raids*!

It was all rather strange . . . being married.

And then, right away, I could tell he was in deep gloom.

Dreadful really. For me it was a great blow, as you can imagine.

You see the poor man thought he had betrayed three people.

Maud, Iseult, and of course myself. Bloody awful.

Well I thought of leaving. Scandal or no scandal.

Voice 1: *[to audience]* Of course the poet himself was a bit off his head in all of it.

And he wrote a poem that summed it all up.

He called it "Owen Aherne and His Dancers."

Owen Aherne? Oh that was just one of his *masks*.

He had lots of them. Masks. His life was a kind of play.

He'd pretend to be someone else.

Safer that way. Wouldn't give offense like.

Though the Missus mightn't think so.

Here it is anyway:

Overvoice: *["WBY voice"]*

A strange thing surely that my Heart, when love had come unsought
Upon the Norman upland or in that poplar shade,
Should find no burden but itself and yet should be worn out.
It could not bear that burden and therefore it went mad . . .

The Heart behind its rib laughed out. "You have called me mad," it said,
"Because I made you turn away and run from that young child;
How could she mate with fifty years that was so wildly bred?
Let the cage bird and the cage bird mate and the wild bird mate in the
wild."

"You but imagine lies all day, O murderer," I replied.
"And all those lies have but one end, poor wretches to betray;
I did not find in any cage the woman at my side.
O but her heart would break to learn my thoughts are far away."

George: Yes. It *was* rather a shock to read that.

But then, eventually, I did meet Maud. And Iseult.

I mean WB had told me about them. I knew the *situation*.

But to have it spelt out like that . . . well . . . you can imagine.

But they seemed to like me. And that meant a lot you see.

Though perhaps they laughed in private.

I may have seemed a comedown from their lofty romantic heights.

Voice 1: Still, the *honeymoon*, if you don't mind my saying so—
that must have been a bit on the strange side.
The *automatic writing* and so on. How was that for yourself?

George: Well yes. The writing and all.
I began it as a bit of a scheme really: something to do
on our rather . . . *strained* . . . honeymoon.
But then I found myself quite taken over—
and something outside myself simply moved my hand.
As if I'd been hypnotised.
I realise it's hard to "get," as they say. But there you are.
The writing said Iseult (*the bird*) was all right and would be.
So WB was relieved. And we went on from there.
And a great deal about our life,
especially its *centre of intimacy*, as they say,
worked out, for a while. For him you see
it (oh you know, the *sexual*) had to be central—
and that mattered very much to me too, that *intimacy*.
And I'm glad to say we *were* compatible.
It was, well, so *good* to discover that.
The *writing* you see, the spirits, *instructed* us.
They told us not to . . . hold back . . . as it were.
I was glad of that of course, and so was he.
I became, if you like, a new *sort* of Muse.
It wasn't a case of *unrequited* love. No.
A heady mix really—sex, our love-making, these *visitations*—
all that curious knowledge. . . .
Yes, we did have a strange beginning. Beyond what he imagined.
You see he actually had had visions
of coming home after a day's writing
and finding me making *tea* . . . that sort of thing. *Christ!*
Common interests of course, yes. But *ordinary life*.
But it really wasn't ever going to be that. How could it be?
But we did share so much, despite our ages.

And it was what we shared in the area of . . .
you know . . . *mystery* . . . that really mattered.
And that not only kept us together then, but kept us happy.
Well, it all seems a long time ago now. I suppose it is.
But it happened. Yes. And I am glad. And yes, I still believe
that in the five first years or so of our marriage
some *mystical state* was leading us on.

Voice 1: And there were the poems too, weren't there?

George: *[with enthusiasm]* Oh yes. I liked many of the poems he wrote then.
That one . . . about our studies and . . . well, you'll know it yourself:

Voice 1: I do. "Solomon to Sheba":
[recites] To Solomon sang Sheba,
Planted on his knees,

George: *[enjoying poem]*
"If you had broached a matter
That might the learned please,
You had before the sun had thrown
Our shadows on the ground
Discovered that my thoughts, not it,
Are but a narrow pound."

Voice 1: *[joining her, a duet]*
Said Solomon to Sheba,
And kissed her Arab eyes,
"There's not a man or woman
Born under the skies
Dare match in learning with us two,

Both together: *[looking at each other, enjoying it]*
And all day long we have found
There's not a thing but love can make
The world a narrow pound."
[Voice 1: small laugh]

George: My *Arab eyes* . . . well I suppose maybe I had.
And there were others, other poems I mean, in the same vein.
To tell the truth I most loved his poems

that were rooted in the *personal*.
I always said there was nothing in his verse
worth preserving but the *personal*.
Much better than all that
pseudo-mystico-intellecto-nationalistico stuff.
He wrote oh . . . not *so* many *poems* for me—
but, do you know, each day of our married life, almost,
he wrote me a letter. Imagine! Yes. *Bloody exhausting*!
And then in one poem
(it was called "The Gift of Harun Al-Rashid")
he gave thanks for my being the *kind* of Muse I was.
He said I was a *gift*, that could
. . . shake more blossom from autumnal chill
Than all my bursting springtime knew.
He often thought of his age you see, of growing old.
And in that respect (others too) I was good for him.

Voice 1: And didn't that poem say too—
Were she to lose her love,
All my fine feathers would be plucked away
And I left shivering.

George: Yes, I'm glad he wrote that. Oh, he was my whole world.
And he knew he was because I told him.
And I his for a time too. And we had our two children.
Not many poets, you see, have children with their Muse.
Of course he was an odd sort of father.
He'd meet one of them—Anne or Michael—on the stairs
and look puzzled and ask "Who have we here?"
He could be vain too. Once he rinsed his hair with dye,
and for a while it was quite *blue*. He wouldn't change it.
Funny, yes, but one daren't laugh.
And of course he won the Nobel Prize. In 1923.
We ate at one in the morning when we heard of it.
Sausages in the kitchen.
Poet and his Muse celebrating, you see!

	And next day we bought new carpet for the stairs!
Voice 1:	*[to audience]* But things changed. Of course they did.

Eventually there was no more automatic writing, spirits visiting, or the like.

And *other things* too, if you know what I mean, came to a stop.

[to George] And you got unhappy, and had to struggle, you said,

to keep yourself in good spirits, to go on.

[to audience] I suppose that might have been when he began having affairs.

With younger women. Margot, Ethel, Dorothy. And Edith.

Amorous adventures, his wife called them.

George: But of course I knew all about them.

And in the end they *amused* me.

Amorous adventures indeed! In *England*?! *Muses*, you understand.

I think by then *I* had lost *my* interest in all *that* side of things.

But he was always happy to come back to Dublin.

To the comforts of home. To our house in Rathfarnham—

Riverdale, which we both loved.

As to the *amorous adventures*, well . . . I spoke to him about them.

"After your death," I said, "people will write of your love affairs.

But I shall say nothing—because I will remember how proud you were."

To tell you the truth,

I *wanted* him to have these *adventures*.

I wanted him to die *happy*, and not an invalid.

They made him happy. That was it.

I became an out-of-work Muse, I suppose.

But I still had a *wife's* work to do.

And he was very much in love with his new Muse . . .

[a bit ironic] whoever she might be! . . .

and *I* simply couldn't provide the *physical* side he desired.

Margot . . . then Ethel . . . both at the one time for a while.

Dorothy. On reflection, his whole life was,

I suppose you might say, *Muse-stricken*.

[slow] Yes, of *course* it hurt. . . . He was so . . . self-centred.

But he craved freedom, you understand. He said to me once:

"As age increases my chains, my need for freedom grows."

I couldn't cure that. Why should I try? *[rise, back to chair centre]*

Voice 1:   *[to audience]* True for her. That was it. *[rising, walking]*

And those late lovers,

maybe they were just the poet shaking his chains.

Margot, for example. Margot Ruddock.

He was in love with her. She the same. Infatuated anyway.

For a few years. Chased him to Majorca she did.

Turned up at six in the morning, waving her verses at him.

Mad she was.

Off she went when he wasn't enthusiastic enough.

Of course some of this coincided with him having an *operation*.

To restore his . . . *manly vigour* I suppose you'd call it.

Well he thought 'twas successful, though the doctors didn't.

Still he thought he'd come into what he called a *second puberty*.

Sex went hand in hand with creative power, he'd say.

And sure maybe it does. Who's to say?

Wild things he wrote in these moods. Things like

Down limb and breast or down that glimmering belly

move his mouth and sinewy tongue.

Like I say, he wasn't one to mince the words, or hold back.

And 'twas then he met Margot. Young. Twenty-seven.

More than a touch of Florence Farr in her too.

Actress. Lovely voice. Erotic possibility. Muse.

And maybe a memory of Iseult was part of it.

Margot was a dancer too, don't you see. *[sit chair left]*

Well, even great men, great *poets*, repeat themselves, I suppose.

Margot: *[putting on scarf, coming forward; another good English voice—a bit rapid-fire breathless; each sentence a distinct unit. Speaks to Voice 1, to audience. Sits, stands, walks, sits, tangles with her scarf. Serious, sometimes scatty, perplexed, emotional; sympathetic too.]*

True. But at the start he *did love* me.

He did yes. I was his Muse then. Of course I was!

"Then almost I tasted ecstasy," I said that.

And did he not say of himself in a poem
Let me be loved as though still young
Or let me fancy that it's true.
Though at first he well, he was *not* still young.
But I told him it wouldn't matter.
And it didn't. But maybe I was a *Siren* too.
Poor darling he was just a little bit transfixed.
But there was sweetness too oh there *was*.
Although he did call it *foolishness*.
Of course I did go a little overboard . . .
And a lot of quite *crazy* things happened after that.
But always I have to say my beloved Yeats darling
looked after me with his concern ill as he was himself.
His wife too, very kind. Though she *was* exasperated.
Couldn't really bear hearing my name.
I lost my poor Pekingese dog too oh well.
Then I said his poems on the wireless.
But of course his ardour cooled why shouldn't it.
I was a short-term Muse that was enough.
But I know I worried the poor darling.
Emotional excitement that was it.
He said I was *wild and unbalanced* well I *was*.
When I grew wilder than usual I was locked up.
That's all. . . .
But he gave me a lovely epitaph he did really.
He said "She was a tragic and beautiful creature."
He said that and I suppose I was.
And those lovely poems he wrote for me.
In one he said I was a *beautiful lofty thing*
in desperate music wound.
And he *did* like my poems . . . well *some* of them.
He even stole a line from me imagine! *Yeats!*
O, sea-starved hungry sea.
Yes. We were kin in some way I suppose.

He saw me. Dancing. Yes. Just listen.

[stand centre; slowed down, quiet; performing voice]

The girl goes dancing there

On the leaf-sown, new-mown, smooth

Grass plot of the garden;

Escaped from bitter youth,

Escaped out of her crowd,

Or out of her black cloud.

Ah, dancer, ah, sweet dancer!

Voice 1:   Oh yes. And how's this it goes on?

[recites]

If strange men come from the house

To lead her away, do not say

That she is happy being crazy;

Lead them gently astray;

Let her finish her dance,

Let her finish her dance.

Ah, dancer, ah, sweet dancer!

Margot: Of course it was my *crazy* side that inspired him too wasn't it?

Oh I think so . . . poets are like that.

Though he worried a bit about that too. *[sit chair right]*

He wondered poor darling,

Did words of mine put too great strain

On that woman's reeling brain?

[Rise, perplexed, holds head; different voice]

Reeling brain indeed!

[quiet] Love? Oh I don't know.

Kindness and desire yes. Pity too perhaps.

Well he was kind. And then he died. *[sit]*

I myself died young. I believe he knew I would.

[stand centre; slow, decisive]

She was a tragic and beautiful creature . . .

Thank you . . . *darling* Yeats! *[back to chair centre]*

Voice 1:   *[to audience]* Very touching yes. He stayed kind, he did.

There was that side to him too, no denying.

"All I can do for her," he said,

"is get her poems published and find her work if possible."

Of course by that time he was adoring Ethel Mannin—

another short-lived Muse was Ethel.

She *warmed* him, if you follow me,

in ways beyond worry—when *Love's anxiety,* as he said,

Made his eyes dim / Made his breath fail.

She took him beyond that heartache so she did

and into what he called *love's levelling bed.*

A touch of the Goddess in her too.

Mother Goddess, he'd say, *[hand to lips, miming] I put your hand to my lips.*

Then there was another lady writer—

Lady Dorothy Wellesley. A poet. Rich too.

They'd talk sex and poetry they would.

Of course with Dorothy being a lesbian and with her own lover, like,

the Muse thing had to take another twist. *[sit chair right]*

Dorothy: *[putting on scarf, rising from chair, voice aristocratic, a bit mannish, languid, condescending to Voice 1]*

Yes indeed! He said the *man* in me brought out the *woman* in him.

His Muse, he'd say, was connected to the woman in himself.

[stand at chair left, foot on chair, leaning]

Voice 1: *[to audience, sceptical]* And sure maybe it was. He even thought

he could share her desire, the woman's kind of desire.

Imagine. . . . Or don't.

Dorothy: And he thought well of my work. Perhaps too well.

He admired what he called its mysterious rhythm.

It was, he said, like *talking in a dream.*

My poems, you see, were a mix of passion and deep thinking.

Voice 1: He relished that. Had a great appetite for it.

Then, at that time, his own poems would have sex on the brain.

This sort of thing:

Overvoice: *["WBY voice"]*

I am in love

And that is my shame.
What hurts the soul
My soul adores,
No better than a beast
Upon all fours.

Dorothy: Oh very direct.

He was wrestling during it all, you see,

with ideas about body and soul.

Of course. . . . Body. And oh yes, Soul.

Voice 1:   He wanted to get it right and Lady Dorothy helped him there.

She too was a different sort of Muse you see.

This sort of thing he'd be at:

Bird sighs for the air
Thought for I know not where,
For the womb the seed sighs.
Now sinks the same rest
On mind, on nest,
On straining thighs.

As Iseult said, *strong drink*. Muse-concocted.

Dorothy: Yes. Lust and rage were what drove him, he said.

Voice 1:   And didn't he share all this with Lady Dorothy.

Dorothy: *[to audience]* Yes he did. He knew I understood him.

With me, you see, he could share his wildest desires and imaginings:

A coarse old man am I,
I choose the second best,
I forget it all a while
Upon a woman's breast.

I nourished that side of his genius, I suppose.

"My house is yours," I told him,

"to work in, at peace, at any time, all yours."

And he wrote me one great poem. He called it by my name.

Remembering the house and everything—

[to Voice 1] even my dog, Brutus. *[sit chair left]*

Voice 1:   *[to her]* I recall the last bit. Powerful piece of poetry it is. Listen now.

Overvoice: *["WBY voice"]*

        Climb to your chamber full of books, and wait,

        No books upon the knee, and no one there

        But a Great Dane that cannot bay the moon

        And now lies sunk in sleep.

        What climbs the stair?

        Nothing that common women ponder on

        If you are worth my hope! Neither Content

        Nor satisfied Conscience, but that great family

        Some ancient famous authors misrepresent,

        The proud Furies each with her torch on high.

Dorothy: *[rising, lifting arms]*

        The proud Furies each with her torch on high.

        Oh . . . so . . . heroic, isn't it?

        In his way he was . . . yes . . . magnificent. *[turn back, sit]*

Voice1: *[rising, to audience]* Well, as I said. A strange lot.

        I suppose he was right, though,

        when he called himself a *wild old wicked man.*

        Or he wanted to play at it anyway.

        And then? Well, in 1937 didn't he meet his last lover, and Muse.

        She took him all the way to the end.

        Edith. Edith Shackleton Heald. Famous journalist. Drama critic.

        He said she had "that kind of understanding, or sympathy, which is peace."

        About fifty she was. . . . Not a young thing.

        Though younger by years than the man himself.

        Mister Yeats was not improved in looks neither—

        with a bit of a paunch and his wild hair streeling all over the place.

        Not really romantic, you'd say. *[walk towards chair left; sit after "Edith" comes forward]*

Edith: *[putting on scarf, coming forward to chair right; educated English voice, intellectually alert and poised, at ease]* Oh he was romantic enough. And to tell the truth,

        I never minded about his fat or his hair.

        Of course he worried about the *sex* and all that.

        He said he was happy and at peace with me, but he worried.

"I worry that I may not please you," he said.

So innocent really. But indeed he did please me.

While in England, he'd move between my house and Dorothy's.

Hers much the grander of course.

I always thought he was tired after his visits to her and her great ladies.

Then he'd get happy and, well, easy with me.

He kept nothing from his wife, you know.

That was good. And she understood. She was happy to have us together.

And he wanted that, wanted her blessing, as it were.

In truth, she and I shared him in that last year or two.

A curious enough arrangement really.

He'd stay with me in one place or another,

and then George would arrive as I left.

All very civilised.

She showed goodwill towards me, and this pleased him.

[a touch humorous] I remember once she had to write to me

to know his digitalis medicine.

So she could send on some more.

"He needs," she said, "the intellectual stimulus that you and others can give.

But unfortunately he also needs that very mild heart stimulus."

She saw and understood that I kept him happy.

Of course she and I could never be friends.

It was my quiet personality and my talk he liked.

He'd visit and stay a while.

Sussex, and in winter the south of France.

He'd write to me too. Such lovely letters!

Full of desire, yes, but also with a longing for peace, stillness, sleep.

In one he said "I am happy and . . ."

Voice 1:   *[seated]* Oh I've read it, I have.

"I am happy and at peace.

What is left me in life is yours.

I long for you body and soul."

Edith: Sad really.

And yet such wonderful words to hear spoken to you, don't you think?

Of course he did not lose his humour either.

Once he said, among his endearments,
"I want to say all those foolish things
which are sometimes read out in breach of promise cases."
His letters always began and ended with *oh my dear.*
It moved my heart. Of course it did.
He was, he said, my lover and friend.
He wrote many fine poems during those two years we were
in our own way, together.
None of them to me actually.
So was I a Muse? Was desire in words only?
Since he was himself silent on that score, I shall follow suit.
But I can say that without me
those last years would have been very different.
And desire was the spur, whatever he did, we did, about it.
And *desire does not end*, he said. True.
Desire. Peace. Sleep . . . I suppose it was a question, in the end,
of Eros and Thanatos—desire and death, you see—
lying down together. At last.

Voice 1:   *[sigh of agreement]* At last. *[rise, walk]*
And then death, real death came. In France.
Dorothy was there. George was there. You were there.
All his Muses trying, as his wife said,
"to light the flame." And strange to say,
hadn't Olivia Shakespeare died only a little while before that.
Woeful saddened by that he was.
He said she'd been "a lovely young girl when they met
and when she died she was a lovely old woman." *[sit chair left]*

Edith: Yes. So terribly sad that. And then there he was himself—
so very ill, dying indeed, in France.
I barely made it, I was delayed.
They told me he was unhappy because of that.
But such were the circumstances we lived with.
Still, thankfully, I did get there in time—
with George and Dorothy, of course.
Though only his wife was with him at the moment of . . .

the moment of his passing.

Well, I suppose that was fitting.

But it was all so quick. I find it difficult to think about.

His wife suggested I share the vigil.

I watched him—alone, so—until four in the morning.

His wake, I suppose.

Then the funeral. Dorothy, George, a few others.

And then—he was gone.

And that short circumscribed life we had, *our* life, was over.

Later, his wife gave me his fountain pen.

And his Oxford dictionary.

And a manuscript of one poem, "Are You Content?"

It was, perhaps, a curious choice.

But I did give him some peace, of that I am sure.

Peace to his mind and body, yes.

And to his spirit too, I suppose.

[stand] Yes, to his spirit.

For a little while. *[start to exit, turn back]*

A muse can do that too, you see. *[back to chair centre]*

Voice 1: *[rising, to audience]*

And so, at his death, wasn't the poet

just where he wanted to be?

At the centre. Surrounded by his Muses.

They took turns holding his hand.

Only days before that he'd seemed happy.

Full of energy. Putting his affairs in order.

Even composing a last poem.

Thinking of death and after-death. Heroic.

Old bones upon the mountain shake.

He knew his time would not be long.

And he said to someone then:

"Man can embody truth but he cannot find it.

I must embody it," he said, "in the completion of my life."

And I suppose—more than anyone else you'd think of—he did.

"You can refute Hegel," he said once to his wife George,

[sit chair right, slow] "but not the saint or the song of sixpence."

George: [putting on scarf, coming forward] Whatever he meant by that, indeed!
Such things he'd say! Mad some of them! Quite mad.
[flippantly] Of course Maud was mad too.
Well, a fanatic. Next door to mad she was. [sit chair left]
And Iseult was a little mad.
And Margot was . . . well . . . crazy, wasn't she?
Even little Laura Armstrong, God help us,
had a *wild dash of half-insane genius* . . .
But of course Olivia . . . Olivia was sane, yes. Edith too, I suppose.
But then there *I* was—in touch with, yes, and taking *dictation*
from the *spirit* world. *Christ!*
One way or another, I suppose, we were all a bit mad.
WB too—mad in his own way. *Muse-mad.*
[slower] But yes, we three were there: Edith and Dorothy and I.
At the end. I suppose that *was* fitting.
But when he died (half-past-two in the afternoon it was),
I was alone with him. I could hear his breathing.
Then I heard . . . the silence. Such silence. So *deep.*
I took his signet ring, and cut a lock of hair from his forehead.
He still had a damn fine head of hair. Leonine.
And he lay there, with the suspicion of a smile—
as if he'd just had some humorous thought.
I recall the moon was in conjunction with Saturn.
I kept the ring. Hawk and butterfly. Venus and Saturn.
We had been married for twenty years. And they were over.
But no, I could not grieve too sharply or too deeply.
I missed him of course.
Such a huge, in ways a . . . monumental . . . presence.
I missed his voice. But there was . . .
a feeling of no sorrow, but of the new beginning of death.
Of course sometimes it shocks people if you say so.
But it was, over the years, what we both believed.
Death for him, you see, well, it was an adventure.
Like life.

Voice 1:   And weren't you only . . . forty-six. . . . What at all did you do then?
George: Well, I lived with his work. I was in charge of that.
           It was a post-Muse life, if you like. It lasted thirty years.
           I was always Mrs. WB. It suited me. I felt it.
           Any other questions?
           Drink? Yes. Jameson Green Stripe.
           Yes I smoked. Enjoyed it.
           Loved his poems. Didn't care for the criticism.
           Didn't understand the half of it. And WB wouldn't have either.
           There. *[rising, to audience]*
           For me too, death was a *portal*, you see, not a . . . dead end.
           We believed, you see, in reincarnation.
           One way or the other. *[back to chair centre]*
Voice 1:   And there you have it.
           Life, death, sex, love . . . and poetry, poetry, poetry.
           Well—maybe 'twas the wife who described him best—
           when she said to him once:
George: *[seated chair centre]* "What a strange, chaotic, varied,
           and completely unified person you are."
Voice 1:   And she should know, shouldn't she.
           And then, as she says, the silence.
           But just think of all those voices. All silent now.
           His wife had a strong, musical, magnetic voice.
           Then Florence and Margot were actresses, he loved their voices.
           And Maud's voice . . . well that sent a shiver
           through the Dublin theatre audience
           when she played Cathleen Ni Houlihan, early on.
           And Iseult too. And Edith. And Olivia.
           Special voices they must have been.
           "Hound Voices" he said himself.
           Listen to him now
Overvoice: *["WBY voice"]*
           The women that I picked spoke sweet and low
           And yet gave tongue. "Hound Voices" were they all.
           We picked each other from afar and knew

What hour of terror comes to test the soul,
And in that terror's name obeyed the call . . .

Voice 1:   Well anyway, their listener, their lover, their poet—
rapt and ravished as he was by all those voices—
was gone. Leaving his poems behind him.
They were sort of his own marrowbone stew, so they were.
To keep the rest of us warm.
[rising, walking] Muses . . . oh he had them alright.
And every one he called *beloved,* or *oh my dear.*
And why wouldn't he, for they were, weren't they?
Wasn't it they that spurred him into song.
But what about *Crazy Jane?* I can hear you say, or Lady Gregory itself?
Well, Lady Gregory, for all her importance to the poet,
was more a sort of mother than a muse.
But as for Crazy Jane. . . .
Well I suppose she was another kind of Muse.
Strange old countrywoman he remembered from early on—
talking her own blue streak. Another "hound voice" surely.
I reckon now Mister Yeats would like us to hear that one too.
Here she is, so, talking with the Bishop. Any bishop I suppose.
He wouldn't have been too fond of bishops now.

Crazy Jane: *[shawled, coming forward; wildish, low, whisperish country voice, eyes*
  searching audience]
I met the Bishop on the road
And much said he and I.

Voice 1:   *[hard "Bishop's" voice]*
Those breasts are flat and fallen now,
Those veins must soon be dry;
[point up, then down] Live in a heavenly mansion,
Not in some foul sty. [sit chair left]

Crazy Jane: *"Fair and foul are near of kin,*
And fair needs foul," I cried.
My friends are gone, but that's a truth
Nor grave nor bed denied,
Learned in bodily lowliness

And in the heart's pride.
  [chants]
Oh a woman can be proud and stiff
When on love intent;
But Love has pitched his mansion
In the place of excrement;
[singing, turns to Voice 1, no style]
For nothing can be sole or whole
That has not been rent.
[turns to exit, then turns back and speaks, hissing her words]
"For nothing can be sole or whole
That has not been rent." *[back to chair centre]*

Voice 1: *[rising]* And that's fair enough for a final word, I suppose . . .
Foul rag and bone shop of the heart. Aye!
Well I could go on. But time, as the poet says, *runs on.*
He's gone. They're all gone . . . Poet, Muses, Voices, the lot.
And now I have to go myself.
But his poems . . . they stay . . . alive as ever . . .
His Muses too, indeed. Their memory is, well, as the song says,
Alive, alive-o . . . [sits chair left]

Singer: *[with kerchief as at start coming forward from chair centre to chair right,*
  sit, smiling, alternating singing and humming verses of "The Salley
  Gardens" as at start]
Down by the Salley Gardens my love and I did meet;
She bid me take life easy, as the grass grows on the weirs;
But I was young and foolish, and now am full of tears.

[as she sings her last line, Voice 1, seated, and Singer say in unison last line of "Politics"]
And maybe what they say is true
Of war and war's alarms,
But Oh that I were young again
And held her in my arms.

[Blackout]

END

Curlew Theatre Company
Presents

NORAMOLLYANNALIVIALUCIA

The Muse & Mister Joyce

Performed by
Tegolin Knowland

Written and Directed by
Eamon Grennan

Noramollyannalivialucia: The Muse and Mr. Joyce

Ho! Talk save us!

—*Finnegans Wake*

Introduction

Noramollyannalivialucia: The Muse and Mr. Joyce is a one-woman "play for voices" in which Joyce's wife, Nora Barnacle, in her sixties and living, around 1950, in Zurich, is the sole character. We imagine her living at the Pensione Neptune, and she is being visited by a group of people—perhaps a "literary tour": the audience will fit nicely into this role—eager to hear something of her life with Joyce. And she is pleased to satisfy their curiosity, as she remembers the joys and difficulties of her life with her writer-husband, Jim, with whom she had two children, Giorgio and Lucia.

Interspersed among her memories are snatches from Joyce's own works. These are spoken either by Nora or by audio overvoices. So we visit with Nora as she offers a varied, surprising, lively, and above all entertaining "Portrait of the Artist's Wife as an Older Woman."

Nora Barnacle—a middle- to working-class Galway girl through and through—became Joyce's major "muse" throughout his writing life. The play gives Nora her place at center stage in her own voice—a voice that has been described as "low, resonant, strong, and rich with the tones of the Irish West." She lets us into an extraordinary life played out peripatetically both in Ireland and Europe, a fact that led to a rich collection of letters between them. Joyce and Nora met in Dublin on June 16, 1904, a day later memorialized as the day on which the action of Joyce's epic novel, *Ulysses*, takes place, a day of monumental importance to the lives of two of its main characters, Molly and Stephen, but also one that changed the history of the novel.

At this time James Joyce was a brilliant university student in Dublin and Nora a worker in Finn's Hotel. Shortly after their meeting, they left together for Trieste, where Joyce had a teaching position. Although they were a couple, they did not get married until 1931. Their daughter, Lucia, was born in Trieste in 1907. Joyce's and Nora's troubled and differing relationships with Lucia, who suffered from mental illness, variously diagnosed as a form of schizophrenia or bipolar disorder, is a major element in the play. She was committed to a mental institution near Paris in 1936 and transferred to an institution in Northampton, England, in 1951, where she lived until her death in 1982.

Joyce and Nora moved with their children to Zurich at the outbreak of World War I because Switzerland was a neutral country in the war and their safe haven. Although they left Zurich to live in France between 1920 and 1940, they often returned to Zurich, and James Joyce died there in 1941. Nora decided to remain in Zurich after his death, where she died in 1951. They are both buried there.

In researching Nora's life for the play, I consulted various biographies, most importantly that of Brenda Maddox, *Nora: A Biography of Nora Joyce* (Hamish Hamilton, 1988) and Richard Ellmann's rich biography of Joyce: *James Joyce*, new and revised (Oxford University Press, 1982). I also read the letters of Joyce (many of them, to Nora, sexually explicit) in *Letters*, edited by Stuart Gilbert and Richard Ellmann (Faber and Faber, 1957–66). I also consulted a useful review in the *New Yorker* (December 8, 2003) by Joan Acocella, of Carol Shloss's book *Lucia Joyce: To Dance in the Wake.*

The first production of the play by Curlew Theatre Company took place in Ireland at the Renvyle House Hotel in November 2014 and in the United States in April 2015 at Vassar College, Poughkeepsie, New York.

For the original production

SET

    Bright-lit stage with a park bench stage left

    Little table beside it for water jug and glass

    A small round outside-table and chair stage right. This too will have a glass of water on it.

    An open book (*Finnegans Wake*) on it, and a pair of reading glasses

    Bright outdoor summer light

CHARACTER

    Nora—Fashionable 1950s dress or skirt and top. Cardigan. Brimmed summer hat.

    She is slow, leaning on walking stick, arthritic. In her sixties.

    Her voice is Galway-soft, humorous, measured, shrewd, straightforward.

    She's capable of shifts of mood—humorous to melancholy—as her memories come to her. She takes life as is. She's resilient.

    She is at ease with the audience, addressing them directly, as if they are visiting her (maybe a group of curious "literary" people?)—where she lives at the Pensione Neptune in Zurich.

    Circumscribed though she is, being seated almost throughout, her small movements while seated are often animated, always expressive.

    The time is around 1950.

Voice off: *[Italian] Signora Joyce! I visitatori son' arrivati.* Nora, your visitors . . . they are here!

    [song ("The Salley Gardens," John McCormack) playing as Nora walks on]

    [Nora enters, walking through audience and talking]

Nora: *[song continuing to a fade as she speaks]* Oh my God there's that song! *The Salley Gardens!*

    [hums along with the song, sings a snatch, song fades]

    Yeats wrote it, you know. But Jim loved it.

He'd sing it to me when we were first walking out.
Sang it in a concert with John McCormack once.
Lovely voice he had, Jim had.
Listen to what was in the paper:

Overvoice: *[posh] Mr. Joyce possesses a light tenor voice,*
which he is inclined to force on the high notes
but sings with artistic emotionalism.
One of his selections "Down by the Salley Gardens"
suited his method best . . .

Nora: *Artistic emotionalism,* no less!
Sometimes I'd say to him, "Jim," I'd say,
"you should have stuck to the singing
and given up the old writing."
Even when he got famous I'd say it to him.
Just, you know, to get a rise out of him.
He'd only laugh. *Give up the writing?!*
Sure the sun would as soon give up rising in the morning
as James Joyce would give up the writing.
Married to it, he was. Though I say so myself.
There . . . I'm settled.
By the way you're very good to sit with me—
for a little bit. I don't get around much, you see.
The arthritis . . .
This is my favourite bench. Times I come out here . . .
and just sit and look and . . . think . . .
Oh about this that and t'other, as we'd say at home.
[pause]
But that was a grand song. Still is. Yeats, aye.
Man of many Muses *he* was, wasn't he?
Maud Gonne, yes, oh and a few others. . . . Muse-mad!
But Jim? *Muses?* God no. He wasn't the type.
Not like Yeats anyway. . . .
Of course when he was a young fellow in school
he'd get a crush on a girl all right—
and that might stir him to writing a poem.

Like that girl on the strand young Stephen sees
in *Portrait of the Artist as a Young Man.*
You know the bit I mean? *[listens]*

Overvoice: *[male, Irish, but not "Oirish". . . a narrator]*
A girl stood before him in midstream, alone and still,
gazing out to sea. She seemed like one
whom magic had changed
into the likeness of a strange and beautiful seabird . . .
Her thighs, fuller and softhued as ivory,
were bared almost to the hips,
where the white fringe of her drawers
were like featherings of soft white down. . . .
She was alone and still, gazing out to sea—
and when she felt his presence and the worship of his eyes
her eyes turned to him in quiet sufferance of his gaze,
without shame or wantonness.
Long, long she suffered his gaze
and then quietly withdrew her eyes from his
and bent them towards the stream,
gently stirring the water hither and thither. . . .
—Heavenly God! cried Stephen's soul,
in an outburst of profane joy . . .

Nora: That one seems a sort of Muse all right.
The way a poet might have one. An inspiration like.
Of course he was young then.
Later . . . things got more . . . complicated . . .
And the Muse thing . . . it did too.
Well, there was myself, to start with. *[small laugh; a bit ironic]*
And there were the ones he made up.
Out of lots of women, yours truly included.
Molly Bloom, yes. Then Anna Livia—
wife and mother she was, and Dublin's River Liffey too.
Think of that!
And then our own daughter, poor Lucia.
When he was writing *Finnegans Wake*

his head was full of Lucia—
her dancing and her drawing and her ways of talking—
and her . . . sickness . . . and all.
The poor thing . . . mad in the end . . . *[pause]*
In a Home she is now . . . in England . . .
I . . . I never see her. . . . *[pause]*
Oh *[brighter]* I was in those books too—*Ulysses, Finnegans Wake.*
In Molly, in Anna Livia.
He'd put bits of me into them, you see—
things I might say or do. . . .
Whenever it concerned a woman
I was never very far from his mind.
And he was a sort of a magpie—
making his books from all sorts of scraps.
Sure wasn't his head full of rubbish he'd pick up:
"Broken matches," he'd say, "bits of glass."
And God knows, and I know, bits of Nora! *[laughs]*
And he'd be scribbling it all down
in those little wee notebooks he had,
or on scraps of wine bills, backs of envelopes, torn cigarette packets.
Oh many's the time I'd have to say to him:
"Will you give over your scribbling now Jim
and come and have your dinner."
But his poems from early on now . . .
There was a Muse in them all right.
Of course she was mostly a sort of *ideal,*
if you know what I mean. Not *real.* No.
Though some of them he wrote just for me . . . he did, yes. *[pleased]*
Lovely simple poems they were, nearly songs.
I used learn them by heart. Listen to this one: *[recites with eyes closed]*

> *I would in that sweet bosom be*
> *(O sweet it is and fair it is!)*
> *Where no rude wind might visit me.*
> *Because of sad austerities*
> *I would in that sweet bosom be.*

I would be ever in that heart
(O soft I knock and soft entreat her!)
Where only peace might be my part.
Austerities were all the sweeter
So I were ever in that heart.

Lovely isn't it? And he *was* "ever in that heart."

Well . . . *nearly* always.

As for austerities . . . in time we had our share of them.

Being penniless, hungry sometimes,

and poor Lucia, of course . . . and his drinking and all.

His brother Stannie was a help to us those times.

Very devoted to Jim he was. And to me too.

Though I have to say Jim didn't treat him so well.

"A brother is as easily forgotten," says he,

"as an umbrella." . . . Cruel . . .

He could be that too, you see—self-centred.

Oh yes . . . yes indeed . . .

But some of the places we had to stay those times—

flats, like . . . they weren't fit to wash a rat in.

Of course, those poems of his were very early on.

In Dublin in June of nineteen o four that was.

When we met first. I was working in Finn's Hotel then.

And we walked out together. And—as they say—

fell in love. Almost on the instant. Yes. Odd . . .

So different we were, him being so intelligent

and well-educated and all.

And me, well, I wasn't all of that.

But I wasn't just a country gom, no!

I knew a bit of the world.

Though the things *he* knew . . . and had *done,*

God, they frightened me sometimes. . . .

And they weren't good for him either.

Anyway, love it was . . .

and that was the be-all and end-all of it.

We'd write letters every day. We would.

My precious darling, I called him,
and he called me his *dearest.*
And he said my soul—yes, my *soul!*—
Was "the most beautiful and simple soul in the world."

Overvoice: *[Dublin middle-class; young] When I am with you*
I lose my contemptuous and suspicious nature.
I wish I felt your head over my shoulder now.
Will you write something to me?

Nora: Well of course I wrote back to him so.

Overvoice: *[Nora young, country, all in a rush] Dear Jim . . . I feel so tired tonight I can't*
say much many thanks for your kind letter when the postman came I ran off
to one of the bedrooms to read your letter it is now half past eleven and I can
hardly keep my eyes open and I am delighted to sleep the night away when I
can be thinking of you so much when I awake in the morning I will think of
nothing but you. . . .

Nora: Oh yes—that was how I wrote my letters.
Just rushed off. Why bother with commas and full stops?
I wrote what I felt and out it came.
He remembered that too—when it came to Molly Bloom—didn't he?
Well anyway, one thing led to another . . .
and Jim . . . he wanted to leave Ireland, you see . . .
for he hated what it was like then,
the meanness, the narrowmindedness, the hypocrisy,
and the Church and all.
And so 'twasn't long after . . . we set off together.
In October it was. Nineteen o four. Eloped I suppose.
On the boat from Dublin's North Wall!
God what was I thinking!
Not thinking at all I suppose . . . just saying *Yes!*
when he asked me to go with him.
Off we went so. Emigrants.
Only for us 'twas an *adventure* too.
We had breakfast in London, I remember, in the train station.
An *English Breakfast* as they say.
"English Breakfast!" says Jim:
"Danish bacon, Irish eggs, American sugar, French milk,

Canadian marmalade, Scotch porridge, New Zealand butter.
Here's your *'English Breakfast!'"* says he.
Oh he was a caution, and he missed nothing.
Of course he wasn't over-fond of the English either.
Then it was on to the Continent with us.
Paris, Trieste, Rome, Zurich. Like gipsies.
He left me sitting once that time, waiting for him in a park . . .
where was it? . . . In Paris maybe, near the station,
or was it by the harbour in Trieste?
Sitting solitary on a bench . . . like this one.
God I felt so . . . alone . . .
strange-looking people, foreign languages, different clothes . . .
and me in the frock I wore and I leaving Dublin.
Twenty I was, and him all of twenty-two.
Think of it. And not even married. Oh no!
I was a while waiting for that indeed. . . . .
Twenty-seven years if you want the truth of it—
till we got to be legally Mr. and Mrs. James Joyce.
He wasn't entirely for it even then. Oh he had his reasons.
But that's another story.
Though we always said we were married. *[pause]*
Where was I? Muses. . . .
Well, I was one I suppose . . . in a sort of a way.
Jim, you see, would put things I told him
into the stories he'd be writing.
You'd tell him something and it'd stick.
You'd never be safe telling him anything. *[humorous]*
One minute it's yours, and the next . . .
there it is in a *story* he's written.
Like my boyfriend when I was young in Galway—
and who died—Sonny Bodkin that was . . .
I remember telling Jim that—*The Lass of Aughrim*, aye. *[strains of "*Lass
of Aughrim," *just melody. Fading. She goes dreamily into her memory—
humming for a beat.]*

Overvoice: *[her younger self, light, country, with a bit of reverb, slow]*

"I am thinking about someone long ago
who used to sing that song, the Lass of Aughrim . . .
a young boy I used to know, . . .
He used to sing that song. . . . He was very delicate . . .
Such eyes as he had: big, dark eyes!
I used to go out walking with him
when I was in Galway.
He died when he was seventeen.
. . . I think . . . he . . . died for me. . . .
It was about the beginning of the winter
when I was going to leave Galway
and come up to Dublin. And he was ill at the time
and wouldn't be let out. He was in decline,
or something like that. I never knew rightly.
Poor fellow. He was very fond of me
and he was such a gentle boy. . . . "

Nora: *[in present voice: brisker, leaning forward, confiding in audience]*
We used to go out together, walking, you know,
the way they do in the country.
When it came time for me to leave
he was much worse and I wouldn't be let see him
so I wrote him a letter.
Then the night before I left,
I was in my grandmother's house in Nuns' Island, packing up,
and I heard gravel thrown up against the window.
So I slipped out into the back garden . . .
and there was the poor fellow out there shivering.
I implored him to go home at once
and told him he would get his death in the rain.
But he said he did not want to live.
I can see his eyes as well as well!
He was standing at the end of the wall
where there was a tree.
In the end he went home as I asked him—
but when I was only a week in Dublin

he died . . . and he was buried in Oughterard
where his people came from. Oh,
the day I heard that, that he was dead! . . .

Overvoice: *[male, soft, reciting] Rain on Rahoon falls softly, softly falling,*
        Where her dark lover lies.
        Sad is his voice that calls her, sadly calling,
        At grey moonrise.

Nora: *[practical, matter-of-fact]* Anyway, that was my story he used there.
I'd be telling him all sorts of things you see—
about my life in Galway and beyond in the country.
And sure didn't he call me
his *beautiful wild flower of the hedges,*
his *dark-blue rain-drenched flower,*
his *little strange-eyed Ireland.*
I suppose that does sound like I *was* his Muse all right.
He had this idea, you see, I was, well . . . everything.

Overvoice: *[male, deep] She is the earth, dark, formless, mother.*

Nora: Of course he called me a lot of other things too.
My Godalmighty, didn't he connect me to Mary Magdalen!
Oh I couldn't keep up with him! You'd think I was an actress—
the parts he imagined for me!
[confiding whisper to audience]
A streetwalker one minute, a Madonna the next.
O Maria Santissima! . . .
Of course I did act once myself.
In that play by Synge that Jim liked—
Riders to the Sea. I was Cathleen.
Jim persuaded me. Here in Zurich that was . . .
near thirty years ago, my God!
And didn't he train the other actors—English they were—
to follow my accent
and get the sound of the Aran Islands from it.
Afterwards they said I was brilliant . . .
that I had the perfect brogue. So there.
I still remember some of it.

That little bit about the mother at the end:
[in stylized, low, country voice, very rhythmic] It's getting old she is, and
   broken
an old woman will soon be tired with anything she will do,
and isn't it nine days herself is after crying and keening,
and making great sorrow in the house.
Oh yes . . . that was it.
[pause] But Muses now. . . .
Well, like I was saying . . .
aside from myself . . . *[little pause]*
there was Molly Bloom.
[many shifts of tone in this speech]
Made up as she was, she *was* a sort of Muse too.
She was sort of like a . . . an *Everywoman,*
if you know what I mean.
And once he created her in his mind, like,
she sort of inspired him.
He'd say, just to annoy me, *she was his type*!
Oh I often said I didn't like her.
That old book of his, I called it, *with a big fat*
horrible married woman as the heroine.
She wasn't me, no. She was much fatter for one thing—
and I had women friends like she didn't,
and I wasn't jumping in and out of bed
with other men or even thinking about it—
the way she seems to spend her time doing.
But to tell you the truth and aside from all that,
there's plenty of myself in her too . . .
though mind you I'd not boast of that—
fat and unfaithful as she is, and full of herself.
But she had good sense too, at times. I'll say that for her.
Like . . . very practical about, you know, sex and all.
She didn't make too much of it.
If thats all the harm ever we did in this vale of tears, says she,
God knows its not much doesnt everybody only they hide it

and what else were we given all those desires for Id like to know . . .
And then there's that bit she says about men and women
and war and all —oh Jim could stick up for the women too—
I dont care what anybody says itd be much better for the world
to be run by the women in it, says she,
you wouldnt see women going and killing one another
and slaughtering . . .
Oh I agree I agree! and good for her!
But of course she was a mixed bag too—
like the rest of us I suppose.
And like me she loved opera, being a singer and all.
And she was a bit religious into the bargain . . . in spite of all.
I liked how she seemed so . . . *open* . . . to . . . well . . . everything. . . .

Overvoice: *[deep-voiced "Molly"—middle-class Dublinish—a singer, breathy; Nora closes*
            eyes listening]
            I love flowers Id love to have the whole place
            swimming in roses
            God of heaven theres nothing like nature
            the wild mountains and then the sea and the waves rushing
            then the beautiful country with fields of oats and wheat
            and all kinds of things
            and all the fine cattle going about
            thatd do your heart good to see
            rivers and lakes and flowers
            and all sorts of shapes and smells and colours
            springing up even out of the ditches
            primroses and violets
            nature it is . . .

Nora: And doesn't she go on then to say something
            I think I may have said to Jim myself one time:
            [continues in her own voice, brisk, pragmatic] as for them saying there's no
                God, says she,
            I wouldn't give a snap of my two fingers
            for all their learning
            why don't they go and create something . . .

atheists or whatever they call themselves
go and wash the cobbles off themselves first
then they go howling for the priest and they dying
and why why because theyre afraid of hell
on account of their bad conscience ah yes I know them well
who was the first person in the universe
before there was anybody that made it all who
ah that they dont know neither do I so there . . .

Ah no, you'd have to like her for that wouldn't you?
Because that's what I'd be feeling too. . . .
Of course Jim never prayed to God or anything, no.
We'd have the arguments but there was no shifting him.
He'd cross the street to avoid a nun he would.
Sure didn't he say 'twas a nun invented barbed wire?
I'd say a Hail Mary in thunder while he'd just shiver.
Black magic! That's all Irish Catholicism was, he'd say,
nothing but black magic.
And here I am now, saying my rosary at bedtime.
And going to Mass when I can—in St. Anthony's beyond there.
But as for Molly . . . well . . . I did like her last bit all right—
And I felt there was something of myself in that too, God knows,
the way she remembers the loving and all.
Memory, that's it. First love . . . there's nothing like it.
Like myself and Sonny Bodkin. . . .
And Molly recalls so much then . . .
the jumble of it and she falling asleep—
the way I sometimes do the same myself—
and she thinking all sorts of things,
Gibraltar and all where she'd been a girl . . .
the way I was a girl in Galway—going about
among its narrow streets and along the bay . . .

Overvoice: *["Molly"] The sun shines for you he said*
              the day we were lying among the rhododendrons
              on Howth Head . . . the day I got him to propose to me yes . . .
              he said I was a flower of the mountain yes . . .

so we are flowers all a womans body yes . . .

and I gave him all the pleasure I could

leading him on till he asked me to say yes . . .

and I was thinking of so many things he didnt know of . . .

the Spanish girls laughing in their shawls . . .

and the Greeks and the Jews and the Arabs

and the devil knows who else from all the ends of Europe . . .

and the wineshops half open at night . . .

and O that awful deepdown torrent O

and the sea the sea crimson sometimes like fire

and the glorious sunsets and the fig trees

in the Alameda Gardens yes

and all the queer little streets

and pink and blue and yellow houses . . .

and Gibralter as a girl where I was a Flower of the mountain yes . . .

and how he kissed me under the Moorish wall . . .

Nora: Oh that's her alright. . . . And doesn't she go on then . . .

[remembering, reciting it rhythmically, eyes closed] and I thought as well him as another, says she,

and then I asked him with my eyes to ask again yes

and he asked me would I yes to say yes my mountain flower

and first I put my arms around him yes

and drew him down to me

so he could feel my breasts all perfume yes

and his heart was going like mad

and yes I said yes I will Yes.

[in her ordinary voice] Like a poem that is.

And of course that could have been Jim and myself, yes,

in our first days of walking out that summer—

In nineteen o four. Oh yes . . .

the kissing and the thinking and all of that.

But as for Molly . . . . Well . . .

she's full of life and colour all right, and contradictions—

I'll say that for her—and spirit . . .

and her own class of humour that was a bit like I had myself—

practical like, seeing the odd side of things—
and straightforward about sex and all,
not beating about the bush or anything.
And even that song she sang—"Love's Old Sweet Song"—
Jim liked to hear me sing that too. *[she sings a verse, savouring it] Love's old
sweet song* . . .
She loved life and I did too, Jim knew that.
Ordinary life. Isn't that what he put into her?
And wasn't that what he wanted in me too?
"Nora," he'd say, "you're ordinary . . . . *extra* ordinary . . . *Extraordinary!*"
[laughs]
Though I must say what sometimes went between us
when we were young wasn't all that ordinary. No.
Those letters we wrote when we were separated
back in . . . when was it? . . . 1909 or thereabouts . . .
I was alone in Trieste. He'd gone to Dublin on his own
with our Giorgio—seeing a publisher about *Dubliners* . . .
and visiting with his father and all.
And wasn't he driven near demented by jealousy—
when he heard bad things about me . . . with men like.
Just Dublin gossip—you know the Irish way of it.
But it maddened Jim all right, and I could do nothing.
So then the letters were our way of patching things up.
We were needing one another, and we put it all in the letters.
Oh I blush now to think all the things we said—
All those four-letter words . . . *arse* and . . . well . . . you know . . .
and about our bodies and all,
the things we'd do with one another.
Two weeks of it . . . back and forth, back and forth.
I gave as good as I got—or as bad, I suppose. *[laughs]*
Oh I'll not burn your ears with the like.
But God in heaven and may God forgive us
they were . . . well . . . *filthy* I suppose.
But I mean . . . 'twas only natural wasn't it?
We were young and we had bodies hadn't we?

And apart for the first time in five years. . . .

He was very . . . *inventive,* Jim was. And I was too.

And I told him he could write what he liked.

Well that opened a door it did, in the both of us.

"Nora, my faithful darling," he'd say one minute,

"my sweet-eyed blackguard schoolgirl . . . ,

I feel I would like to be flogged by you" . . .

But next thing then—"you are always my beautiful wild flower

of the hedges, my dark-blue rain-drenched flower."

Very . . . *vivid* we were. Lord! And *needy* too. . . .

That's, now, a side of the Muse you mightn't think of . . . *[laughs, then*
    pause]

But Jim was always sickened, you see, by what he called

the *lying drivel about pure men and pure women*

and spiritual love and love forever.

And why wouldn't he be?

For he didn't like, he said,

the big words that make us so unhappy.

Though he did say too . . . that . . . our sex

was *a kind of sacrament.* Well I suppose it was.

Though I remember there were times

he wanted me to go with other men.

Not all the way mind, but, you know, close.

So he'd have something to write about.

Can you credit that? And he as jealous as the Devil.

I didn't of course. 'Twould have killed him.

Though I did have my . . . well . . . admirers.

Nothing serious mind. Though nice in its way.

Nice to hear a man tell you the sun rises for you,

as one did: *Il sole si'e levato per Lei, Nora.*

Prezioso that was. In Trieste.

Yes. I remember that all right.

And then he did stray a bit himself, Jim did.

A couple of flirtations and fantasies anyway.

Young lady students he'd have and the like.

Writing to them too in that way of his.
Didn't last long any of it.
He knew what was good for him, you see. *Me.*
And in the end we managed so we did.
Took things as they came. We had to.
Stayed together till the end. Love that was.
And of course my name wasn't Barnacle for nothing.

PAUSE

But Jim could be, you know, very *direct* . . .
about things about the body, body things.
Frilly knickers he loved too. Drawers
with crimson bows. Not a word of a lie.
Mother of God, he'd want me to be
all frills and lace and the like . . . and ribbons.
Mad too he'd be, saying all sorts of things
to make you laugh.
Sure didn't he say once (you'll excuse me now,
or cover your ears if you like)
he could tell the *sound of my fart*
in a roomful of farting women. *[laughs]*
That doesn't sound much like a Muse now, does it?
[sings] I hear you . . . calling . . . me . . . !
All sorts of mad things he'd be saying in those letters.
My little strange-eyed Ireland he called me.
But then he'd say Ireland was my *native dunghill,*
with its *tricolour of peas, rice, and eggyolk.* . . .
Oh he had as many twists and turns to him
as an old boreen out the back of beyond.
But in truth he was mostly happy if I was happy.
And god love him how attentive he was
when I was sick in hospital one time.
Slept beside me in the next room he did—
I couldn't stop him.

He'd go off then in the daylight for cigarettes . . .
and he'd sit in an empty church so he would.
I suppose he was sort of praying . . .
For me to be cured like.
Myself sometimes, I'd pray for him.
When he'd have a pain or anything.
O my God take away Jim's pain, I'd pray.
He'd only laugh, and say his own prayer went like this:
[mimics him] O Vague Something Behind Everything! . . .
Go on, I'd say, you can do better than that!

PAUSE

Of course once he'd finished with *Ulysses*
he didn't waste much time getting started on another book.
And sweet Mother of May! what a book! *Finnegans Wake*!
He said he made *Ulysses* out of next to nothing.
But this one he said he made . . . out of nothing at all.
Like God made the world, says he.
Nothing, is it? And everything too.
The whole history of the world indeed.
And more. More. Just like one big huge world-dump!
And word dump too.
For he rightly banjaxed the English language with that one.
Seventeen or eighteen years it took.
Jesus Mary and Joseph it near killed him,
not to mention the rest of us—myself and Giorgio and Lucia.
"If only I had married a ragpicker or a farmer,"
I'd say, "or anything but a writer."
"For the love of Mike," I said when I saw a bit of it,
"why don't you write sensible books people can understand
and give up that chop suey you're writing?"
In the end, though, I did think it was . . . well . . . great.
People would be blathering on about *Ulysses*—
"What's all this about *Ulysses*," I'd say,

"*Finnegans Wake*, that's the important book."
Anna Livia Plurabelle . . . he put bits of me in *her* all right.
I once heard him reading from it—
the part about the washerwomen and all—
and I thought the music of it was lovely.
"If you have trouble understanding it," Jim'd say,
"just read a passage aloud." And it does help, I swear.

Overvoice: *[recording of James Joyce reading]:*

Well, you know or don't you kennet or haven't I told you
every telling has a taling and that's the he and the she of it.
Look, look, the dusk is growing!
My branches lofty are taking root.
O, my back, my back, my bach!
I'd want to go to Aches-les-Pains. Pingpong!
There's the Belle for Sexaloitez! And Concepta de Send-us-pray!
Pang! Wring out the clothes! Wring in the dew!
Will we spread them here now? Ay, we will. Flip!
Spread on your bank and I'll spread mine on mine. Flep!
It's what I'm doing. Spread! It's churning chill. Der went is rising.
I'll lay a few stones on the hostel sheets.
A man and his bride embraced between them.
Else I'd have sprinkled and folded them only.
And I'll tie my butcher's apron here. It's suety yet . . .

Nora: Odd, yes, but still you can sort of get it can't you?
And you know, I think he popped a hint of me in there too.
Though I wasn't ever a washerwoman no—
except for that once I took in washing . . .
after our Giorgio was born. Oh I did! Merciful hour!
Muse and all, there I was . . . taking in washing!
Of course a book like that
couldn't have a simple Muse now could it?
And given the tricks he was up to, indeed,
maybe the language itself was his Muse then too. . . .
English to start with, that was natural—
but *Dio mio*! the one he made up himself out of it!

Twist your tongue and bamboozle your brains, it would.

Times I'd say to him,

"Jim," I'd say, "I think that's your own class of revenge—

on the English like—for that being their language."

For didn't he say himself once:

| Overvoice: | *[male]* "My soul frets in the shadow of their language . . ." |
| Nora: | That's right. Revenge. |

The English took away our language you see,

except in parts of Connemara and the west.

Well you all know that. So he couldn't write in Irish.

So maybe he was attacking English itself—

if you know what I mean. Of course,

it's hard to think of my husband as a . . . a patriot,

or any class of nationalist even—but there you are. . . .

Well anyway—Anna Livia . . .

[reads in book, telling a story at first, then more lyrical; speedy enough, plenty
   of variety, to decisive finish]

Ah, but she was the queer old sekowsha anyhow,

Anna Livia, trinkettoes!

And sure he was the quare old buntz too,

Dear Dirty Dumpling, . . .

Gammer and gaffer we're all their gangsters . . . .

My sights are swimming thicker on me

by the shadows to this place. . . .

Can't hear with the waters of.

The chittering waters of.

Flittering bats, fieldmice bawk talk . . . .

Can't hear with bawk of bats,

all thim liffeying waters of.

Ho, talk save us!

My foos won't moos.

I feel as old as yonder elm. . . .

Dark hawks hear us. Night! Night!

I feel as heavy as yonder stone. . . .

Night now! . . . Night night!

Tellmetale of stem or stone.
Beside the rivering waters of,
hitherandthithering waters of.
Night! . . .

[voice shifting to normal, serious] Of course, truth to tell . . . whatever about me,
'twas poor Lucia he mostly had in mind
and he writing that book. . . .
She was, as Professor Jung said once—
(Carl Jung himself that was, yes)—
she was his *anima inspiratrix*—his Muse, right—
with her weird ways of saying things and all.
And all the time Jim lamenting and lamenting
and never giving up thinking she'd get better.
He blamed himself, you see.

Overvoice: *[male]* "Whatever spark or gift I possess,
has been transmitted to Lucia
and it has kindled a fire in her brain."

Nora: *[her voice in this long speech shifts between modes]* But she would do crazy things.
Once she went to Ireland, to relations in Bray,
and didn't she start a fire in her room . . .
and she slept rough in Dublin, didn't eat, talked suicide . . .
frightened the life out of the relations.
Such a weight on us the poor thing was.
So many doctors, all of little use. No cure.
I find it hard even to think of it. . . . *[pause]*
She flung a chair at me once, right at my head.
And God knows I was fearful always after that.
That was sad. About twenty-five she was then. A young woman.
And you can't imagine the terrible letters
she wrote to me from that time in Ireland. . . .
It would take me days to get over the hurt of them.
And oh the scenes, such scenes . . .
The howling out of her once at the train station in Paris,
so we'd all not leave for London. So we didn't.
Even worse, wasn't she up to all sorts of tricks—

sex I mean—dreadful. I'm no prude, as you know,
but they'd put the heart across me.
She said a load of young men had seduced her . . .
But of course a lot was in her imagining only.
How could she help it? She couldn't, that was it.
Even Sam, poor Sam Beckett—she loved him . . .
and hoped for more. But God knows
that was never to be a match made in heaven, how could it be?
For he had his own troubles, hadn't he?
But that hurt her so it did, no doubt about it. Poor thing—
and the engagement with that Alex Ponisovsky
that he broke off. A disaster pure and simple!
She was scarcely made for this world at all.
She thought I didn't approve of her. . .
But I couldn't really understand her. . . .
And jealous, oh don't . . . Of me, of Jim.
"C'est moi qui est l'artiste," she'd shout at him.
Doctors, psychiatrists, the lot—we had them.
Even Professor Jung. She didn't like him.
"A big fat materialistic Swiss man," she called him,
"trying to get hold of my soul!"
Jim was drinking his way through it all too.
Awful. He'd be carried home. It near broke us up.
I'd get depressed myself, of course I would, and angry too—
his drinking—he'd get absolutely blithered—
and his silences, endless silences. Days on end
and he'd not toss a word my way, not a word.
It was a hard time. And every so often
I'd just have to explode a bit at him—
"Why don't you go and drown yourself," I said once—
we were living in Paris that time—
"go and drown yourself in the bloody Seine!"
Of course he didn't and we made up after.
But I suppose his heart was breaking for the child—
for his *rainbow girl* as he called her.

In the end we had to send for the straitjacket
and get her into an Institution. And that was that.
1936 that was, how could I forget? . . . and I've not seen her since.
That crucified my heart . . . but what could we do?
Everyone thought it for the better.
Jim would visit every Sunday.
Teaching her Latin, and bringing her
those little Italian cakes, the dolci, she liked.
Sometimes they'd sing and play together.
And dance, yes, oh all wild and abandoned they'd be then.
But he'd come home and just weep and weep and weep.
God of Heaven it brings tears to my eyes now
just thinking of it . . . and to think of how she'd
imitate Charlie Chaplin—his funny walk and cane,
his moustache, his bowler hat—and make us all laugh.
And I can scarcely bear to think at all
of the wee lullaby Jim'd sing to her when she was little:
[sings lullaby] C'era una volta
    Una bella bambina
    Che si chiamava
    Lucia. . . .
    Dormiva durante il giorno
    Dormiva durante la notte . . .
[stops, small silent weeping; pause]
But there he was [back to normal] . . . writing Finnegans Wake.
And his poor eyes playing hell with him.
Times he had to write with a coloured crayon
on a great big sheet of white paper.
How he did it only God knows.
All the operations! But the eyes only got worse.
Near blind he was in the end.
But nothing would stop him, he was that driven. . . .
And all the ways he got Lucia into it . . .
She was a dancer you see.
And very good she was too. Modern dance.

Recitals. In Paris even. They loved her,
Bravo Irlandaise! they shouted at her one time.
Poor Jim was so pleased by that.
But in the end she gave that up too.
But 'twas a bond between them.
For what was *he* at, he'd say,
only the music and the dance of words—a *sounddance,* he'd say . . .
In the end it was her strangeness that drove him, you see.

Overvoice: *[male]* "Everybody else thinks she's crazy,
but her mind is as clear and unsparing as the lightning.
She's a fantastic being,
speaking a curious abbreviated language of her own.
I understand it, or most of it . . ."

Nora: And maybe he did.
But into *Finnegans Wake* she went anyway.
He wasted nothing, you see.
Everything was grist to that mill of his.
One bit especially she was in—
that one about the young girl, Nuvoletta.
He wrote it not long after she gave up the dancing.
Oh a month of tears we had that time. . . .
And once I heard her say it out loud—
in that funny mixed accent of hers:
a *pasticcia* of Italian, I'd call it, with a *soupçon* of French,
a dollop of German and a chopped sausage of Triestino.
But she had a nice voice too . . .
a friend of ours said
"'twas like it bubbled up from a deep country well."

Overvoice: *[Lucia; low, European-inflected; storytelling, a child's story]*
Nuvoletta in her nightdress, spun of sixteen shimmers,
was looking down on them, leaning over the bannistars
and listening all she childishly could. . . .
She was alone.
All her nubied companions
were asleeping with the squirrels. . . .

Nuvoletta listened as she reflected herself,
though the heavenly one with his constellatria
and his emanations stood between,
and she tried all she tried to make the Mookse
look up at her . . . and to make the Gripes hear
how coy she could be . . .
She tried all the winsome wonsome ways
her four winds had taught her . . .
and she smiled over herself
like the beauty of the image of the pose of the daughter
of the queen of the Emperour of Irelande . . .
But sweet madonine, she might fair as well have carried
her daisy's worth to Florida . . . .

Nora: Oh *sweet madonine* indeed!
I can hear her now, singing it out of her.
Here's how it goes on:
[recites by heart in a speedy storytelling manner, with expression]
Then Nuvoletta reflected for the last time
in her little long life and she made up
all her myriads of drifting minds in one.
She cancelled all her engauzements.
She climbed over the bannistars;
she gave a childy cloudy cry: Nuée! Nuée!
A lightdress fluttered. She was gone.
And into the river that had been a stream
(for a thousand of tears had gone eon her
and come on her and she was stout
and stuck on dancing and her muddied name
was Missisliffi) there fell a tear a singult tear
the loveliest of all tears . . . for it was a leap tear.
But the river tripped on her by and by
lapping as though her heart was brook:
Why, why, why! Weh, O weh!
I'se so silly to be flowing but I no canna stay!
Oh the poor child, our misfortunate Nuvoletta.

	Our little tear-filled cloud, Lucia.
	Lord above, she was so close to him.
	Like that time she wrote to him:

Overvoice: *[Lucia] Father if ever I take a fancy to anybody*
I swear to you on the head of Jesus
it will not be because I am not fond of you.
Do not forget that. . . .
Who knows what Fate has in store for us?
But if ever I should go away, it would be
to a country which belongs in a way to you,
isn't that true father?

Nora: That broke my heart, the innocence of it.
Of course some say I abandoned her.
It wasn't the way I felt. No.
But it was all so hard. I think back
and wonder could I have done . . . other than I did.
But then I mind the time she was his *rainbow girl* . . .
just a whisk brisk sly spry spink spank sprint of a thing . . .
and not the way she got to be—
the way she broke her own heart and all our hearts too,
the creature. . . . And I swear to God, you know,
I don't think . . . I could have done. . . . *[pause]*
Well anyway . . . poor Lucia was a Muse to him that time.
He learned from her ways, you see,
and from her dancings and her mishmash language.
[pause, then a practical voice] Of course I had my own part in there too.
Isn't it a book about a family after all? Wife. Mother.
But then the end, O God in heaven the end of it . . .
and the lot of us—Lucia, myself, and Jim too, the fatherchild in him,
and of course the old river Liffey itself, Anna Livia—
all run together in what he made of us.
I'll never forget him reading it out to us—Giorgio and myself—
and we feeling . . . such *feelings* . . .
of the thing being done . . . the seventeen years of it over.
Such . . . what was it? . . . oh . . . just *relief* I suppose . . .

like the river itself going back to the sea.

It's a saying goodbye, isn't it, the end of it? For isn't life all partings?

It's the river-woman that says it, Anna Livia Plurabelle.

But I suppose 'tis everybody too. All of us.

Listen.

[She glances at book, then speaks it out; emotional, rhythmic, with power and
a kind of suppressed anger at first, then moving to a lyrical conclusion]

All me life I have been lived among them

but now they are becoming lothed to me.

And I am lothing their little warm tricks.

And lothing their mean cosy turns.

And all the greedy gushes out of their small souls.

How small it's all!...

Home!

My people were not their sort out beyond there...

No! Nor for all our wild dances in all their wild din.

I can see myself among them,

Allaniuvia pulchrabelled.... Loonely in me loneness....

O bitter ending! I'll slip away before they're up.

They'll never see. Nor know. Nor miss me....

My leaves have drifted from me. All.

But one clings still. I'll bear it on me.

To remind me of.... Carry me along, taddy,

like you done through the toy fair!...

Whish! A gull. Gulls. Far calls. Coming, far!

End here. Us then. Finn, again!...

mememormee! Till thousandsthee. Lps.

The keys to. Given!

A way a lone a last a loved a long the

[small pause] And so it goes, back to the start, like a big circle

or a wheel going round and round—

he thought life was a big circle you see....

all the way back to Dublin and

riverrun past Eve and Adam... and starting again...

Just like that strange portrait Brancusi did of him. The spiral.

Abstract, of course, but Jim liked it.

But do you know what his father said when he saw it? *[put on Cork accent]*

"Begod," says he, "the boy seems to have changed a good deal." *[laughs]*

Very humorous his father was. Like Jim.

Jim felt close to him, but of course Jim had left Ireland and all . . .

And then his father was a drinker, not good to his family.

But he liked me, he did, I'll say that for him.

Took account of my name when he heard it.

"Barnacle?" says he *[Cork accent]*. "Oh, she'll stick."

Jim wrote a lovely poem after he died, yes . . .

at the time our grandchild Stevie was born . . .

"Ecce Puer," it's called. "Behold the Child."

Overvoice: *[male] Of the dark past*
A child is born;
With joy and grief
My heart is torn.

Calm in his cradle
The living lies.
May love and mercy
Unclose his eyes!

Young life is breathed
On the glass;
The world that was not
Comes to pass.

A child is sleeping:
An old man gone.
O, father forsaken,
Forgive your son!

Nora: *Love and mercy.* That's about it isn't it?

What we all need.

Well anyway, *Finnegans Wake* was over and finished—

and always starting again, the way it does.

But of course poor Jim couldn't start again.

Mortal tired he was. And it was 1939.

And the war, another war, coming at us again.

And again we're gipsies, stravaguing place to place.

With Giorgio and Giorgio's little Stevie.

And in the end it was back here to Zurich with us . . .

Back to where we'd gone at first all those years ago—

all young and foolish and in love as we were—

the poet and his Muse, how are you!

And here we were again . . . safe at last.

But . . . then . . . Oh Lord! . . . after nigh only a month or so . . .

my poor Jim died on me! Just like that.

The thirteenth of January 1941 . . .

Near half past two in the morning it was.

I remember it like yesterday.

I was hurrying to be with him . . . but he went before I got there.

All alone he was so. . . . Him who loved company. . . .

And there he was in the hospital bed. . . . Gone . . .

. . . all that life . . . all those words . . . Gone . . .

into the big silence filling the room around him.

Not even fifty-nine he wasn't. So young, God in heaven!

Yet old and worn out too . . . by the work . . . the struggles . . . the life.

Poor little Stevie kept crying *Nonno! Nonno!*

And Lucia, oh God it was terrible when she was told,

and her in the Asylum place, in Occupied France that was.

Overvoice: [Lucia] "Cet imbécile! What is he doing under the earth?

When will he decide to leave?

He's watching you all the time. . . .

Tell him I am a crossword puzzle, . . . "

Nora: And indeed she was that and no denying.

As for the funeral, I arranged that.

Not a Catholic one, no, I couldn't do that to him. No.

. . . It was snowing. I shed no tear.

But as they lowered the coffin

I could glimpse his face through the wee glass window in it . . .

and I couldn't help myself . . . for I cried out
"Jim, how beautiful you are!" I just did.
And I was remembering the end of his own story
he'd written so long before, *The Dead*.
He said it was in homage to me he wrote it.
And I was remembering
that little cemetery in Oughterard
we visited together once. . . .

Overvoice: *[male, quiet, fading at end] The snow was falling, too,*
upon every part of the lonely churchyard on the hill
where Michael Furey lay buried.
It lay thickly drifted on the crooked crosses and headstones,
on the spears of the little gate,
on the barren thorns. His soul swooned slowly
as he heard the snow falling faintly through the universe
and faintly falling, like the descent of their last end,
upon all the living and the dead. . . .

Nora: And now here it was—falling on Jim's own coffin.
I could scarcely get my head around that, hard as I tried. . . .
[small pause; start again] He's buried beyond over there, you know, near the Zoo.
You can hear the lions roaring there.
He always thought 'twas like the Zoo in the Phoenix Park.
I think he may like it there so, hearing the lions roaring and all.
Lions roaring indeed!
Of course you know he was terrified of dogs.
Afraid of his life of them.
Coraggio! I'd say to him if one came at us.
Though I suppose for all his fearfulness at some things—
dogs, and any sort of a rough fistfight at all,
and thunder and lightning scared him silly—
still and all, for all that, he was a bit of a lion himself.
King of the jungle! The literary jungle! Indeed! *[laughs]*
But such times we'd had! Indeed we had!
Teems of times and happy returns!
Poet and his Muse. . . . Oh . . . he was a poet alright—

I always said that . . .

And then they were over, those times. Gone. So quick. Gone.

And that, as Jim would say, *is the he and the she of it.*

But do you know what I'm thinking now?

I'm thinking of the time we left Ireland—

for good and all I suppose.

And on our travels we got as far as Paris . . .

or maybe it was Trieste . . .

But wherever it was—we'd just arrived, like I said . . .

and Jim left me sitting . . . in a park there—

near the station or the harbour, on a bench—

yes, just like this one—

while he went off looking for a place to stay.

And I'm thinking now of that young woman,

only a girl of twenty she was—O Madonna!—

all of forty years ago and more!—just sitting all alone there,

surrounded by such strange foreign goings-on and all.

And her all alone and far from Dublin—

not to mention Galway . . . Bowling Green, Nun's Island and all!

And her, myself that is, thinking all sorts of things—

the life I'd left, the unknown before us,

and how hungry I was, yes, and not a word

of the languages I was hearing could I understand.

And I was thinking too—you know how your mind drifts—

of the gas times I'd have when I was a young one in Galway . . .

Myself and Mary O'Holleran, the tricks we'd get up to . . .

the nights we'd dress up as men—we would!—

and go roaming about Eyre Square. Such divilment! *[laughs]*

And my going up to Dublin then—

after my Uncle Tommy beat me one time too many . . .

and meeting Jim and all . . .

Well anyway . . . that was me just sitting there—

with the memories spilling out of me, . . .

and here we were—in Paris or Trieste or wherever it was—

and Jim was an awful time gone—ages it seemed—

and I just sitting there in my old frock from Dublin . . .

and hoping to God no one would sit beside me and speak to me . . .

you know how it is. . . .

But then God in Heaven the *relief*

when I saw Jim hurrying through the people

and waving at me, and smiling too. That big smile of his!

He'd been held up by some trouble or other,

but he'd found us a place to stay sure enough.

And there she is so, that young girl,

flooded with relief as she is,

and she's thinking, *Well, thank God! There's Jim*

coming back to me! . . . We'll go on from here so . . .

And we did go on . . . and here I am now, look at me . . .

old as I am and none too steady. . . .

all these years and all our lives later . . .

and all that happened in them:

the cities, the sadness, the good times we'd have—

eating out and meeting all sorts of people,

artists, writers, poets—from all over Europe, America too . . .

and the parties . . . and the terrible wars . . .

and the children, and the books . . .

and our grandchild, little Stevie, and poor Lucia . . .

and Jim dying on me so young . . . and . . . oh . . . everything.

It was the odd old *Odyssey* we had, indeed it was—

like the wanderings of Ulysses himself—

with its ups and downs, its ins and outs,

and each and every one of its roundabouts.

As for being a Muse—whatever it might mean . . .

well that was part of it.

One way or the other, that was part of it, wasn't it?

For didn't he say it to me once:

Overvoice: [male] "Let me love you in my own way, Nora,

and have your heart always close to mine . . .

Everything that is noble and exalted and deep

and true and moving in what I write

	comes from you, Nora . . . comes
	only by listening at the doors of your heart."
Nora:	So . . . there you are. He said that. True then,

comes from you, Nora . . . comes
only by listening at the doors of your heart."

Nora: So . . . there you are. He said that. True then,
and God knows I think it stayed true after—
ups and downs and roundabouts and all.
And then he made me that lovely present
of *Chamber Music* long ago—those poems I loved—
wrote them out on parchment, he did,
in his own fine hand—he had lovely handwriting—
had them bound and all—
and with our initials intertwined on the cover.
So it would last, he said,
after our own poor passion-driven bodies, will be no more.
And I suppose he was right.
[recorded sound of a guitar playing slow melody]
I loved this one:

> *Sleep now, O sleep now,*
> *O you unquiet heart!*
> *A voice crying "Sleep now"*
> *Is heard in my heart.*
>
> . . .
>
> *My kiss will give peace now*
> *And quiet to your heart—*
> *Sleep on in peace now,*
> *O you unquiet heart!*

[guitar continues for a beat or two and she speaks over it]
Unquiet heart, . . . well . . . my heart is quiet enough now so it is.
And Jim's is too, I'd hazard.
Chamber Music. Aye . . . I have it still . . .
up in my room there and do often look at it,
and will never let go of it—not for love or money. . . .
For didn't he say too the time he gave it to me:
"The beauty of your soul, Nora, outshone that of my verses."
And that's the why he gave me the book as a present, you see.

It held the desire of his youth, he said.

"And you, darling," he said, "were the fulfilment of that desire."

The fulfilment of that desire.

How could I ever forget he said that? And I never did.

And then the books that came after—

with Molly, Anna Livia, and poor Lucia in them—

and myself—my soul I suppose, yes, and my body too, God knows *[little laugh]*—

always ebbing and flowing through them . . . the way he wanted.

Muses the lot of us so . . .

even if he wasn't the type! *[laughs]*

But . . . as the old mother says in that play I was in once:

[acting voice] What more can we want.

No man at all can be living forever,

and we must be satisfied.

And, you know . . . I suppose that's true too.

But then . . . there's the books! And all of us in them.

Here comes everybody indeed!

[laughs, and then decisively goes on] And isn't that a sort of living forever now?

[pause] Well . . . *basta!* I should be getting along. *[remembers hat]*

Oh Dio mio! my hat!

There! Giorgio will be here soon.

[music: "Love's Old Sweet Song"*]*

Oh sweet Mother of May, there's that song again! *[she hums/sings a snatch of it, breaks off, music continues, soft]*

He's been great, you know, Giorgio has.

All the time I've been . . . not so spry like.

A good son to me he's been, despite his own troubles.

He even gave up the drink . . .

Which God knows . . . was more than my husband ever did.

[laughs, then shakes her head]

Ah . . . Jim . . . sure what could you do? . . .

[She moves slowly off as music fades out to silence, and light fades slowly.]

END

J.M.Synge

The
Aran Islands

A dramatic recital for two voices

performed by
Tegolin Knowland & Sean Coyne

adapted & directed by
Eamon Grennan

J.M. Synge's The Aran Islands

Adapted as a Play for Two Voices

> *Give up Paris. . . . Go to the Aran islands. Live there as
> if you were one of the people themselves; express a life that
> has never found expression.*
> —W. B. YEATS TO J. M. SYNGE, 1897

Introduction

Between May 1898 and October 1901, John Millington Synge, a Dubliner, spent just under four months (over four separate visits) on the Aran Islands lying off the West Coast of Ireland. His first visit was in May–June 1898; his second in September 1899; the third in September 1900; and the last one occurred in September 1901. From the diary and notebooks he kept while there, he composed his volume, *The Aran Islands*, completed in 1901, but unpublished until 1907. It was in this same year, 1907, that his masterpiece, *The Playboy of the Western World*, caused riots when performed for the first time in the Abbey Theatre. Having written a number of other plays (some of whose plots had their originating seeds in material from *The Aran Islands*), as well as prose pieces and a volume of poems, Synge died in 1909, at the age of thirty-seven.

J. M. Synge's The Aran Islands is an adaptation for two voices of Synge's book of the same name. All the selections in the play occur on Inis Meáin, the middle island, where Synge spent most of his island time. In them Synge records the impressions of the natural and human character of Inis Meáin that captured most powerfully his attention and fired his sympathetic imagination.

Reading the book, I've always been struck not only by the *spoken* sense of the prose but also by how multilayered the book is. One layer is anthropological: Synge is investigating and reporting on the nature and habits of the islanders in an almost scientific way, looking at their folk traditions, their work habits, the style of their houses, and the political, social, and cultural realities they embody as a community and within which they conduct their daily lives. Another layer to the text is that of folktale, a tradition carried on by one or two of the islanders who serve as *seanachaí* (traditional tellers of stories in Irish). And then there's the layer composed by Synge's response as a lyric poet to his island experiences—his rapturous entry into the colors and kinetic vitality of the changing weather, his elegiac sense of the islanders' endangered life in a world of sea and storm, his delight in the barren, beautiful rocky terrain.

It was my sense of how these layers relate to each other, to compose the rich texture of *The Aran Islands*, that stimulated how I structured the play. It prompted me to use the male voice to address the more factual side of things, while the female voice not only takes on the various women speakers who appear in the narrative but is also used to express the more lyrical, rhapsodic side of Synge's own narrative persona. For me, what's important and finally, I hope, successful about the piece is the interplay between these two voices, and how between them they achieve something of the feel of the book, something of both its literary and its essentially human texture.

The play was first performed by Curlew Theatre Company at Clifden Arts Festival in County Galway in September 2009. In adapting the text, I consulted the Penguin edition of Synge's work with its fine introduction by Tim Robinson.

For the original production

Voices

One male, one female. Both play Synge/Narrator. When other characters speak, the female voice plays the female parts and the male voice plays the male parts. The male voice is the more factual, scientific, anthropological; the female tends to the lyrical-evocative.

Set

Neutral: sometimes a room in the cottage; sometimes the open air. Black curtains on the three walls of the playing area. The chairs are placed towards the centre or back of a small stage, but not too distant from the audience. A lobster pot and boxes form, respectively, the left and right downstage extremity of the playing area.

Props
    Two kitchen chairs
    A lobster pot and some fishing nets and some rope
    Some boxes to serve as a sitting place
    An audio machine
    A tweed cap
    A blackthorn stick
    A black wool shawl
    A bright-coloured kerchief

Note: The piece is divided into 21 small "scenes," the division between one and the other marked by some sound effect, if possible, or, if not, then simply by a decisive pause. Any performance (for stage or radio) can choose to have more actors, and the various speaking parts can be distributed among them. The idea of two Narrators, however, is integral to my idea of the piece.

Overvoice: *[a "WBY voice" speaking this verse of Yeats's]*
                     And that enquiring man John Synge comes next,
                     That dying chose the living world for text
                     And never could have rested in the tomb
                     But that, long travelling, he had come
                     Towards nightfall upon certain set apart
                     In a most desolate stony place,
                     Towards nightfall upon a race
                     Passionate and simple like his heart.

PAUSE

[Sound of a ship's horn, fading. Sound of gulls.]

First narrator: *[informative tone of voice]* I am settled at last on Inishmaan
                     in a small cottage with a continual drone of Gaelic coming
                     from the kitchen that opens into my room. Early this morning
                     the man of the house came over for me with a four-oared
                     curragh, and we set off a little before noon. It gave me a
                     moment of exquisite satisfaction to find myself moving away
                     from civilization in this rude canvas canoe of a model that has
                     served primitive races since men first went on the sea. *[small
                     pause]*

                     During the thunderstorm I arrived in, I saw several girls
                     with men's waistcoats buttoned round their bodies. Their
                     skirts do not come much below the knee, and show their
                     powerful legs in the heavy indigo stockings with which they
                     are all provided. *[small pause]*

                     My room is at one end of the cottage, with a boarded floor
                     and ceiling, and two windows opposite each other. Then
                     there is the kitchen with earth floor and open rafters, and
                     two doors opposite each other opening into the open air, but
                     no windows. Beyond it there are two small rooms of half the
                     width of the kitchen with one window apiece.

Second narrator: *[lyrical description, as if of a painting]* The kitchen itself, where
                     I will spend most of my time, is full of beauty and distinction.
                     The red dresses of the women who cluster round the fire on
                     their stools give a glow of almost Eastern richness, and the

walls have been toned by the turf-smoke to a soft brown that blends with the grey earth-colour of the floor. Many sorts of fishing tackle, and the nets and oilskins of the men, are hung upon the walls or among the open rafters; and right overhead, under the thatch there is a whole cowskin from which they make pampooties.

Every article on these islands has an almost personal character, which gives this simple life, where all art is unknown, something of the artistic beauty of medieval life. The curraghs and spinning-wheels, the tiny wooden barrels that are still much used in the place of earthenware, the homemade cradles, churns, and baskets, are all full of individuality, and being made from materials that are common here, yet to some extent peculiar to the island, they seem to exist as a natural link between the people and the world that is about them. *[small pause]*

First narrator: *[factual]* The general knowledge of time on the island depends, curiously enough, on the direction of the wind. Nearly all the cottages are built, like this one, with two doors opposite each other, the more sheltered of which lies open all day to give light to the interior. If the wind is northerly the south door is opened, and the shadow of the doorpost moving across the kitchen floor indicates the hour; as soon, however, as the wind changes to the south the other door is opened, and the people, who never think of putting up a primitive dial, are at a loss.

Second narrator: *[enthusiasm, some humour]* This system of doorways has another curious result. It usually happens that all the doors on one side of the village pathway are lying open with women sitting about on the thresholds, while on the other side the doors are shut and there is no sign of life. The moment the wind changes everything is reversed, and sometimes when I come back to the village after an hour's walk there seems to have been a general flight from one side of the way to the other.

In my own cottage here the change of the doors alters the whole tone of the kitchen, turning it from a brilliantly lighted room looking out on a yard and laneway to a sombre cell with a superb view of the sea. *[pause]*

First narrator: *[factual]* Nearly all the families here have relations who have had to cross the Atlantic, and all eat of the flour and bacon that is brought from the United States, so they have a vague fear that, [speak in "islander voice"] "if anything happened to America" their own island would cease to be habitable.

Second narrator: [humorous] Most of the strangers they see on the islands are philological students and the people have been led to conclude that linguistic studies, particularly Gaelic studies, are the chief occupation of the outside world.

One old man said to me:

Old man: [slow, old, islander voice] I have seen Frenchmen, and Danes, and Germans, and there does be a power of Irish books along with them, and they reading them better than ourselves. Believe me there are few rich men now in the world who are not studying the Gaelic.

PAUSE

[sound of a fog horn]

Second narrator: A week of sweeping fogs has passed over and given me a strange sense of exile and desolation. I walk round the island nearly every day, yet I can see nothing anywhere but a mass of wet rock, a strip of surf, and then a tumult of waves.

Now the rain continues; but this evening a number of young men were in the kitchen mending nets, and the bottle of poteen was drawn from its hiding place.

One cannot think of these people drinking wine on the summit of this crumbling precipice, but their grey poteen, which brings a shock of joy to the blood, seems predestined to keep sanity in men who live forgotten in these worlds of mist.

First narrator: I sat in the kitchen part of the evening to feel the gaiety that was rising, and when I came into my own room after dark, one of the sons came in every time the bottle made its round, to pour me out *my* share. [small pause]

Second narrator: But today it has cleared at last, and the sun is shining with a luminous warmth that makes the whole island glisten with the splendour of a gem, and fills the sea and sky with a radiance of blue light.

I have come out to lie on the rocks where I have the black

edge of the north island in front of me, Galway Bay, too blue almost to look at, on my right, the Atlantic on my left, a perpendicular cliff under my feet, and over me innumerable gulls that chase each other in a white cirrus of wings.

[intense meditative lyric voice] As I lie here hour after hour, I seem to enter into the wild pastimes of the cliff, and to become a companion of the cormorants and crows.

PAUSE

[bird cries]

Second narrator:	The old man, Pat Dirane, has been telling me a story:
Pat Dirane:	*[old islander voice]* One day I was travelling on foot from Galway to Dublin and the darkness came on me and I ten miles from the town I was wanting to pass the night in. Then a hard rain began to fall and I was tired walking, so when I saw a sort of a house with no roof on it up against the road, I got in the way the walls would give me shelter.

As I was looking round I saw a light in some trees two perches off, and thinking any sort of a house would be better than where I was, I got over the wall and went up to the house to be looking in at the window.

I saw a dead man laid on a table, and candles lighted, and a woman watching him. I was frightened when I saw him, but it was raining hard, and I said to myself, if he was dead he couldn't hurt me. Then I knocked on the door and the woman came and opened it.

Good evening, ma'am, says I.

Young Island woman:	*[tranced soft voice, which is really in Pat's head]* Good evening, kindly stranger. Come in out of the rain.
Pat Dirane:	Then she took me in and told me her husband was after dying on her, and she was watching him that night.
Young Island woman:	*[same slightly disembodied voice]* But it's thirsty you'll be, stranger. Come into the parlour.
Pat Dirane:	Then she took me into the parlour—and it was a fine clean house—and she put a cup, with a saucer under it, on the table before me with fine sugar and bread.

When I'd had a cup of tea I went back into the kitchen

where the dead man was lying, and she gave me a fine new pipe off the table with a drop of spirits.

Young Island woman: *[same slightly disembodied voice]* Stranger, would you be afeared to be alone with himself?

Pat Dirane: *[responding to her voice, all in his head]* Not a bit in the world, ma'am, he that's dead can do no hurt.

[back to ordinary voice] Then she said she wanted to go over and tell the neighbours the way her husband was after dying on her, and she went out and locked the door behind her.

I smoked one pipe, and I leaned out and took another off the table. I was smoking it with my hand on the back of my chair—the way I am myself this minute, God bless me—and I looking on the dead man, when he opened his eyes as wide as myself and looked at me.

"Don't be afeared, stranger," said the dead man; "I'm not dead at all in the world. Come here and help me up and I'll tell you all about it."

Well, I went up and took the sheet off of him, and I saw that he had a fine clean shirt on his body, and fine flannel drawers.

He sat up then, and says he—

"I've got a bad wife, stranger, and I let on to be dead the way I'd catch her goings-on."

Then he got two fine sticks he had to keep down his wife, and he put them at each side of his body, and he laid himself out again as if he was dead.

In half an hour his wife came back and a young man along with her. Well, she gave him his tea, and she told him he was tired, and he would do right to go and lie down in the bedroom.

The young man went in and the woman sat down to watch by the dead man. A while after she got up.

Young Island woman: *[same slightly disembodied voice]* Stranger, I'm going in to get the candle out of the room; I'm thinking the young man will be asleep by this time.

Pat Dirane: She went into the bedroom, then, but divil a bit of her came back.

Then the dead man got up, and he took one stick, and he

gave the other one to myself. We went in and we saw them lying together with her head on his arm.

Well, the dead man hit him a blow with the stick so that the blood out of him leapt up and hit the gallery.

And that's my story.

PAUSE

[gull sounds]

Second narrator: It is a Holy Day, and I have come up to sit on the Dún while the people are at Mass.

A strange tranquillity has come over the island this morning, as happens sometimes on Sunday, filling the two circles of sea and sky with the quiet of the church.

No one who has not lived for weeks among these grey clouds and seas can realize the joy with which the eye rests on the red dresses of the women, especially when a number of them are to be found together, as happened early this morning.

First narrator: But the women and girls, when they have no men with them, usually tried to make fun with me.

Girl: Is it tired you are stranger?

First narrator: *[playing along] Arra ní hea a chailín, tá uaigneas orm.* Bedad, it is not, little girl, it is lonely I am.

Girl: Here is my little sister, so, stranger, who will give you her arm. *[laughs]*

First narrator: *[over sound of girls' and women's mocking laughter]* And so it went on. Quiet as these women are on ordinary occasions, when two or three of them are gathered together in their holiday petticoats and shawls, they are as wild and capricious as the women who live in towns.

On that occasion the women were over-excited, and when I tried to talk to them they crowded round me and began jeering and shrieking at me because I am not married. A dozen screamed at a time, and so rapidly that I could not understand all they were saying, yet I was able to make out they were taking advantage of the absence of their husbands to give me the full volume of their contempt. Some little boys who were listening threw themselves down, writhing with laughter among the seaweed, and the young girls grew red with embarrassment and stared down into the surf.

For a moment I was in confusion. I tried to speak to them, but I could not make myself heard, so I sat down on the slip and drew out my wallet of photographs. In an instant I had the whole band clambering round me, in their ordinary mood.

PAUSE

[knocking]

First narrator: Yesterday a letter came from the son who is in America, to say that he had a slight accident to one of his arms, but was well again, and that he was leaving New York and going a few hundred miles up the country.

Second narrator: All that evening the old woman sat on her stool at the corner of the fire with her shawl over her head, keening piteously to herself. America appeared far away, yet she seems to have felt that, after all, it was only the other edge of the Atlantic, and now when she hears them talking of railroads and inland cities where there is no sea, things she cannot understand, it comes home to her that her son is gone forever. She often tells me how she used to sit on the wall behind the house last year and watch the hooker he worked in coming out of Kilronan and beating up the sound, and what company it used to be to her the time they'd all be out.

First narrator: The maternal feeling is so powerful on these islands that it gives a life of torment to the woman. Their sons grow up to be banished as soon as they are of age, or to live here in continual danger on the sea; their daughters go away also, or are worn out in their youth with bearing children that grow up to harass them in their own turn a little later.

PAUSE

[sound of sea storm, wind, waves, throughout next episode, played as an emotional duet]

First narrator: *[caught up in vivid memory]* The other day, taken out in a curragh, I felt the full might of the sea. It was a four-oared curragh, and I was given the last seat so as to leave the stern for the man who was steering with an oar, worked at right angles to the others by an extra thole-pin in the stern gunnel.

When we had gone about a hundred yards they ran up a bit of a sail in the bow and the pace became extraordinarily rapid.

The shower had passed over and the wind had fallen, but large, magnificently brilliant waves were rolling down on us at right angles to our course.

Second narrator: *[voice more excited, remembering]* Every instant the steersman whirled us round with a sudden stroke of his oar, the prow reared up and then fell into the next furrow with a crash, throwing masses of spray. As it did so, the stern was thrown up, and both the steersman, who let go his oar and clung with both hands to the gunnel, and myself, were lifted high up above the sea.

First narrator: *[excited voice, "dramatising" the experience]* The wave passed, we regained our course and rowed violently for a few yards, when the same manoeuvre had to be repeated. As we worked out into the sound we began to meet another class of waves, that could be seen for some distance towering above the rest.

Second narrator: *[intense]* When one of these came in sight, the first effort was to get beyond its reach. The steersman began crying out in Gaelic:

Boatman: *[shout]* "Siúil! Siúil!"

Second narrator: "Run! Run!" and sometimes, when the mass was gliding towards us with horrible speed, his voice rose to a shriek. Then the rowers themselves took up the cry, and the curragh seemed to lap and quiver with the frantic terror of a beast till the wave passed behind it or fell with a crash beside the stern.

First narrator: *[explaining]* It was in this racing with the waves that our chief danger lay. If the wave could be avoided, it was better to do so, but if it overtook us while we were trying to escape, and caught us on the broadside, our destruction was certain. *[intense]* I could see the steersman quivering with the excitement of his task, for any error in his judgment would have swamped us. . . . We had one narrow escape.

Second narrator: *[intense]* A wave appeared high above the rest, and there was the usual moment of intense exertion. It was of no use, and in an instant the wave seemed to be hurling itself upon us.

With a yell of rage the steersman struggled with his oar to bring our prow to meet it. He had almost succeeded, when there was a crash and rush of water round us. It felt as if I had been struck upon the back with knotted ropes. White foam gurgled round my knees and eyes. The curragh reared up, swaying and trembling for a moment, and then fell safely into the furrow.

First narrator: This was our worst moment, though more than once—when several waves came so closely together that we had no time to regain control of the canoe between them—we had some dangerous work. Our lives depended upon the skills and courage of the men, as the life of the rider or swimmer is often in his own hands, and the excitement of the struggle was too great to allow time to fear.

Second narrator: *[quiet]* But . . . I enjoyed the passage. Down in this shallow trough of canvas that bent and trembled with the motion of the men,

First narrator: *[concluding]* I had a far more intimate feeling of the glory and power of the waves than I have ever known in a steamer.

PAUSE

[snatch of fiddle music]

Second narrator: Today I walked out with a blind man, old Máirtín. As I led him home through the paths he described to me—it is thus we get along—lifting him at times over the low walls he is too shaky to climb, he brought the conversation to the topic they are never weary of—my views on marriage.

Blind Máirtín: *[confiding old islander voice]* Whisper, noble person, do you never be thinking on the young girls? The time I was a young man, the divil a one of them could I look on without wishing to marry her.

Second narrator: *[humouring voice, in island manner]* Ah Máirtín, it's great wonder you'd be asking me. What at all do you think of me yourself?

Blind Máirtín: Bedad, noble person, I'm thinking it's soon you'll be getting married. Listen to what I'm telling you: a man who is not married is no better than an old jackass. He goes into his sister's house, and into his brother's house; he eats a bit in this place and a bit in another place, but he has no home for himself; like an old jackass straying on the rock. *[laughs]*

PAUSE

[sound of sea; curlew cry]

Second narrator: *[mix of visionary and physical/practical, almost to self]* Lingering late by the sea this evening, I could hear nothing but a few curlews and other wild-fowl whistling and shrieking in the seaweed, and the low rustling of the waves. It was one of the dark sultry nights peculiar to September, with no light anywhere except the phosphorescence of the sea, and an occasional rift in the clouds that showed the stars behind them.

The sense of solitude was immense. I could not see or realize my own body, and I seemed to exist merely in my perception of the waves and of the crying birds, and of the smell of seaweed.

[intense] When I tried to come home I lost myself among the sandhills, and the night seemed to grow unutterably cold and dejected, as I groped among slimy masses of seaweed and wet crumbling walls.

After a while I heard a movement in the sand, and two grey shadows appeared beside me. *[at ease again]* They were two men who were going home from fishing. I spoke to them and knew their voices, and we went home together. *[small pause; intense, quiet, almost in fear]* Now the wind outside is terrific. If anything serious should happen to me I might die here and be nailed in my box, and shoved down into a wet crevice in the graveyard before anyone could know it on the mainland.

PAUSE

[bell tolling]

First narrator: *[practical, descriptive]* After Mass this morning an old woman was buried. She lived in the cottage next to mine, and more than once before noon I heard a faint echo of the keen. *[very low sound of keening]*

I did not go to the wake for fear my presence might jar upon the mourners, but all last evening I could hear the strokes of a hammer in the yard, where—in the middle of a little crowd of idlers—the next of kin laboured slowly at the coffin.

Today, before the hour for the funeral, poteen was served to a number of men who stood about upon the road, and a portion was brought to me in my room. Then the coffin was carried out sewn loosely in sail cloth, and held near the ground by three cross-poles lashed upon the top.

As we moved down to the low eastern portion of the island, nearly all the men, and all the oldest women, wearing petticoats over their heads, came out and joined in the procession.

Second narrator: *[intense, descriptive, lyrical]* While the grave was being opened the women sat down among the flat tombstones, boarded with pale fringe of early bracken, and began the wild keen, or crying for the dead. Each old woman, as she took her turn in leading the recitative, seemed possessed for the moment with a profound ecstasy of grief, swaying to and fro, and bending her forehead to the stone before her, while she called out to the dead with a perpetually recurring chant of sobs.

All round the graveyard were other wrinkled women, looking out from under the deep red petticoats that cloaked them, rocked themselves with the same rhythm, and intoned the inarticulate chant that is sustained by all as an accompaniment,

The morning had been beautifully fine, but as they lowered the coffin into the grave, thunder rumbled overhead and hailstones hissed among the bracken.

First narrator: *[explanatory]* In Inishmaan one is forced to believe in sympathy between man and nature, and at this moment when the thunder sounded a death-peal of extraordinary grandeur above the voices of the women, I could see the faces near me stiff and drawn with emotion.

Second narrator: *[sympathetic, lyrical]* This grief of the keen is no personal complaint for the death of one woman of eighty years, but seems to contain the whole passionate rage that lurks somewhere in every native of the island. In this cry of pain the inner consciousness of the people seems to lay itself bare for an instant, and to reveal the mood of beings who feel their isolation, in the face of a universe that wars on them with winds and seas.

First narrator: *[explaining]* They are usually silent, but in the presence of death all outward show of indifference or patience is forgotten, and they shriek with pitiable despair before the horror of the fate to which they are all doomed. *[keen dying away]*

PAUSE

[snatch of fiddle music: "King of the Fairies"*]*

Second narrator: Old Pat Dirane continues to come up every day to talk to me, and at times I turn the conversation to his experiences of the fairies.

Pat Dirane: *[matter-of-fact]* I have seen a good many of them, in different parts of the island, especially in the sandy districts north of the slip. They are about a yard high with caps like the "Peelers" pulled down over their faces. On one occasion I saw them playing ball in the evening just above the slip, and I said I must avoid that place in the morning or after nightfall for fear they might do me mischief.

Another night I heard a voice crying out in Irish, "A mháthair, tá mé marbh" ("O mother, I'm killed"), and in the morning—

[more "dramatic"] there was blood on the wall of my house, and a child in a house not far off was dead.

Second narrator: Yesterday Pat took me aside and said he would tell me a secret he had never yet told to any person in the world.

Pat Dirane: Take a sharp needle and stick it in under the collar of your coat, and not one of them will be able to have power over you.

PAUSE

[harp music, slow, haunting, quickening]

Second narrator: Some dreams I have had in this cottage seem to give strength to the opinion that there is a psychic memory attached to certain neighbourhoods.

First narrator: Last night, in a dream, after walking among buildings with strangely intense light on them, I heard a faint rhythm of music beginning faraway on some stringed instrument.

It came closer to me, gradually increasing in quickness and volume with an irresistibly definite progression. When it was quite near the sound began to move in my nerves and blood, and to urge me to dance with them.

I knew that if I yielded I would be carried away to some moment of terrible agony, so I struggled to remain quiet, holding my knees together with my hands.

The music increased continually, sounding like the strings of harps, tuned to a forgotten scale, and having a resonance as searching as the strings of the cello.

Then the luring excitement became more powerful than my will, and my limbs moved in spite of me.

Second narrator: *[growing in intensity, but controlled]* In a moment I was swept away in a whirlwind of notes. My breath and my thoughts and every impulse of my body became a form of the dance, till I could not distinguish between the instruments and the rhythm and my own person or consciousness.

For a while it seemed an excitement that was filled with joy, then it grew into an ecstasy where all existence was lost in a vortex of movement. I could not think there had ever been a life beyond the whirling of the dance.

Then with a shock the ecstasy turned to an agony and rage. I struggled to free myself, but seemed only to increase the passion of the steps I moved to. When I shrieked I could only echo the notes of the rhythm.

At last with a moment of uncontrollable frenzy I broke back to consciousness (exhausted) and awoke.

First narrator: *[quiet]* I dragged myself trembling to the window of the cottage and looked out. The moon *[gesture]* was glittering across the bay, and there was no sound anywhere on the island.

PAUSE

[roll of a bodhrán]

First narrator: *[matter-of-fact]* One old woman, the oldest on the island, is fond of telling me anecdotes—not folktales—of things that have happened here in her lifetime.

Old woman: *[storytelling]* There was once a Connaught man who killed his father with the blow of a spade when he was in passion, and then fled to this island and threw himself on the mercy of some of the natives with whom he was said to be related. They hid him in a hole—which the old man has shown me—and kept him safe for weeks, though the pólis came and searched for him, and couldn't he hear their boots grinding on the stones over his head.

First narrator: In spite of a reward which was offered, the island was incorruptible, and after much trouble the man was safely shipped to America.

[lecturer voice] This impulse to protect the criminal is universal in the west. It seems partly due to the association between justice and the hated English jurisdiction, but more directly to the primitive feeling of these people—who are never criminals yet always capable of crime—that a man will not do wrong unless he is under the influence of a passion as irresponsible as a storm on the sea.

If a man has killed his father, and is already sick and broken with remorse, they can see no reason why he should be dragged away and killed by the law.

Such a man, they say, will be quiet all the rest of his life, and if you suggest that punishment is needed as an example, they ask:

Old woman: Would anyone kill his father if he was able to help it?

[small pause]

First narrator: The same old woman once gave me her view of the use of fear.

Old woman: A man who is not afraid of the sea will soon be drowned, for he will be going out on a day he shouldn't. But we do be afraid of the sea, and we do only be drowned . . . now and again.

PAUSE

First narrator:
Two recent attempts to carry out evictions on the island came to nothing, for each time a sudden storm made it impossible to land. (They say the storm was stirred up by a local witch.)

Second narrator:
This morning, however, broke beneath a clear sky, and when I came into the open air the sea and rocks were shining with wonderful brilliancy. Groups of men, dressed in their holiday clothes, were standing about talking with anger and fear, yet showing a lurking satisfaction at the thought of the dramatic pageant that was to break the silence of the seas.

First narrator:
[factual] About half past nine the steamer came in sight, and immediately a last effort was made to hide the cows and sheep of the families that were most in debt.

Till this year no one on the island would consent to act as bailiff, so that it was impossible to identify the cattle of the defaulters. Now, however, a man of the name of Patrick has sold his honour, and the effort of concealment is practically futile.

This falling away from the ancient loyalty of the island has caused intense indignation, and early yesterday morning, while I was dreaming on the Dún, this letter was nailed on the doorpost of the chapel:

Angry Island man:
Patrick, the devil, a revolver is waiting for you. If you are missed with the first shot, there will be five more that will hit you.

Any man that will talk with you, or work with you, or drink a pint of porter in your shop, will be done with the same way as yourself.

First narrator:
About midday, however, a house was reached where there was no pretext for mercy, and no money could be procured. At a sign from the sheriff the work of carrying out the beds and utensils was begun in absolute silence, broken only by the wild imprecations of the woman of the house.

She belonged to one of the most primitive families on the island, and she shook with uncontrollable fury as she saw the strange armed men who spoke a language she could not understand driving her from the hearth she had brooded on for thirty years.

["lecturer" voice] For these people the outrage to the hearth is the supreme catastrophe. They live here in a world of grey, where there are wild rains and mists every week in the year, and their warm chimney corners, filled with children and young girls, grow into the consciousness of each family in a way it is not easy to understand in more civilized places.

Indeed, the outrage to a tomb in China probably gives no greater shock to the Chinese than the outrage to a hearth in Inishmaan gives to these people.

Second narrator: *[subdued]* When the few trifles had been carried out, and the door blocked with stone, the old woman sat down by the threshold and covered her head with her shawl.

Five or six other women who lived close by sat down in a circle round her, with mute sympathy. Then the crowd moved on with the police to another cottage where the same scene was to take place, and left the group of desolate women sitting by the hovel.

PAUSE

[snatch of fiddle music]

First narrator: This evening at a gathering in the cottage, a young man had come up to bring me a copy of the *Love Songs of Connaught,* which he possesses, and I persuaded him to read, or rather chant, me some of them. When he had read a couple I found that the old woman knew many of them from her childhood, though her version was often not the same as what was in the book.

[sound of a woman's voice reciting melodically a few lines from "Bean an Fhir Rua" *in* Dánta Grá*]*

Second narrator: She was rocking herself on a stool in the chimney corner beside a pot of indigo, in which she was dyeing wool, and several times when the young man finished a poem she took it up again and recited the verses with exquisite musical intonation, putting a wistfulness and passion into her voice that seemed to give it all the cadences that are sought in the profoundest poetry. *[fiddle, slow air]*

The lamp had burned low, and another terrible gale was howling and shrieking over the island. It seemed like a dream that I should be sitting here among these men and women listening to this rude and beautiful poetry that is filled with the oldest passions of the world. *[slow air fades]*

First narrator: *[with enthusiasm]* Then I played on my fiddle a French melody, to get myself used to the people and the qualities of the room, which has little resonance between the earth floor and the thatch overhead.

Then I struck up the "Black Rogue" *[fast fiddle music, dance tune]* and in a moment a tall man bounded out from his stool under the chimney and began flying round the kitchen with peculiarly sure and graceful bravado.

Second narrator: The lightness of the pampooties seems to make the dancing on this island lighter and swifter than anything I have seen on the mainland, and the simplicity of the men enables them to throw a naïve extravagance into their steps that is impossible in places where the people are self-conscious. *[dance music fading]*

A little after that the old men went away, and I was left with some young men between twenty and thirty, who talked to me of different things. One of them asked me if ever I was drunk, and another said to me:

Young Island man: Wouldn't you be right to marry a girl out of this island, for they're nice women in it, fine fat girls, who would be strong and have plenty of children, and not be wasting your money on you!

PAUSE

[chord on a fiddle]

Second narrator: *[factual]* A young married woman I used often to talk with is dying of a fever—typhus I am told—and her husband and brothers have gone off in a curragh to get the doctor and the priest from the north island, though the sea is rough.

First narrator: *[intense and quiet]* I watched them from the Dún for a long time after they had started. Wind and rain were driving through the sound, and I could see no boats or people anywhere except this one black curragh splashing and struggling through the waves. Then when the wind fell a little

I could hear people hammering below me to the east. The body of a young man who was drowned a few weeks ago came ashore this morning, and his friends have been busy all day making a coffin in the yard of the house where he lived.

After a while the curragh went out of sight into the mist, and I came down to the cottage shuddering with cold and misery.

The old woman was keening by the fire.

Old woman: I have been to the house where the young man is, but I couldn't go to the door with the air was coming out of it. They say his head isn't on him at all, and indeed it isn't any wonder and he three weeks in the sea. Isn't it great danger and sorrow is over every one on this island?

First narrator: Do you know if the curragh will soon be coming back with the priest?

Old woman: It will not be coming soon or at all tonight. The wind has gone up now, and there will come no curragh to this island for maybe two days or three. And isn't it a cruel thing to see the haste that is on them, and they in danger all the time to be drowned themselves?

First narrator: [quiet] How is the woman doing?

Old woman: [fairly slow] She's nearly lost, she won't be alive at all tomorrow morning. They have no boards to make her a coffin, and they'll want to borrow the boards that a man below has had this two years to bury his mother, and she alive still. I heard them saying there are two more women with the fever, and a child that's not three. The Lord have mercy on us all! [blesses herself]

First narrator: [intense and quiet] I went out again to look over the sea, but night had fallen and the hurricane was howling over the Dún. I walked down the lane and heard the keening in the house where the young man was. Further on I could see a stir about the door of the cottage that had been last struck by typhus.

Then I turned back again in the teeth of the rain, and sat over the fire with the old man and woman talking of the sorrows of the people till it was late in the night.

PAUSE

[sound of rain and wind fading]

First narrator: *[a bit humorous]* A few days ago I had some photographs to show, that I took here.

While I was sitting on a little stool near the door of the kitchen, showing them to the family, a beautiful young woman I had spoken to a few times last year slipped in, and after a wonderfully simple and cordial speech of welcome, she sat down on the floor beside me to look on also.

The complete absence of shyness or self-consciousness in most of these people gives them a peculiar charm, and when this young and beautiful woman leaned across my knees to look nearer at some photograph that pleased her, I felt more than ever the strange simplicity of the island life.

Second narrator: Yet in some ways these men and women seem strangely far away from me. They have the same emotions that I have, and the animals have, but I cannot talk to them when there is much to say, more than to the dog that whines beside me in a mountain fog.

PAUSE

[soft roll on a bodhrán]

First narrator: *[factual]* A man has been washed ashore in Donegal with one pampooty on him, and a striped shirt with a purse in one of the pockets, and a box for tobacco.

For three days the people here have been trying to fix his identity. Some think it is the man from this island, others think that the man from the south answers the description more exactly. Tonight as we were returning from the slip we met the mother of the man who was drowned from this island, still weeping and looking out over the sea. She stopped the people who had come over from the south island to ask them with a terrified whisper:

Old Island woman:	What are they thinking over there?
First narrator:	Later in the evening, when I was sitting in one of the cottages, the sister of the dead man came in though the rain with her infant, and there was a long talk about the rumours that had come in. She pieced together all she could remember about his clothes, and what his purse was like, and where he had got it, and the same for his tobacco box, and his stocking. In the end there seemed little doubt that it was her brother.
Young Island woman:	Ah! it's Mike sure enough, and please God they'll give him a decent burial.
First narrator:	Then she began to keen slowly to herself. She had loose yellow hair plastered round her head with the rain, and as she sat by the door suckling her infant she seemed like a type of the women's life upon the islands.
Second narrator:	For awhile the people sat silent, and one could hear nothing but the lips of the infant, the rain hissing in the yard, and the breathing of four pigs that lay sleeping in one corner. Then one of the men began to talk about the new boats that have been sent to the south island, and the conversation went back to its usual round of topics.

PAUSE

[lazy lap of waves]

First narrator:	I have had another trip in a curragh, this time on a calm sea. We started early in the day. Near the middle of the sound, however, the man who was rowing in the bow broke his oar-pin, so we had only a three-oared curragh, and if the sea had gone much higher we would have run a good deal of danger.
Second narrator:	*[thoughtful, quiet, lyrical]* Our progress was so slow that clouds came up with a rise in the wind before we reached the shore, and rain began to fall in large single drops. The black curragh working slowly through this world of grey, and the soft hissing of the rain gave me one of the moods in which we realize with immense distress the short moment we have left us to experience all the wonder and beauty of the world.

[wave sound fading]

First narrator: But on Inishmaan, even *manufacture* is of interest. The kelp they collect from the rocks, for example, after the storms of autumn and winter, is burnt in a kiln until it is as hard as limestone. The kiln holds about two tons of molten kelp, and when full it is loosely covered with stones, and left to cool. Then it is loaded in batches onto curraghs for transport to Kilronan, on the big island, where it's tested to determine the amount of iodine it contains, and paid for accordingly.

Second narrator: The low flame-edged kiln, sending out dense clouds of creamy smoke, with a band of red- and grey-clothed workers moving in the haze, and usually some petticoated boys and women who come down with drink, forms a scene with as much variety and colour as any picture from the East.

The men feel in a certain sense the distinction of their island and show me their work with pride. One of them said to me:

Island man: I'm thinking you never saw the like of this work before this day?

Second narrator: That's true. I never did.

Island man: Bedad, isn't it a great wonder, then, that you've seen France, and Germany, and the Holy Father himself, and never seen a man making kelp till you come to Inishmaan.

PAUSE

First narrator: *[factual]* The young woman with typhus has died and been buried.

When the coffin had been laid down, near the grave that was to be opened, two long switches were cut out from the brambles among the rocks, and the length and breadth of the coffin were marked on them. Then the men began their work, clearing off stones and thin layers of earth, and breaking up an old coffin that was in the place into which the new one had to be lowered.

Second narrator:	*[fascinated]* When a number of blackened boards and pieces of bone had been thrown up with the clay, a skull was lifted out, and placed upon a gravestone. Immediately the old woman, the mother of the dead man, took it up in her hands, and carried it away by herself, then she sat down and put it in her lap—it was the skull of her own mother—and began keening and shrieking over it with the wildest lamentation.
First narrator:	*[objective]* As the pile of mouldering clay got higher beside the grave a heavy smell began to rise from it, and the men hurried with their work, measuring the hole repeatedly with the two rods of bramble. When it was nearly deep enough the old woman got up and came back to the coffin, and began to beat on it, holding the skull in her left hand. This last moment of grief was the most terrible of all.
Second narrator:	*[spellbound]* The young women were nearly lying among the stones, worn out with their passion of grief, yet raising themselves every few moments to beat with magnificent gestures on the boards of the coffin. The young men were worn out also, and their voices cracked continually in the wail of the keen.
First narrator:	*[fascinated observer]* When everything was ready the sheet was unpinned from the coffin and it was lowered into its place. Then an old man took a wooden vessel with holy water in it, and a wisp of bracken, and the people crowded round him while he splashed the water over them. They seemed eager to get as much of it as possible, more than one old woman crying out with a humorous voice—
Old woman:	"Tabhair dhom braon eile, a Mháirtín." "Give us another drop, Martin."
Second narrator:	There is hardly an hour I am with them that I do not feel the shock of some inconceivable idea, and then again the shock of some vague emotion that is familiar to them and to me. On some days I feel this island as a perfect home and resting place; on other days I feel that I am a waif among the people. I can feel more with them than they can feel with me, and while I wander among them, they like me sometimes, and laugh at me sometimes, yet never know what I am doing.

PAUSE

[roll of bodhrán]

First narrator: *[factual voice]* In the evenings I sometimes meet with a girl who is not yet half through her teens, yet seems in some ways more consciously developed than anyone else that I have met here. She has passed part of her life on the mainland, and the disillusion she found in Galway has coloured her imagination.

     [almost to himself] As we sit on stools on either side of the fire I hear her voice going backwards and forwards in the same sentence from the gaiety of a child to the plaintive intonation of an old race that is worn with sorrow. At one moment she is a simple peasant, at another she seems to be looking out at the world with a sense of prehistoric disillusion and to sum up in the expression of her grey-blue eyes the whole external dependency of the clouds and sea. *[factual]* Our conversation is usually disjointed. One evening we talked of a town on the mainland.

Young Island woman: Ah, it's a queer place; I wouldn't choose to live in it. It's a queer place, and indeed I don't know the place that isn't.

First narrator: Another evening we talked of the people who live on the island or come to visit it.

Young Island woman: Father McGlinchey—is gone, he was a kind man but a queer man. Priests is queer people, and I don't know who isn't. *[pause]*

     Do you know *[between coy and surprised]* . . . I'm very fond of the boys.

First narrator: One evening I found her trying to light a fire in the little side room of her cottage, where there is an ordinary fireplace. I went in to help her and showed her how to hold up a paper before the mouth of the chimney to make a draught, a method she had never seen. Then I told her of men who lived alone in Paris, and make their own fires that they may have no one to bother them. She was sitting on a heap on the floor staring into the turf, and as I finished she looked up with surprise:

Young Island woman: They're like me so, would anyone have thought that!

First narrator: I have never heard talk so simple and so attractive as the talk of these people. Another evening they began disputing about their wives, and it appeared that the greatest merit they see in a woman is that she should be fruitful and bring them many children. As no money can be earned by children on the island this one attitude shows the immense difference between these people and the people of Paris.

["lecturer" voice] The direct sexual instincts are not weak on the island, but they are so subordinated to the instincts of the family that they rarely lead to irregularity. The life here is still at an almost patriarchal stage, and the people are nearly as far from the romantic moods of love as they are from the impulsive life of the savage.

But below all that sympathy, there is still a chasm between us.

PAUSE

[roll on bodhrán]

First narrator: And now, sadly, I've had my last evening on my stool in the chimney corner. I had a long talk with some neighbours who came in to bid me prosperity, and lay about on the floor with their heads on low stools and their feet stretched out on the embers of the turf.

The old woman was at the other side of the fire, and the girl I have spoken of was standing at her spinning-wheel, talking and joking with everyone.

Young Island woman: *[half mocking and joking, half not]* When you go away now you are to marry a rich wife with plenty of money, and if she dies on you, you're to come back here and marry myself for your second wife! *[laughs; little pause]*

First narrator: The next day . . . I left with the steamer.

[Exit]

[sound of steamer, gulls]

END

CURLEW THEATRE COMPANY
PRESENTS

The Loves

of

Lady Gregory

A PLAY FOR VOICES

Performed by
Tegolin Knowland

Written and Directed by
Eamon Grennan

The Loves of Lady Gregory

Introduction

The Loves of Lady Gregory offers a sketch of Lady Augusta Gregory (1852–1932). It presents the various aspects—private and public—of a long, creative, and productive life. She was a witness to and direct participant in much of Ireland's modern history, living at the heart of the most important historical events in Ireland's advance from the early days of the Cultural Revival through the Easter Rising, the War of Independence, and the Civil War, to the new Ireland.

In this play for voices, Lady Gregory herself narrates the story of her life, looking back at it after her death. As well as her plays and translations of Irish sagas and folktales, she concentrates on certain intimate relationships: her marriage; a couple of affairs; the death of her son, Robert, in the Great War; her love for the trees on her estate at Coole Park; her friendship with Yeats and collaborative creative partnership with him in the composition of some of their plays. She also remembers the founding and establishment of the Abbey Theatre with its various travails and difficulties. All these are brought to life in her own distinctive speaking voice, as she mulls over and comments on her personal life and her artistic career. An overvoice speaks passages from her poems, letters, and plays.

My intention in writing the play was to create an immediate and memorable self-portrait of a woman who is often confined to the margins of literary history and cast in the shadow of her male contemporaries. In truth she was the cofounder with Yeats and Synge of the Abbey Theatre. In addition, as well as writing her own plays, she collaborated with Yeats in the writing of a number of plays—most memorably *Kathleen Ni Houlihan*—which are often attributed to Yeats alone. Her worth as a collaborator was not always fully acknowledged even by Yeats himself, a fact that left her with a sense of being ill-treated, especially as she supported him financially and personally, as well as creatively. They did, however, remain close and loving friends (as testified by some of Yeats's later poems) until her death.

Born into a family of the Anglo-Irish Ascendancy at Roxborough, her family's estate in County Galway, she married Sir William Gregory, a member of the Irish Parliament, in 1880. His home, Coole Park, was a neighboring estate. In the struggle for Irish independence she, being of the upper class, was in a complicated position. She backed the nationalist cause (she was a good friend of Michael Collins, for example), and she understood that her own class might not be a part of Ireland's future. But her family home was burned down, and she herself was threatened by some local nationalists. She died from breast cancer at age eighty at home in Coole Park.

In researching material for the play I relied especially on:

Elizabeth Coxhead, *Lady Gregory: A Literary Portrait*. Harcourt Brace, 1961.
Lady Gregory's Diaries, 1892–1902 (Colin Smythe Publication), edited by James Pethica. Oxford University Press, 1996.
Mr. Gregory's Letter-box, 1813–1830 by Sir William Henry Gregory. Oxford University Press, 1982.
Seventy Years, 1852–1922: Being the Autobiography of Lady Gregory. Macmillan, 1976.

The first production of the play, by Curlew Theatre Company, took place in the National Library in Dublin in January 2018.

For the original production

SET
    Bench; chair; backdrop

[Fiddle playing slowly "She Moves through the Fair" *as lights come up. Last verse hummed, then softly sung by Lady Gregory as lights come up to full. She's seated on bench.]*

Lady Gregory *[upper-class Irish, refined]*:
> *Last night she came to me,*
> *My dead love came in.*
> *So softly she entered,*
> *Her feet made no din.*
> *She laid her hand on me*
> *And this she did say,*
> *"It will not be long love*
> *Till our wedding day"*

[music fades]

Love and death. . . . Yes. I always loved that song.
She's a ghost of course. There are . . . so many of us.
Yeats once said that after his death Coole would be his
most visited earthly place. I loved Coole. Its trees.
[litany] Chestnut ash beech birch . . . elm and oak . . . catalpa, sycamore.
Norway spruce, juniper . . . larch and laurel . . . weeping willow. . . .
I would look after them. When one died or was
toppled by storm, I would plant two saplings in its place.

Loving life, you see, making sure it went on.
And whenever I was angry at some public news
I took my little hatchet and chopped and slashed at
the choking ivy and woodbine, and that calmed me.
Sometimes I would think I could sit here forever—
any sunny day—and dream of coming back as a tree.
Not one of the great ones, mind you: those tall
masterful guardians—elm, oak, chestnut, sycamore—no.
Something . . . ladylike . . . neither shy nor overbearing.
A silver birch, perhaps, standing ghostly
in a grove of shadows. But distinctly there.
Today I shall think of what I loved.
Not just the trees, no. All sorts of loves.
"The Loves of Lady Gregory." A rather odd idea,
Doesn't quite fit with my "image."
Didn't Maud Gonne describe me once as
That queer little old lady who looks like Queen Victoria.
Perhaps she was jealous at my hold over
her unrequited lover, Willie Yeats. Well, no matter.
Of course *Maud's* wasn't the only such description.
Someone else once portrayed me as *That monumental widow*
swathed in widow's weeds and crape
as if she were Queen Victoria's understudy.
Understudy indeed. What cheek!
Sometimes it was a kind of praise:
One night of Abbey rioting over Synge's *Playboy,*
a friend said I stood at the door of the Green Room
as calm and collected as Queen Victoria
about to open a charity bazaar!
Poor old Queen. But how callous towards Ireland.
I was presented to her as a bride, you know,
and had to kiss her hand. I did so. In later years
I fear I might have bitten one of her royal fingers.
But on . . . to *The Loves of Lady Gregory.* . . .

I said once that my life seemed a series of enthusiasms.
It might better be seen as a series of loves.
Adding up, I suppose, to simply . . . myself.
Isabella Augusta Persse Gregory. 1852 to 1932.
My being in the world.
I did *not* love my parents. Not really. I loved
the house I was born in. Roxborough. The estate.
Adored my older brothers. For a while.
Their horses, their hunting, their wild exploits.
But . . . I did not love my parents. I tried to be
dutiful, yes of course. But not much more.
Does that shock you? Oh dear. But it's true.
My father was a gruff, remote, big-voiced presence.
Always upright in his wheelchair, giving orders.
We never had a conversation. Not one. The Master.
I'd watch and listen. Unnoticed. From the shadows.
My mother—the Mistress—didn't like me.
She was a beauty and knew it. Was given to self-praise.
I was her ninth child. Probably unwanted.
A girl. Not pretty. Very quiet. Very . . . watchful.
She was violently attached to her rules, and her strict,
unforgiving religion: Protestant. Evangelical. Proselytising:
[clipped, polite, decisive voice]
Sit up straight, Augusta! Remember:
Religion, Courtesy, Posture! Your holy trinity.
And why, may I ask, should we not endeavour
to turn our heretic servants into proper
God-fearing members of the true *Church?*
Very well, have it your own way. Stubborn girl!
Augusta is the plain one, you know. Yes!
No one will have her. No! She reads books!
No one will have her!

But I did love—my first real love, I suppose—my Nanny. Mary
Sheridan.

A paid servant. Yes, I knew that. But I loved her.
Her stories and her country voice. She was a native Irish speaker.
I could hear the difference that made. Her English—
with its small, distinct heartbeat of Irish in it. It was different.
It brought to my eager ears a different world.

[country voice]
Oh Augusta pet, could you only have heard
the great clapping and shouting of the people
one time I was a child—at a play I was—and
all of a sudden wasn't there this big noise and
everyone shouting: "The French! The French!
The French have landed at Killala!
Glory be to God! The French! The French have landed!"
In 1798 that was, pet. The Rising of '98.

She'd tell stories, too: faeries, heroes, strange beasts.
And read me poems. Irish poems. Not Moore's melodies, no.
Rebel poems. I'd listen and learn some by heart.
And spend my weekly sixpence (which I'd earned by
memorising passages from the King James Bible)
on poetry books. At the bookshop in Loughrea.
So the old bookseller would always say:
"I look to Miss Augusta to buy all my Fenian books."
Fenian books. Yes. Thomas Davis.
I would stand on a chair and recite. *[stand, arms out]*
[child's "dramatic" voice]
"DID they dare, did they dare, to slay Owen Roe O'Neill?"
"Yes, they slew with poison him they feared to meet with steel."
"May God wither up their hearts! May their blood cease to flow,
May they walk in living death, who poisoned Owen Roe."

Of course *I* wasn't a rebel.
I was—like all my kind—a Unionist.

Well, that was Roxborough, which I did love,
with its rambling house, its streams, fields, gardens.
A deer park even. Its view of Slieve Echtge.
My brothers. Sisters. And of course the Farm.
The workers. The servants. Two worlds.
And there I was—the listener—alive and all ears between them.
The different sounds of them.
I would not have known how to say it then, but yes,
I loved those other voices, the world they offered.
Well . . .
as it turned out, my mother proved a false prophet.
Someone *did* want me. Our neighbour, William Gregory.
Master of Coole. Everyone was astonished.
How did that little thing get the big man?
How did *that little thing get the big man?*
Governor of Ceylon. Member of Parliament. Big man indeed!
Even Sarah Bernhardt admired his *esprit*, his fine spirit.
My mother, of course, took it as a compliment to herself!
I was twenty-eight. He was sixty-three. 1880 that was.
Yes . . . old enough to be my father.
But . . . he loved me, admired me. Found me . . . interesting.
We did have things in common. Love of books. Conversation.
Politics. Interest in the big world.
He was very fond of me. As I was of him.
Though I was not the love of his life. No. That was his dead wife.
But our marriage was one of . . . ever-increasing affection.
And love. Yes. William opened a new world for me—
suddenly entering into society after my quiet years.
Kissing the queen's hand, having an audience with the Pope.
England. Europe. The Empire. The salons of London.
We lived there, William and I, and our Robert,
when Parliament was in session—
He as an MP. Me with my charity work. We with our social life.
Oh the gossip, the politics, Gladstone, the Irish question.

Famous poets and writers. The artists.

All those so very English voices.

Aristocratic, upper-class voices ringing in my ears.

Our friends and acquaintances called me their "Irish rebel."

Funny yes. But condescending too, I always felt.

But I did . . . luxuriate in all that. In a way. For a while.

In London I was good at drawing out conversation. A listener.

Though perhaps I didn't *love* that life.

Not the way I came to love Coole. No.

After London, or Paris, or Athens, or Egypt, even Venice

I would always be glad to get back to Coole.

To its silences . . . its cloudy, sunny, wet western weather.

And its Irish voices.

In Coole I was the Lady of the Big House.

The poor people came daily to the door.

I'd mix their cough cures and dye their flannel

with madder, in an iron pot. But they believed

I could cure them of all diseases, including poverty.

But how? I could not see that. For in that answer

would lie my own and my class's extinction.

The Ascendancy. The great Estates.

Mostly, though, I remained in tune with my husband's politics.

He was a good Irish MP of course—friend of Daniel O'Connell.

And in his own way an enlightened landlord.

When his own father had died from Famine fever,

William told me that when he had returned to Coole

to take over the estate, he had been stricken:

Overvoice: *[Sir William Gregory, upper-class Irish]*
By the sight of all those poor wretches
housed up, starving,
against our demesne wall
Their wigwams of fir branches.
Their skin drawn tight as a drum.
Their hollow voices. I can never forget any of it.

Perhaps for this reason he proposed a notorious bill in Parliament:
the buying up of small farmers' lands—a sort of clearance really—
steering some to the workhouse, others to emigration . . .
those nightmares for so many.
Still his tenants liked him. What he wanted
was a contented peasantry, and a yeoman class.
Things to remain the same. Only improved, made better.
It was old-fashioned. And very English.
But with such palpable inequality
how could there be content? I grew to know that.
I suppose—kind and understanding as he was—
he couldn't fully . . . *imagine* . . . those other lives.
Later, thinking of such things, I could not avoid
hearing a small inner voice—whispering:
It will all go, Augusta, every colonised stick and stone. . . .
We are, no doubt about it, a doomed class.
And deep down I would sense the justice in that.
For our class had planted sour grapes so often,
it was inevitable our own teeth would eventually
be set on edge. But, as I say,
I remained a Unionist until my husband died.
After twelve mostly happy years of marriage.
I took care of him in his last illness. With love, yes.
I went without sleep for nineteen days. He was delirious.
On the last evening, fully conscious, he took my hand.
The tie that has bound us, he said,
is going to be loosed at last.
I have loved you very much . . . I know
you will be a good mother to our son.
Weeping, I said, *Who knows but we may meet again.*
Oh and who knows, he said, *but we may not.*
And then he died. The 6th of March, 1892.
I sat there all night alone with him.
And slept all the next day. I never forgot him, ever.

His decency. His loving me. His skill and intelligence
and essential humanity as a statesman. His love for Coole.
And, indeed—Unionist or not—for Ireland.
I wore widows' black for him for the rest of my life.
Then it was Coole:
The empty house. The tenanted grave. Our young son.
When he died I was barely forty.
My sheltered days were over. I had to begin a new life. . . .
And I did. . . . A widow in my widow's weeds.
My . . . penitent's widow weeds.
Penitent's?
Well . . . that brings me to . . . another kind of love.
One that struck me like lightning, when—
two years into my marriage—I fell in love—
with my husband's close friend and colleague, Wilfrid Blunt.
Dearest Wilfrid. English. Poet. Libertine. Adventurer.
Romantic rebel. Practicing "amorist." And married.
And the handsomest man in England. We met in Egypt.
He was breathtakingly gorgeous in his Arab regalia.
More than anyone I knew he seemed at home anywhere—
in palaces, prisons, the desert, the drawing rooms of London.
A masterful man. I was breathless with . . . oh with
passion, surprise (*How did that little thing get the big man?*)
We became lovers. For a little while. Heady joys. Such talk.
His poems had nobility, I thought.
To do some little good before I die, said one,

Overvoice: [*Wilfrid Blunt, upper-class English*]
  To take my place in the world's brotherhood
  As one prepared to suffer all its fate;
  To do and be undone for the sake of good,
  And conquer rage by giving love for hate;
  That were a noble dream, and so to cease,
  Scorned by the proud but with the poor at peace.

His eyes, his arms, his kisses. His . . . everything.

I was smitten. It was my first *emancipation.*
We were, he said, . . . co-conspirators.
Talking Irish politics, Arab nationalism, books, his poetry.
"Blunt and Augusta talk more nonsense between them,"
my husband said, "than any two people I know."
He was amused. And remained, happily, unaware.
Oh . . . always the rebel, Wilfrid went to jail in Galway
during the Land League troubles. Demonstrating
against a landlord. Two months' hard labour.
Proud to be the first Englishman, he said,
to be jailed for Ireland. Being a landlord's wife, of course,
I did not approve, and neither did my husband.
Still I ached for Wilfrid when I visited him in prison.
I was imprisoned myself in a way.
Helplessly hovering between duty and desire—
in our own little walled-off world of love.
Betrayal, of course, did not come easily.
Our affair quickly became a great weight dividing my life.
I knew we had to part. So I wrote poems, love sonnets.
Of course I couldn't publish them myself. The scandal!
So Wilfrid put them in a book of his own poems,
and we called them *A Woman's Sonnets.*
Of course he "re-remodelled" (as he said) some of them.
Toning them down. Just like a man.
But they still carry, I believe,
the sound of my own young voice.

Overvoice: *[Lady Gregory, young]*
  I lead a double life—myself despise
  And fear each day to have my secret read.
  . . . In thy dear presence only have I rest,
  To thee alone naught needs to be confessed.
  Thou wert my all, my dear, and too soon I knew
  How small a part I could be in thy life . . .
  I staked my all upon a losing game

Knowing thy nature and the ways of men. . . .
Wild words I write, wild words of love and pain
To lay within thy hand before we part,
For now that we may never meet again
I would make bare to thee my inmost heart. . . .

Oh dear. Such . . . helpless . . . innocence really.
Wilfrid, of course, had a different view of it all.
"Duty is pleasure, pleasure duty," he said. . . .
"Love is a little thing, for one short day."
But no. I wanted it to last and last. Besotted, yes.
After our "liaison," however, we did become loving friends.
For life. After I went back, that is—
good wife as I was—back to my good husband.
Back, too, to being—despite my lover's ardent nationalism—
a good Unionist. But Wilfrid always remained
in my heart. To his death. We wrote such letters.
And when I myself . . . went . . .
I asked for the Bible he'd given me to accompany me at the end.
Oh dear, nothing is ever really simple, is it?
While I'm on the subject of—what shall I call it?—
romantic love and . . . well . . . sex . . . I should mention
one more such . . . interlude. Yes, one more.
And that was all.
Not much of a record, really,
to judge by my London friends.
Certainly I was no Molly Bloom . . .
It happened many years later.
An Irish-American.
John. Dear John Quinn. Friend to Yeats
and to all of us engaged in the Cultural Revival.
Lawyer, art collector, cultured man. And, like Wilfrid,
John was very . . . very . . . masterful. Yes. I liked that.
An amorist, too. Always with one mistress or another.
I knew that. But he won me with his enthusiasm—

for our work, and for me. He said I was *wonderful*!
I was all of sixty at the time—and he was forty-two.
It does sound rather like a music-hall song.
A younger man! And guilt-free! Such a relief!
I wrote, then, the most passionate letters of my life.
My John, my dear John, I said in one . . .

Overvoice: *my own John, not other people's John—*
I love you, I care for you, I want you, I believe in you.
How I long to be alone sometimes
that I may think only of you.

And in another, I said to him:
Something impetuous and masterful about you
satisfies me!
Well yes, a little on the torrid side I agree.
I blush. Queen Victoria? Not quite.
When I returned to Ireland, of course, things . . .
cooled. Isn't it always the way? The fear of scandal—
of anything that would tarnish
our theatre, our movement, our national hopes.
And of course John—being of an amorous, masterful disposition
had another mistress. Indeed he seemed to be
seldom without one. And yet, there he was,
telling *me* I was wonderful. Heady joys indeed.
We began our affair in America. The Abbey on tour—
Even President Roosevelt admired us. Admired *me*!
And in spite of the troubles over Synge's *Playboy*,
I liked America very much. So unlike Ireland really.
The newspapers adored my being "a Lady."
They thought that was "pretty darn great."
And although our affair lasted but a little while—
still, as with Wilfrid, Quinn and I remained close
until his (oh dear!) so early death. He was only fifty-four.
After that, America seemed very distant—
without what we had been to one another.

So . . . there you have it: my confession.
Wife and guilty lover; widow and not-at-all-guilty lover.
My short but very sweet amorous saga.
Let us hope I am forgiven.
But by now, I suppose, some of you may be wondering . . .
What about Yeats? Were we lovers?
No. Absolutely not.
We were from the time we met—1896 that was—very close.
He every inch the poet—his voice magnetic, hypnotic—
me his . . . hostess and . . . carer . . . at Coole.
But no—it was never, . . . the other.
Willie was muse-mad, of course, as you know,
and—whatever about my amorous interludes—
I never ascended to the rank of *anyone's* Muse.
And I suspect I was the happier for it.
So, no, never a muse for Mister Yeats was I.
Muse-mad as he was. With Maud his Muse-in-chief.
Rather comical at times. There I'd be—ensuring Willie's
comfort at Coole so he could get on with his work—
feeding him his earthly meat and potatoes,
serving him the best wine, while he'd be
agonizing and rhapsodising
over his absent, unrequiting Muse. Do not disturb!
Tread softly, for you tread on my dreams. . . . Indeed!
So no. We were never lovers.
I was more a . . . a mother really. . . . In fact
he said I was mother, friend, sister, and brother to him.
I gave *him* space, peace, sustenance.
And he gave *me*—beyond any lover—the gift
not only of lifelong friendship, but the gift, too,
of a purpose in life. He enabled me to embrace
a *new love.* I'd been a writer before, but it was he
who gave me encouragement, the wings to fly.
Already I had learned some Irish, been to Aran,

and I loved the stories in his *Celtic Twilight*.
So when he suggested I myself might collect folklore
around Gort, Coole, Kiltartan,
it was a sort of fresh falling in love.
I listened with renewed purpose, so,
to all those country voices lodged in my head
since I'd listened to the voice of Mary Sheridan.
Among farmers, potato diggers, old men in workhouses
I found what I was looking for: stories that opened a window
into the inner life of the country people.
I would bring small gifts. And listen. And record
what I heard—feeling the strange contrast
between the *poverty* of the tellers and the *splendour* of the tales.
Swans turning into kings; talking bulls; lovers' flights
on the backs of eagles; music-loving water witches.
And the tellers! Such voices they had.
Here's how one ended the story of Deirdre:

Overvoice: *[man, country] So at last all of them fell by each other's hands.*
And when Deirdre saw they were dead,
she took up a sword or a dagger
that was lying on the ground, and she fell dead
along with them. And she was buried
on one side of a dry stone wall
and her husband on the other side.
And a briar grew up on his grave, and a briar on hers.
And they met over the wall and joined with one another.

Lovely, isn't it!
After all that—when Yeats suggested I translate the old Irish sagas—
I felt I had stumbled not only into another love,
but into a life's work. I was happy, so,
and I leant myself to it as intensely, I believe,
as I would to any lover.
And so there I was, day after day, in the reading room
of the British Museum—with the noise of London buses

and all the English voices of London about me,
putting those ancient Gaelic stories into an English I made
out of the language of the King James Bible
and the language I heard spoken around Coole—
in Kiltartan and the other villages and townlands:
Glenbrack, Rineen, and the rest. A language
the local people would recognise. A language
to bring those legendary and mythological characters—
masterful men like Cuchulain, Naoise, Ferdia, Diarmuid,
and tragic heroines like Deirdre and Grania—
down to earth. Heroic, yes, but human too—
with all their human loves, jealousies, needs, hates,
strengths and ideals, weaknesses and sorrows—all their
complicated passions. And all those feelings and passions
spoke through me as I worked.
And I do believe that such an ideal world had its place
in what would happen later in Ireland.
Didn't Pearse, after all, hang Cuchulain's words
on the wall of St. Enda's? And didn't Yeats say
it was Cuchulain who stood beside Pearse in the Post Office?
I also loved this exchange between Finn and Grania:

Overvoices: *[Grania starts; Finn responds]*
What is whiter than snow?
    The truth
What is the best colour?
    The colour of childhood
What is the best of jewels
    A knife
What is sharper than a sword
    The wit of a woman between two men
What is quicker than the wind
    A woman's mind . . .
What is the best music?
    The music of what happens.

The music of what happens. How lovely!
I especially loved those many laments
that bind love and death so tightly together.
In them I could hear an echo of my own heart.
Strange, is it not? . . . how Gaelic literature
contains so many laments in the voices of women.
Douglas Hyde's *Love Songs of Connacht,* his translations,
taught me a great deal. I even tried some myself.
This one was my favourite:
Donal Óg, or *The Grief of a Girl's Heart.*

Overvoice: *[woman]*

> *It is late last night the dog was speaking of you;*
> *the snipe was speaking of you in her deep marsh.*
> *It is you are the lonely bird through the woods;*
> *and that you may be without a mate until you find me.*
> *When I go by myself to the Well of Loneliness,*
> *I sit down and I go through my trouble;*
> *My heart is as black as the blackness of the sloe,*
> *It was you put that darkness over my life.*
> *You have taken the east from me,*
> *you have taken the west from me;*
> *you have taken the moon,*
> *you have taken the sun from me.*
> *And my fear is great*
> *you have taken God from me!*

Such . . . courage. Such suffering. No self-suppression.
It was such a release to be speaking such words,
as if they were my own.
Beside them, my own long ago love poems
seemed pallid, thin, conventional.
So I felt happy and fulfilled—it was 1903—
when I'd finished *Cuchulain of Muirthemne.*
And how pleased I was at the praise it received.
When Synge told me it was his *daily bread*

and that I had found the dialect he was in search of—
I was overjoyed. Yeats said it was
"The best book that has come out of Ireland in my time."
A little excessive, yes. That was his way. Still . . .
one forgives such excess in a friend, doesn't one?
I should add that praise was not universal.
The younger generation, in the person of James Joyce,
was far from complimentary.
And, though I had given him some money to get to London,
while there he reviewed my folklore collection
by saying it was woeful, dreary, and untrue.
He also, of course, much later, parodied unmercifully my Cuchulain
tales in his own modern epic, *Ulysses.*

Overvoice: *[heroic, grand]*
          The figure seated on a large boulder at the foot of a round tower
          was that of a broadschouldered deepchested stronglimbed
          frankeyed redhaired freelyfreckled shaggybearded
          widemouthed largenosed longheaded deepvoiced
          barekneed brawnyhanded hairylegged sinewyarmed ruddyfaced hero.

Amusing, no doubt. Even *I* was inclined to laugh.
But isn't parody a form of flattery? I like to think so.
And I do remember with a smile the limerick he wrote
after I had given him that gift of money.
Overvoice: *[Dublin accent]*
          There was an old lady named Gregory
          Who cried, "Come, all ye poets in beggary."
          She found her imprudence
          when hundreds of students
          Cried, "We're in that noble category."

Category indeed! Oh dear.
Well, rebellious youth—
especially if it has genius—has its rights of free speech.
And he was such a handsome, sweet-voiced, petulant boy.
Aside from my translations of the myths and the sagas

I also, as you probably know, wrote plays.
Comedies, farces, tragicomedies, tragedies.
I loved discovering I could do that, and with pleasure.
I had, as they say, a certain facility.
And whether sad or merry, deep or shallow,
I loved the people I filled them with,
loved their voices, their local speech—
all full as a ripe apple with local flavours.
In my comedies I loved all those garrulous villagers
with their eager, ordinary hungers—
for news or gossip, quarrels or companionship,
for stories—endless stories.
Most of all I loved their sense of . . . of *community*.
Of being, no matter how they'd quarrel or bicker,
so at one with themselves and with each other.
And such talk they had.
Listen to this. *[Irish country accent:]*
It's too much talk you have, Bridget Tully. A rope is it, you're wanting?
It isn't much of a rope was needed
to tie up your own furniture the day you came into Martin Tully's house,
and you never bringing as much as a blanket,
or a penny, or a suit of clothes with you
and I myself bringing seventy pounds
and two feather beds. A rope, is it?
I tell you the whole of this town is full of liars and schemers
that would hang you up for half a glass of whiskey.
By bringing their voices to life like that,
I could feel—at least in my imagination—
that I too belonged to that world—
its humours, and griefs, its colours and its complex politics.
Oh yes, I did not avoid politics. Alongside farces
like *Spreading the News, Workhouse Ward, The Jackdaw,*
I touched deeper and more pressing issues.
The Rising of the Moon was my favourite.

I loved the rebel with his bravado and his song.
Remember this?
Oh now tell me Seán O'Farrell
where the rising's going to be. . . .
But I also loved the Sergeant
with his perplexity and his crisscrossed loyalties.
It was a humorous treatment of something very serious
in our often so very mixed-up political life.
Rebel and Policeman, both Irish.
I suppose—given my own divided life—I understood both.
Well goodnight now comrade and thank you, says the Rebel.

Overvoice: *You did me a good turn tonight and I'm obliged to you.*
Maybe I'll be able to do as much for you
when the small rise up and the big fall down. . . .
when we all change places at the Rising of the Moon.

Then the *Sergeant* who has let him escape says:

Overvoice: *A hundred pounds reward! A hundred pounds!*
I wonder now, am I as great a fool as I think I am?

It all ends in laughter, yes, but serious laughter too.
At first both Unionists and Nationalists disliked it.
But, whatever about the Unionists, the Nationalists
soon found its true spirit, saw the truth of it.
Gaol Gate too—another favourite—draws its ending
away from tragedy and lamentation
to a celebration of national loyalty.
To the martyr's sense of sacrifice—
that one would give one's life for a cause:
Did they ever hear in Galway
such a thing to be done,
a man to die for his neighbour. . . .
It was not a little thing for him to die,
and he protecting his neighbour.
Yes, I *felt* that as I wrote those words—
words that would take on greater, more tragic weight

some years later. I myself, of course, was never one
to storm the barricades—like Maud, or Con Markievicz.
No, mine was another way. But my heart
was lodged in such sentiments.
As it was in *Kathleen Ni Houlihan*.
So I was rather annoyed when Yeats
claimed the latter as his own, since I had contributed
such a large part to it. All the ordinary speech, indeed.

Overvoices: *[Michael]*
Have you no one to care you in your age, ma'am?
[Old Woman]
I have not.
With all the lovers that brought me their love,
I never set out the bed for any.
[Michael]
Are you lonely going the roads, ma'am?
[Old Woman]
I have my thoughts and I have my hopes.
[Michael]
What hopes have you to hold to?
[Old Woman]
The hope of getting my beautiful green fields back again.
The hope of putting the strangers out of my house.

That sort of thing, you see. Ordinary speech.
I loved that. And had a good ear for it too.
Which Yeats, oddly enough, did not.
I suppose, unlike me, he never really listened.
Too busy, I suppose, talking to himself.
But when he said later in a poem—
Did that play of mine send out
Certain men the English shot?—
he should really have said *that play of ours.*
Yes, that would have been correct.
I felt the sting of that, being a woman, erased like that.

No matter. One way or another, it was said that between them
The Rising of the Moon and *Kathleen Ni Houlihan*
made more rebels than a hundred nationalist pamphlets.
We were all rebels, you see. In our *different* ways.
And as Kathleen herself says:
They shall be remembered for ever,
They shall be alive for ever,
They shall be speaking for ever,
The people shall hear them for ever.
Rather a pity *Yeats* himself did not remember
who'd written most of that play.
By the way, do you know I played Kathleen once?
Yes. Much later. At the Abbey. Three nights in a row.
Maire Walker couldn't appear, so with great trepidation
I volunteered. After all, I said, what is needed
but a hag and a voice. I wonder did Maud know I said that.
(Her playing of Kathleen so long before had been
a wonderful and stirring thing.)
But all those years later, I was terrified.
Still, for three nights I did it.
Oh the sweat I sweated! I was soaked!
But I did get a couple of curtain calls each night.
That was pleasing. Of course Yeats, as was his way,
could not entirely enthuse. "Very nice," he said. "Of course
if I had directed you . . . it would have been much better."
Of course! Such modesty! Still, he was my encourager too.
I described him once as *good praiser, wholesome dispraiser,*
heavy-handed judge, open-handed helper of us all . . .
Simply put—he taught me my trade.
And I suppose he was right when he said
We were the last romantics—chose for theme
Traditional sanctity and loveliness;
Whatever's written in what poets name
The book of the people. . . .

Curiously enough—speaking of my plays—
in another one—a tragedy dealing with the love of
Diarmuid and Grania—I came close to something
more intimately *personal* than elsewhere.
For in it I touched on something very near
my own most intimate self. It concerned
love and infidelity. Passion and shame. The divided heart.
Too revealing, I thought, to be played in our Abbey,
so it wasn't. But in it I revisited
all that tempest of feeling roused in me
all those years before by Wilfrid.
Strange are the ways of art.

Overvoice: *[Grania]*
Diarmuid help me. I cannot wed with Finn.
I cannot go to him as his wife—
for you came in and my heart started like a deer.
There is something gone astray. . . .
What way would I live with Finn and my heart
gone from him? . . . What name might I be calling out
in my sleep? It would be a terrible thing,
a wedded woman not to be loyal—to call out
another man's name in her sleep.

A poet once told me that a poem
is the only place one can confess with dignity.
Well, I suppose that may be true for a play too.
Well, anyway, in addition to giving me a purpose in life
and pleasing myself, it was out of my sense of *duty*—
duty and love, really—that I did all that writing.
And to assert my own independence.
I wanted to belong, on my own terms, you see,
to have a sense of belonging.
To what was, I felt, I knew, my country too.
To truly feel that sense of belonging.
Yeats, Synge, Maud, the Gore-Booths, Hyde, and others—

we all felt it. Ached for it. For in the depths,
what I loved was Ireland, the possibility of a new Ireland.
That was my guiding light then, as it was for all of us.
Even Pearse said, once, we were all allies.
Of course I feared that, even as I welcomed it.
Welcomed the thought of a new world.
Yet knew—with some trepidation—I was welcoming
my own disappearance, or at least the vanishing away
of what in so many ways I represented.
The Ascendancy. The Big House. We Privileged Few. Our tiny
    minority.
For wasn't my own divided life an image of it all?
Even as I'd worked to maintain Coole for Robert
(all my economising to pay off the mortgage),
I knew I was both the *end* of something—
my class, our place, all that—
and the beginning of something new.
We wanted to achieve an Ireland, as Yeats said,
that the poets have imagined. We all worked to that end.
But of course in the end we were all of us
caught in the iron toils of history.
Trapped inside the whirlwind that was, first,
the Great War—the so-called war to end war—and then
our own Easter Rising, and all the violence that followed.

I must draw a moment's breath here in my tale.
For I am brought again to that heart-wrenching proximity
of love and death. I had so often noted this,
in so many of those laments I'd written or translated.
But at last I found myself under that great shadow
darkening the world—not only during the years of
the Great War, but in Ireland
between 1916 and 1923 and beyond.
The nightmare years.
It was in 1918, however, that there fell upon me —

as on any mother—there were so many of us
in that War's slaughterhouse of mindless savagery—
fell upon me that grief that is unlike all others:
the death of a son—my only son.
January 23, 1918. How can I ever forget it?

Earlier that month I'd been putting together a book of poems
translated from the Irish. It seemed strange to me, then,
that the laments so outnumbered the songs of joy.
But before that same month was out, I received news
that made the keening of women for the brave
and for those left lonely after all the dead young men,
seem but the natural outcome and expression
of all human life.
To my Robert
—who was always a Unionist, like his father—
loving the idea of the Empire as most of his kind did—
it seemed right and good to join up when war broke out.
Although he was over thirty, married, a father.
He had a purpose you see. He was doing his duty.
And he loved flying. So he went. It's an old story.
For me, however, it was a new nightmare.
Only half of me was there while he was in danger.
I used to wake up as if some part of me
was crying in another place. So I would try not to wake up.
Every morning I prayed for his safety,
while I might spend the day playing with his children—
my grandchildren, my chicks. Carrying on our ordinary life.
It seemed the right thing to do.
I wrote to him, *Oh what a happy world it might be*
with you back and the war at an end. God bless you, my child!
I went on, so, planting broom, and trees that would have pleased him.
He was fighting for Empire, yes. But in his heart
I knew he carried Coole and Kiltartan.

But he *was* happy, I knew that, too. He told me so.
And told Bernard Shaw that his time on the Western Front
had been the happiest months of his life.
To hear that made me glad of course, but sad too.
But what could I do but support my son?
And worry for him. Days and agonised nights of worry.
Part of me was not in Coole at all, but where *he* was—in Italy.
Then, at last, the awful knock on the door.
The sound I feared more than any other.
The Gort postman. The telegram. My shaking hands.
I could not stand up. *We regret to inform you* . . .
The world going black. So much to do.
I had to bring it to his wife. The news. To Margaret.
By cart. By train. Shivering all the way.
Clenching my fists. My teeth. No talk. *Robert!*
Till I got to Galway. *It's Robert!*
was all Margaret said when she saw me.
I sank to the floor, then, and wept and wept.
I wept in great speechless waves of grief, a sea of salt tears.
Sitting and rocking there on the floor. Weeping.
Like any grief-stunned old woman. A mother.
Speechless. Empty of everything but his name.
Calling it out. Keening. *Robert! Robert!*
He was such a wonder. Athletic, thoughtful, brave.
A cricketer, he played for Ireland. A good boxer.
Fine horseman. Painter. Designer. Writer. One of *us*.

Overvoice: *["WBY voice"]*

> *We dreamed that a great painter had been born*
> *To cold Clare rock and Galway rock and thorn,*
> *To that stern colour and that delicate line*
> *That are our secret discipline*
> *Wherein the gazing heart doubles her might. . . .*
> *Soldier, scholar, horseman, he,*
> *As 'twere all life's epitome.*

What made us dream that he could comb grey hair?

Yes he was all that. But most of all he was . . . *my son!*
Lost in Italy. So strange. Buried in Padua.
Italy where we had often visited together.
Decorated in the war. The Military Cross. Legion of Honour.
But what are medals to a mother's grief?
I was like that queen in Shakespeare grieving for her son:
Grief fills the room up of my absent child,
Lies in his bed, walks up and down with me,
Puts on his pretty looks, repeats his words,
Remembers me of all his gracious parts . . .
And then Yeats wrote that poem of his. Imagining Robert's voice:

Overvoice: *I know that I shall meet my fate*
Somewhere among the clouds above;
Those that I fight I do not hate
Those that I guard I do not love;
My country is Kiltartan Cross,
My countrymen Kiltartan's poor,
No likely end could bring them loss
Or leave them happier than before.
Nor law, nor duty bade me fight,
Nor public man, nor cheering crowds,
A lonely impulse of delight
Drove to this tumult in the clouds;
I balanced all, brought all to mind,
The years to come seemed waste of breath,
A waste of breath the years behind.
In balance with this life, this death.

Oh it is of course, in itself, a fine poem.
But not a true portrait of my Robert. No.
For surely he was motivated too
by what he thought of as his *duty.*
A touch of Yeatsian mythmaking, I suppose.
But how could I think of the years behind

as *a waste of breath*. All those years when he had been
the apple of my eye. How could these be a waste?
A child all curiosity. A lonely boarding school boy.
My endless fretting, over his marks, his health, his behaviour—
for he had no father then.
His young manhood, university, marriage,
and becoming a father. Being an artist! One of *us*.
All those years so vivid in my mind each day.
No, surely not a waste.
[pause] Poetry is not always life.
But in truth, my heart was broken.
Then all those laments I had written or translated—
all seemed so scarifyingly real, so immediate, so terribly right.
And then to be buried so far away. Near Padua.
I never visited. I so wish he might have been buried
in Coole, among the woods he loved.
I could have walked to him often.
Planted flowers there, too—spring flowers.
Seen the daffodils and primroses coming back every spring.
It would have been something.
A kind of . . . resurrection, I suppose.
Oh, how love and mourning—love and death—
can be such near neighbours.
That was the worst, yes. My widow's mourning dress
felt more appropriate now than ever.

PAUSE

Of course—although it was very different—
my heart had been in anguish before that:
when our own History took us and all our plans
into its tight and tragic grip. Easter 1916 . . .
The Rising, the executions. The horrors of it all.
In Coole, we were far from Dublin. But around us

the world was all armed men, police activity.
Fears, roads blocked, lootings. Kidnappings and killings.
No news by telephone or telegraph.
Guns landing at Kinvara. Police barracks attacked.
Martial law proclaimed. We lived in fear.
Kilcolgan, Clarenbridge, all the villages disturbed.
Public houses ransacked. Barricades on the roads to Galway.
Sinn Feiners polite. Redmond volunteers perplexed.
Which side were they on?
Families divided. Friends against friends, brother against brother.
My own son fighting for the Empire.
A week's siege. Intense anxiety.
In truth we were locked in
and the key was turned on our uncertainty.
Then the news of the slaughter in Dublin.
Before I knew everything, I called the rebels "the disturbers."
Felt, as many did, they were destroying
not only Dublin but the hope of Home Rule.
But my view widened, my sympathies deepened.
Then the terrible week of executions.
The news that Pearse and the other leaders had died splendidly.
MacDonagh like a prince, they said, and Plunkett
whistling the soldier's song, *Amhráin na BhFiann.*
Pearse and MacDonagh, I knew them, they were enthusiasts.
They could have been part of our movement.
Then, with the executions, *all changed, changed utterly—*
as Willie said in his poem. How right he was!
And while I did not love Pearse, MacDonagh, Plunkett
as I loved my own son, I did feel deeply their idealism,
loved what *they* loved and died for.
Indeed, *a terrible beauty* had *been born.*
So . . . the Rising was over. But no rest even then:
Robert's death, and the European War dragging on

to November 1918; and then,
the Rising's awful aftermath.
Oh those nightmare years of the Black and Tan war.
Our own War of Independence.
Guerrilla warfare. How else could the rebels fight?
The country I loved
dismembered by licensed ruffians in uniform.
They came to Gort, shooting and destroying.
Black and Tans, Auxiliaries.
Roaming about drunk, seeking drink and women.
A young girl shot by a lorry-load of soldiers.
Shooting young boys for nothing.
Dragging bodies behind their terrible lorries.
Torturing, imprisoning. Unspeakable violence.
My neighbour poor Malachi Quinn's young wife
shot dead with her child in her arms.
He was bewildered. They were so happy, he told me:
had just saved the hay, dug the potatoes, threshed the corn
and were ready for winter. Their ordinary world, so,
shattered by those uniformed murderers.
"My God it is too cruel," he said.
"She could play every musical instrument."
Monsters in uniform spreading terror and ruin.
Two young women raped before their father and brother
and the family wishing it to be hushed up. The horror of it!
A *rough beast*, indeed, slouching through the land.
In church I could not say the prayer for the King.
For where was God in all this?
I could do no more than pray for peace.
One of the Psalms we would sing in church haunted me:
They range all night on slaughter bent
Till summoned by the rising moon . . .
From fields and villages and towns

Commissioned vengeance flew.
And in the midst of all this mayhem and horror
I would be looking after the chicks, my grandchildren,
while they did their lessons, or played in the garden.
Part daily life, you see. Part deathly nightmare.
And the sense of dread everywhere.
The destruction of our ordinary world. Until . . .
until a Truce was called.
When, in time, the Tans left Dublin, as you know—
there was no booing or applause from the crowd that had gathered.
Just a sort of delighted murmur, a triumphant purr.
I understood that . . .
First the Truce. Then the Treaty.
The poisoned chalice of the Treaty.
And then, alas, the Split:
Between those for and those against the Treaty.
Free Staters against Republicans.
our own misbegotten blood-letting, the monstrous Civil War.
All of that I saw, *sidelined* then,
but caught irrevocably between both sides—
with one harrowing atrocity following another.
In truth those days were, as Yeats said, *dragon-ridden.*
And the nightmare did indeed *ride upon sleep.*

I hated it all—hated that they could not agree
on the stumbling block of the Oath—how to deal with it.
But that it should lead to such carnage, hatred,
viciousness, and deaths defied my understanding.
Christ's teaching, I felt, was blurred by such horrors.
As a Republican, I liked de Valera. Another masterful man.
But Collins too, I liked. The Free State, after all,
was the Government. I had to make room for that too.
So there were apples from Coole for the Free State soldiers.

But succour, too, for the republicans on the run.
On that uneasy threshold I was waiting it all out.
Loving the country. Fearing for it. And for all those who—
on either side—risked and lost their lives each day.
Yes, I *was* afraid. I was not, after all, Joan of Arc.
Yet when I was threatened once
I let it be known that I would sit each evening
by my big window, reading. Happily, nothing happened.
I took comfort, too, from our tenants telling me
no stone of Coole nor hair of my head, would be harmed.
Though Roxborough, alas, was burned to a shell.
Heartbreaking the forlorn sight of it. My childhood
in ruins. Gone up in smoke. So sad to witness that.
Once, too, there was a terrible loud knocking
at our hall door in Coole.
The servants trembling. Men's rough voices.
Open up or twill be the worse for you!
I went down and stood there but didn't open.
Eventually they went away.
That shook my nerves, yes. Yet I felt it was right
that I myself should know what others suffered.

And still, even in the midst of that unspeakable time,
Coole Park was radiant through spring and summer:
the great white horse chestnuts in bloom;
the crimson and white hawthorns; lilac and laburnum
and our big copper beech with its famous signatures—
all flourishing. And all the leaves so fresh after rain,
sunlight making them glisten. And I would remember
Yeats's lines about *the woods in their Autumn beauty.*
The woods that now I held in trust for my grandson.

And *still* the terrible happenings persisted.
Once I went to see Georgie Yeats over at Ballylee.

She said Mrs. Gogarty had told her, in tears,
that Renvyle House had been burnt down.
Other big houses, too, were put to the torch—
the countryside became a chain of bonfires.
Then poor Erskine Childers was executed,
leaving his wife—my friend, Molly—to grieve.
And so on . . . on to the ambush and death of Michael Collins.
What a terrible blow! I liked and admired him.
Strong as he was, he was a human being, not a Messiah.
Like de Valera he was masterful, but in so different a way.
Passionate, down-to-earth, humorous—
Where de Valera was colder, more calculated, remote.
I had *prayed* for them *both*. . . .
But I had such high hopes for Collins. His future. Ours.
When I heard he was dead,
I went and sat in the garden—alone—for a long time.

At last, when de Valera's Republican surrender order
ended the Civil War, it was a great relief. Everywhere.
Still, I told my friend, Fr. O'Kelly, that one should not be
more angry with the Government or with the Republicans
than with different sections of one's own mind—
tilting to good or bad, on one side or the other.
That is what I felt, hoping for peace. And I felt
that that very thought was the image of my self.
For it seemed I had always stood—as steadily as I could—
between things: between demands, between worlds,
between classes, religions, languages, and so on.
Even between those who loved me and whom I loved.
But now . . . now I hoped good feeling would come—
now the fight was over—and they would all shake hands.
In 1924 that was.
But in face of such bitter memories—

of murders, reprisals, executions, hunger strikes—
a quick forgiveness was doubtful.
And whatever about the cities, I knew
it was the countryside that always remembers—
has such a long, long, unforgiving memory.

As for me—I simply wished the ground I loved
could be healed. The Scripture verse
that sang forlornly in my head then was
Love worketh no ill to his neighbour.
And when, in 1924, I read and then heard
Juno's lament in O'Casey's play, that verse came back.
For I always loved how, in his great plays for us at the Abbey,
Seán caught all that awful, awful time
with such truth, such vigour, compassion, understanding.
From his brave account of the tragically complex
horrors of the Rising, to the tragically avoidable
wounds of the Civil War.
His people so deeply humanised.
The ordinary tragicomic humanity
of their voices, their wonderful Dublin voices
obliging us to hear them out.

So there stands poor Juno—her own son dead—
lamenting how she hasn't grieved enough
for her neighbour, Mrs. Tancred,
whose son has died serving the other side:
Ah why didn't I remember when her own poor son
was found like me own son Johnny's been found now—
she says, keening her own lament:

Overvoice: *because he was a Die-Hard! Ah why didn't I remember*
that he wasn't a Diehard or a Free Stater, but only a poor dead son!
It's well I remember all that she said—and it's my turn to say it now:

What was the pain I suffered, Johnny, bringin you into the world
to carry you to your cradle, to the pains I'll suffer
carryin you out o' the world to bring you to your grave!
Mother o' God, Mother o God, have pity on us all!
Blessed Virgin where were you
when me darlin son was riddled with bullets?
Sacred Heart o' Jesus, take away our hearts o' stone,
and give us hearts o' flesh! Take away this murderin hate
and give us Thine own eternal love.

Every night at the Abbey, I would listen to those words
in the darkened theatre, and my tears would freely fall.
For Robert, and for every one of those poor mothers' sons,
wherever they had fallen.
Oh it was all such a tangle of love and death,
hope and fear, big world and small,
bittersweet memory and each passing, ordinary day.
And through it all—all those bad days and nights—
indeed in spite of it all—we tried our best
to keep things at the Abbey going.
Writing. Encouraging. Organising.
Helping it become in time our National Theatre.
I devoted myself to that task. *That* was *my* duty.
And I did, with all the difficulties it brought,
I did love the task.
But all that—important as it is—is another story.

Well, that was the end of the most dangerous, I suppose,
and difficult time of my life. A time
filled with the urgencies of love
and the sad recognitions of death, tragic deaths.
I felt how right they were now, my dark widow's weeds.
For through all that terrible time I was truly in mourning,

not just for my son, or my husband, but for the country itself,
for Ireland. And though it was a far cry, I felt,
from Mary Sheridan's memory of the French at Killala,
I knew that for me the line from there
to the end of our Civil War was unbroken.
And knew my love that had been roused back then for Ireland,
my feeling for it as my own country,
was somehow unbroken too.
No doubt you'll smile and say
oh it is all more complicated than that,
and you'll be right. But through it all,
what remained quite clear to me was the fact
that running under so much of my life
with its series of enthusiasms, there ran—
like the underground stream that runs
between Thoor Ballylee and Coole Park—
there ran a single unbroken thread of love.
A thread that for all its twists and turns
still wound its own deliberate, determined way.

And so there I was, in the New Ireland.
Our own independent Irish Free State.
And I suppose I *can* say
that I had played my part in bringing that about.
Although it did not match exactly what I had dreamed of.
No. For the hatreds spawned by the Civil War
had a long life still to run. We all know that.
And indeed, I'm afraid the New Ireland
did, in time, let us down somewhat—
and not only those of us in the minority.
Marriage, divorce, birth control, education—
not to mention the more socially enlightened elements
of the Proclamation itself—all were to become

issues that could divide us. That was a pity.

And so we hoped that it still might, in time, happen—

that the Ireland we imagined: Free State Ireland—

Independent Ireland—Republic of Ireland—diverse Ireland—

even a United *Island of Ireland*—would become

not simply the country we loved,

but the country we had dreamed of.

But all that, too, is another story.

Of course, even after the war ended, and even

after reaching the allotted *three score and ten,*

I wasn't one to slow down too much.

Many of my loves had still to be attended to.

Coole itself, for one. It was finally sold to the State—

with the agreement I could rent the house and gardens,

and live there for life. What a relief that was.

Simply to remain . . . at home.

And my grandchildren, the chicks, to be cosseted.

And the Abbey, oh yes the Abbey . . .

with all its problems, its in-fightings and jealousies.

Its complicated cat's-cradle of needs, policy debates, arguments.

I was still at its always excitable nerve centre.

Either as its *[laughs]* "charwoman" (as Bernard Shaw described me)

or as its Old Lady saying Yes or No to scripts, actors, directors.

Always in a struggle against slackness.

Slackness I could never abide, no.

But then all those opening and closing nights marked with parties—

the entire company tucking into my famous Coole barm-brack.

Celebrating the simple fact of Our Irish Theatre. A theatre of our own

I always felt so proud and satisfied then.

In the Abbey, too, I was something of a peacemaker.

The actors could be like quarrelling children.

I had to be their mother . . . though one with a steely nerve,

which—as you know—I had.

Of course some thought that in those roles
I could be condescending . . . a snob.
Was I? Well, yes . . . no . . . yes . . . Oh very well, yes.
I did make the occasional . . . remark.
As when I said that John Redmond—leader of the Irish party
in Westminster—*looked uncomfortable in a clean shirt.* Oh dear.
Or that the riotous fights over Synge's *Playboy*—a play
I never much liked really (a little too *overt* for my taste)—
were *between those who used a toothbrush
and those who didn't.* That sort of thing.
Or that to appeal to a popular audience we at the Abbey
had to be *baptised of the gutter.* Silly really.
But such remarks, if made by a politician—or even by a man—
would have garnered little or no notice at all.
But it's hard to get away with much if you are a Lady!
My remaining years were also punctuated
by one abiding, dutiful love.
A love I pursued—alas fruitlessly—to the end.
For I had always fought and would continue fighting
for the return of the paintings my nephew, Hugh Lane,
(who went down with the *Lusitania*) had willed to the nation.
But which by a legal quibble ended up in England's keeping.
Oh dear, one more reason to cry *Perfidious Albion!*
(You know, I defy anyone to study the history of Ireland
and not develop a deep dislike for England!)
Over and back across the Irish Sea I scuttled, so,
like a busy yo-yo: speaking to English officials,
haranguing newspaper people, politicians, friends, lords, ladies.
Pursuing that end. But that is yet another story.
Of course, in the end, I did have to slow down.
(Though I'm proud to say that even at seventy
I could still run to catch a tram or a train—
my long black dress, black veil, and big black hat

all flapping in the breeze. Quite a sight! Not Queen Victoria!)
I still loved life, you see.
As an old Scottish acquaintance once said to me—he was over eighty:
"Yes, I'd like to keep going. Things are so . . . interesting."
But when I became ill I was obliged to take things more slowly.
And at times, sitting surrounded by the lonely silences of Coole,
or with a storm shaking the shutters and rattling the big windows,
I knew age had come upon me.
And I would read over again
my translation of Raftery's *An Cailleach Béara. The Old Woman of Beare.*

Overvoice: *[Irish country voice]*

> *Ebbtide is to me as to the sea.*
> *Old age brings me reproach.*
> *I used to wear a shift that was always new,*
> *today I have not even a cast one.*
> *The summer of youth where we were*
> *has been spent along with its harvest.*
> *Winter age that drowns everyone,*
> *its beginning has come upon me.*
> *Though many are my company in the darkness,*
> *a hand has been laid upon them all.*

"Though many are my company in the darkness,
a hand has been laid upon them all. . . . "
Indeed!
Through all that time, however, my dear Yeats
was a bright light of friendship,
a loving companion among those gathering shadows.
He would come over from Ballylee and I would read to him.
That was such a comfort. Not to be too much alone. . . .
For there was no evading old age. Or illness.
I had to be operated on. While under the anaesthetic,
I revisited the streams of Roxborough and Coole.

Walked there in my mind, named over to myself
the landmarks, the woods, the trees. My early loves.
I recited the litany of the sacred places.
And I whispered Willie's poem, hearing his voice:

Overvoice: *["WBY" voice]*
    I have heard the pigeons of the Seven Woods
    Make their faint thunder, and the garden bees
    Hum in the lime-tree flowers; and put away
    The unavailing outcries and the old bitterness
    That empty the heart. . . .
    I am contented, for I know that Quiet
    Wanders laughing [there], eating her wild heart.

I liked to think of that wild heart, even if my own
was never *truly* wild. Yet it too found *Quiet*. At last.
Once, during those final months, I said to Yeats,
"It may be the time has come for me to slip away . . .
I don't want to become a burden and give trouble.
I have had a full life and—except for the grief of
parting with those who are gone—a happy one."
And then, in time, it was over. The play was ended.
The mask of life was lifted and laid aside.
With all its loves and deaths, its griefs and hilarities,
its wisdom and its folly, its . . . everything.
Laid aside. As an actor removes her cloak, her paint,
the voice she has worn, the loves she has mimed.
And says, as I say: that was me: my life. That was it.
I too had to resign my part in that casual comedy.
All my adult life I suppose I played a part. Had a role.
Was a character: "Lady Gregory." That was my calling.
My vocation. My duty. My love.
And I stuck to it. Black widow's weeds and all!
And though I only acted once in the theatre—

perhaps you might still call me a . . . *Leading Lady. [amused]*

Of course *I* was not the *end* of the *larger* journey.
Ireland's own journey.
No, I was simply a stage along the way.
Like Yeats, Synge, O'Casey, Shaw,
Maud, the Countess, Pearse, MacDonagh,
and all those many others.
Even Joyce—though he took his own, different, path.
We were all stages along the way.
The way of the Word. In the beginning was the Word.
And in the middle too. The Word, the words.
The words that would make sense of the country
all of us wanted, had dreamed of, worked towards, fought for.
Making sense of it and of our selves—
of our own ways of being in the world,
in our own changing world . . . *[small pause]*
One day, close to the end, I rose from my bed.
It was rather painful, yes. But I knew what I was doing.
I visited each of the rooms in turn.
Gazing on the paintings, the furniture, the curtains,
the windows, even the doorknobs.
All those things I had lived with for fifty years.
That had given me my most profound sense of belonging.
I walked slowly about among them, visiting them.
I was saying goodbye to the house, that life.
And then . . . I returned to my bed.
And waited.
Through my bedroom window, I could catch glimpses
of how the trees were bending and shivering in the breeze.
How the light was working among the leaves:
its shivery quicksilver glittering.
And I lay there naming over again those trees

that had been my care for so long.
How's all your care? The country people say.
Oh, for the moment, all is well, I would reply.
All my care:
my actors, writers, tenants, servants, workers, grandchildren.
All my care.
Robert, William, Wilfrid, John, Hugh.
Yeats, Synge, O'Casey, and others . . .
I cared for them all; they all knew me.

Overvoice: *[Dublin accent, "O'Casey"]*
Blessed Bridget O'Coole! How did she of the grandees
manage to come so close to the common people?
She trotted fearlessly and listened to tales, and songs.
Made merry and was sad with the ordinary people.
Rare wine and homemade bread were hers.
Out of her plush and plum
she came to serve the people, body and mind,
with whatever faculties God had given her.
And were we not all the luckier for it?

And the trees . . . yes of course . . . the trees were my special care.
[litany as at start] Chestnut ash beech birch, elm and oak, catalpa,
sycamore.
Norway spruce, juniper, larch and laurel, weeping willow.
The trees, you see—great ones in their prime, injured ones
after tempests, saplings in their fresh young life—the trees
were my companions all those years. My guardians too.
Through bough-breaking winter storms, sunny summer calms,
and in, of course—as Willie would say—*in their Autumn beauty.*
So . . .
if ever one day you visit Coole . . . yes, the House *is* gone
(and that is, as they say, *a crying shame*) . . . but the woods endure.
And that's where you may find a tiny fragment of my soul.
Not in that great copper beech
where the great names of the Irish Revival are carved.

No. But in a slim silver birch, standing ghostly
in a grove of shadows.
Do stand a silent moment there, won't you?—
and reach, and touch, its shining bark.
[music, "She Moves through the Fair," and slow blackout*]*

Curlew Theatre Company

PRESENTS

Peig: An Ordinary Life

A Play for Voices

Adapted by Eamon Grennan from *Peig: the Autobiography of Peig Sayers*
Translated from the Irish by Bryan MacMahon

Performed by Tegolin Knowland and Sean Coyne
Directed by Eamon Grennan

Peig: An Ordinary Life

adapted from Bryan MacMahon's translation of
Peig: The Autobiography of Peig Sayers of the Great Blasket Island

Introduction

Peig (Margaret) Sayers, Ireland's best-known female Seanachai (traditional teller of stories, myths, folktales), was born in Vicarstown, Dunquin, County Kerry, in 1873. She came from a big family, but only four of her siblings survived. She inherited, as she tells us herself in her dictated autobiography (*A Scéal Féin*), her storytelling gift from her father, Tomás Sayers.

Peig could neither read nor write English. But she had an uncanny mastery of spoken Kerry Irish. Visitors, from Ireland and elsewhere, came to listen to her stories, her language, and her accent. The English scholar and translator Robin Flower (whom she called Bláithín, "little flower") said "her words could be written down as they leave her lips, . . . with no savour of the artificiality of composition."

As a young woman, Peig worked twice in domestic service in Dingle. Having been disappointed in her attempt to emigrate to America, she spent the rest of her life in Kerry. Like many other women of her time, place, and station Peig's marriage in 1892 was an arranged one, but she loved her husband, Pádraig (Peats) Ó Guithín, a fisherman and native of the Great Blasket Island, where she went to live. Five of her children predeceased her: three in infancy, others from sickness or accident. Her husband died early, from a cold caught while out fishing, and her remaining children emigrated.

When the Irish Department of Education put her book on its Leaving Certificate curriculum in the 1970s, the book and its author got a reputation for gloom and doom among those who felt forced to read it.

What I have tried to do, however, in this "play for voices" is capture a number of Peig's own voices—courageous, sad, humorous, compassionate, angry, and always dramatic at root—great storyteller as she is. My hope is to illustrate Peig's uncanny powers of observation and recall, as reflected in Bryan MacMahon's fine translation, from which I have adapted passages to create her voice in the play. This "voice collage" adds up to a life: a full life in which her simple yet complex power of character turns the ordinary into the extraordinary, makes it memorable beyond the often monochromatic picture that many people may have had of her. We hear and see her in her simple, richly experienced love of life and of the world around her. It is a voice bringing Peig herself into our world as an ordinary yet extraordinary, living, audible, and brave human being in her own particular time and place and, most importantly, in her own voice.

In late 1941 Peig moved back from the Great Blasket to Vicarstown. She died in Dingle in 1958 and is buried in Dunquin.

The play is adapted from the translation of Peig's autobiography (dictated in Irish to her son Mícheál) by Bryan MacMahon, playwright and author, and former lecturer in Paul Engel's School of Creative Writing, Iowa. His translation, *Peig: The Autobiography of Peig Sayers of the Great Blasket Island*, was published in the United States by Syracuse University Press in 1974. This adaptation is being published with the kind permission of Maurice MacMahon.

Peig: An Ordinary Life was first performed by Curlew Theatre Company on September 11, 2022 at the Blasket Center, Dún Chaoin, Co. Kerry.

For the original production

SET
    Plain black neutral backdrop
    Kitchen chair and small armchair

PROPS
    Walking stick; coloured shawl; black shawl

[stage in blackout; low fiddle tune, slow air]

Overvoice: *[brief recital of Peig's own voice reading in Irish the beginning of* "St. Brendan and His Book" *("Naomh Breandán agus a Leabhar Aifrinn");* then fade into *Peig's voice in English; Kerry accent; low, aged, halting]*

What ever did I want . . . ?

I wanted no more . . .

than to give . . .

an accurate account

of the life I had . . .

the people I knew . . . .

so we'd be remembered . . . .

when we'd moved on . . .

into eternity . . .

I thought always . . .

my life was no way important . . .

that all I could say about it . . .

was guesswork and blind groping. . . .

But whether that's so or not . . .

It's there now anyway. . . .

Many a thing I saw . . . .
and I never let anything go astray . . .
for people like us . . .
will never be there again . . .
and that old world . . .
will have vanished . . .

[sudden full light up on Peig; voice stronger, normal, rhythmic; quickish, but words carefully enunciated (as native Irish speakers do when speaking English). She has different moods: feisty, humorous, reverent, reminiscent, nostalgic, sad—depending on subject matter.]

Peig: Ye're welcome all. *Fáilte.*

Are ye comfortable? Proper seats and all?

When I'd be telling stories in my house on the Island,

the neighbours and children would come in to hear them.

Others too: strangers, educated people, scholars and the like.

And I'd be telling them stories, I had a gift for that.

Stories from the myths and legends of Ireland, and all that.

But today 'tisnt such stories I'll be telling ye.

But the story of myself, aye. My own life. *Mo Scéal Féin.*

Nothing grand like legends or myths, no—

but my own story, ordinary as it is.

But oh 'twas a *distinguished* audience I had back then. Like this one . . .

I'd wet my lips, so, settle myself on the stool in the corner,

and brace myself for talking.

They'd be sitting there on stools and benches

and on the floor itself . . . listening,

But ye lot have gathered *here* now,

and I see ye're comfortable. That'll do ye fine so.

[settles herself, readying for "storying"]

I was born twice, d'ye know that?

Not that I was drawn twice

from the womb of my poor mother, no.

But two lives, aye.

And very *different* lives they were too.

The first from when I was born (1873 that was)

to when I was about nineteen. My childhood.
At home with my people first—
in a small spot called Vicarstown outside Dunquin.
Twice then in service, starting when I was twelve or thirteen
and serving my time in the town of Dingle.
Domestic service. Twice, aye: one good, the other bad:
like life itself I suppose.
I escaped all that, anyway, at nineteen years of age—
when I agreed to a match being made, and a marriage following.
'Twas then I began my second life—
away from Dingle, Dunquin, and Vicarstown. . . .
away even from the island of Ireland—
and onto the big island of the Blaskets off the coast of Kerry.
Right so. Two lives. Two different lives. . . .
But aren't there millions like that—with two lives?
Like our own emigrants—
off in their droves and shiploads
from the time of the Famine
right up to my own time, and yours indeed.
My own children among them.
A life here; leave; then a life
wherever their journeys take them.
They say I was a fine talker and storyteller.
I suppose I was.
Like my father, Tomás Sayers, before me,
who had more tales than any man of his time.
Margaret Peig Brosnan was my mother.
'Twas after her I was called.
Her thirteenth child I was. The last.
"The scrapings of the pot,"
I heard my father say once . . . oh yes, very nice. *[laughs]*
But of that thirteen, 'twas only myself
and three others before me lived.
For after the first three, didn't the others—

one after another—all die.
Nine children they buried, my mother and father did.
Nine. Common enough those times.
But small wonder my poor mother, God help her,
was often sad and distracted.
Being last, of course, I was everyone's pet . . .
well, ye know how it is.
My people hadn't much:
all the land they possessed was the grass of two cows.
Poor, yes, but wasn't everybody that time—
out there in the townland of Vicarstown near Dunquin.
At four I started school. In the Babies Class.
Right away, d'ye know, I loved books—
the lovely coloured pictures in them!
The Master it was gave me my first book. It had a red cover.
I was as delighted as if I'd been presented with . . . a *cow*!
When I was seven my brother Seán
married a girl from Ventry, who moved into our house.
Cáit Boland was her name.
Fiery-tempered, apt to flare up,
she gave my poor father little peace in his own house.
Being a quiet man, he'd only say:
"You'd be better off with a bit of sense, my cailín."
But you know the old *sean-fhochail*:
Advising a rough-spoken woman
is like striking cold iron with a rib of hair.
Well, the years went by
and I'd be doing little jobs about the house,
and sometimes I'd be herding the cattle.
When I'd get home them times
I'd be as hungry as a ploughman.
Then potatoes out of the embers, roasted fine and hot,
was my fare—with a lump of butter
and a drop of new milk. You'd never bate it!

Of course that time 'twas in Irish
we were bred, born, and reared.
But in school they taught us a bit of English too:
Bó bán, a white cow; gamhain breac, a speckled calf.
All well and good so.
Still, we got a new master one time
and he had such a foreign accent on his speech
he could have been a big bucko of an Englishman
over from the city of London!
We kept on wanting to soften that terrible cramp
he had on his tongue, using the Irish, the poor man.
Oh we'd read some English too, we would,
and I learned a poem off by heart, I did.
'Twas about emigration and it made me sad.
[recites, carefully enunciating]

> *Erin my country! Though sad and forsaken,*
> *In dreams I revisit thy sea-beaten shore;*
> *But alas! In a far foreign land I awaken,*
> *And sigh for the friends who can meet me no more!*

I sore pitied that man, I did,
for he could be any Irish emigrant at all—
in America or any place foreign.
At school I was never very wild or anything.
Oh, but I did do a few divilish things. Only a few, mind.
Once, I stole a lovely loaf of apple cake
from our neighbour Ould Kitty
when I was selling her six eggs. Disgraceful, oh aye!
But sure I was young, and the divilment
is in the young, and harmless enough too.
Here's how it happened:
[settles herself for a "story"; quick tempo, no hesitations]
I was needing a schoolbook and it cost thruppence,
so I got six eggs from our hens and off I went to Ould Kitty.
In her cabin, she was, squatting on her hunkers,

and the little place black with smoke around her.
Well, I gave her the eggs and asked for the thruppence
and while she was foostering for the pennies
didn't I spy a loaf of bread inside on a shelf.
'Twas a cake made of snow-white flour
with apple filling in the middle and sugar on top.
Well, to see a bit of white bread that time
was something of a marvel, so is it any wonder
I was taken by an unmerciful desire to taste the cake,
and the temptation struck me to snatch some of it
so I dug my talons into the cake, I did,
and made two halves out of it
and stuck one of them under my oxter.
Then didn't Ould Kitty hand over the pennies.
"Is it going to school you are now, pet?"
Says she sweetly. "'Tis indeed," says I,
and off I legged it out the door—
stolen sweet cake and all!
"Lord above in Heaven," says my friend Kate Jim,
when I met her and took the lump of cake
out of my armpit. "Where did you get that?"
"Stole it from Ould Kitty, girl," says I.
"and 'tis a fine big piece of flour-loaf sweet as honey—
made of apples and sugar and other stuff."
Good enough so. All well so far. . . .
But, even then, couldn't I feel a kind of remorse
starting up inside of me.
"But what'll I do," says I to Kate, "if Ould Kitty finds out?"
"But sure she wasn't watching you," says she.
"But there was Someone," says I,
"watching me alright, and now I'd prefer
not to have touched it. For God save my soul,
but won't Ould Kitty be out cursing me,
and my father will be worse if he hears it."

"Cut the sign of the Cross on yourself," says Kate,

"and ask God to protect you from her."

"Oh girtl," says I, "isn't it fine and easy *you* have the cure?"

Howanever . . . in the heel of the hunt

there was never any mention of the stolen loaf.

My sin, so, stayed in the dark. . . .

So there:

that was the first roguery ever entered my head,

and just look at how I gave into it.

But sure I suppose lots of young ones do the like.

Harmless enough. Except for Ould Kitty!

On with my life so . . . *[slows down a little]*

One evening—I was twelve or thirteen at the time—

I heard my father's voice. Angry he was.

Overvoice: *[father] A woman is more stubborn than a pig, and a pig is more stubborn than the devil!*

Peig: He was saying this to his daughter-in-law, Cáit.

Later, I heard him whispering to his friend Muiris:

Overvoice: *[loud whisper] If I got any suitable place*

I'd put that unfortunate girl there in service.

Peig: 'Twas me he meant, I knew that.

To save me from the fights.

Overvoice: *For she'll have food and clothing,*

cause no dissatisfaction.

Peig: But Lord God in bed that night, I had such thoughts!

What would I do when I left my own home?

Who'd do a hand's turn for my mother?

For I was the sole consolation and comfort she had.

'Twas a bad night.

Still, when I woke up next morning

the dark was gone and the sun was shining.

"God direct me," I said to myself then.

"Nothing for it now

but to put the evil day on the long finger."

Life had to be lived in its own moment, you see, that was it.

But there were good times in it too, of course there were.
Like I remember my first time
going to the Races on Ventry Strand.
Well, *[readying for a "story"]*
on the morning of the Races I was
out of bed all excited at the crack of dawn.
My mother didn't know what was happening.
[speedy back and forth dialogue]
"What's pinching you now, Featherhead?" says she.
"I'm off to the races, girl," says I.
"Who'll be with you," says she.
"My Father and Kate Jim," says I.
"Well well," says she, "dependin' on your Da, is it?
And he the biggest ninnyhammer in the country
when he has a drop taken!"
"But sure he won't get drunk at all," says I,
"for Jim and old Muiris will be with him."
"God help your wit, child," says she,
"isn't one of them as lightheaded as the other. . .
But God prosper your day anyway."
So off we went.
When we reached Ventry Strand,
every square inch of it was covered
with stands and platforms and tables—
all laden with sweet cakes and confections.
Thimble-riggers and food people with their tables too.
Well anyway, the men started in drinking:
gallon cans of porter were set down in front of them,
and from drink to drink they went
until not one of them knew
if he was standing on his head or his heels.
Oh then the hullaballoo and noise began in earnest!
One man was praising, another dispraising,
a third going clean out of his mind with singing.

My father was a fine singer and did his bit too,
gripping onto the hand of the man beside him.
Keeping their spirits up, they were, I suppose.
Well, like that, time was slipping away
and I was getting weary—
for I had a headache from all the noise.
"Wasn't I a fool," says I to Kate Jim,
"not to listen to my mother when she told me
'twas the most foolish thing in the world
to depend on my father."
I went over to him, so.
Crying, I was, sort of pettish-like.
"Are you going home at all Dad?"

Overvoice: *Home we'll go with the help of God, girl.*
Don't be one bit uneasy about that.

Peig: "But whisper Dad," says I,
"*When* will you go home?"

Overvoice: *[cheerful] I'll go home girl when I have enough drank.*
If you see your brother Seán, let you go home with him,
and don't be depending on me.

Peig: So there I left him, and he in the height of his glory—
chanting *Dónal na Gréine.*
'Twas then I met my brother Seán.
"Where's your father?" says he.
"Inside over there," says I,
"and a proper noody-naddy he is."
"Oh God girl," says Seán,
"isn't that the way he generally is.
We'll be going home straight so."
So then I bought sweets for the lot of us . . .
and we started on the long road home.
Well, home at last, my mother was waiting:
"You must have a great load of news from the Races," says she.
"Did you see the horses run?"

"'Pon my very soul but I didn't," says I,
"nor even a piece of a horse . . .
for from start to finish that day
I never laid eyes on horse nor jockey,
but inside in a tent all the while
listening to the addled old music of those men—
and my father, who is not in Heaven."
   "And where did you leave the Forest Ranger?" says she.
"He was merry, I suppose, if running true to form."
"Sure everyone there, girl, was on his ear," says I.
But listen to me now: Soon after that
didn't I hear a *tatata-rara* up the road,
and in the door came my father
and he as light in his head as a puck goat, and singing.
"Now bad scran to you!" cries my mother.
"How well you never lost the old habit!"
But he moved up to her then and out of his pocket
didn't he draw a half pint of whiskey and held it out to her.
"Well, may I never lose you," says she then.
"You never forgot me!"
And she poured a lively drop for herself.
'Twas all good cheer so, and my father
raising every second bar of a song . . . .
Sure, Lord above, 'twas just like being at a wedding:
dancing and music, and singing all the old Irish songs.
My mother was the finest singer ever sang a verse,
and with a little drop on board
she sang, and sweetly, "Gráinne Mhaol,"
and after that a man sang "An Clár Bog Déil,"
and on like this they carried, till well after midnight.
And ye know, I think that was the most entertaining night
I ever spent, at the start of my days.
Well, as I always say, there's never a bright
without a dark, an up without a down,

a tide coming in without a tide flowing out . . .
So 'twasn't long after that merry night
that the music of my life changed, yes, changed utterly.
One day, my father spent the whole day in Dingle
and when he came home he told my mother
he'd found a place for me there.
I remember my mother then:
she put her head down and cried bitter tears
and, young as I was, the heart in my breast was broken.
For what would she have to go through
when I was far away from her?
I sat in the garden so, and cried my fill.
I was jealous of Kate Jim and all the other girls
who were happy as the days were long.
The turns of the world are very strange, I thought:
some people sorrowful, others full of joy. . . .
That night I couldn't eat. . . .
I just said my prayers and went to bed—
thinking bad thoughts the whole night long.
For I knew my schooldays were surely over.
But 'twas a bright morning when I woke up:
a sunbeam was shining through the window
and a thousand midges or *cuilleógs*
were flitting about in it.
I saw a spider, too, spinning a thread of silk
out of his own body—and lowering himself
from the tie beam of the rafters.
Birds were singing outside the window—
and I could hear the cock crowing too.
And I said out to myself:
The High King of Creation be praised and thanked,
Who ordained a livelihood
for every creature according to nature.
Whatever God has in store for me now,

that will come to pass. . . .
But that morning, as I left with my father
I could see my mother—
all huddled up by the fire and crying to herself.
I ran up to her, so, and put my two arms tight around her—
till my father had to come and take me away.
Well, I'd never been to Dingle, so 'twas like a new world
and it filled me with wonder.
Grand tall buildings on all sides
with people hurrying past each other
and sure I couldn't understand one word
of what they were saying.
And the two eyes popping out of my head with fright.
God of Miracles! I told myself.
I won't live one single day here.
We went to the house then where I'd be working,
and there my father left me.
"The blessing of God be with you," he said.
And then *[amazed]* he was gone . . . and I was alone.
Alone in a strange house where I knew no one.
Worse still, I knew no English—
save for an odd word here and there that made no sense.
But the woman of the house was Nell Curran:
a cousin of my father's she was,
and a generous, hospitable, pleasant woman.
And her husband Seamas
every bit as good as she was herself.
And they had me sleep, so, in the one room
with Granny Nan, who lived with them.
And since the old lady had but little English,
we spoke Irish all the time, the two of us.
I was glad of that, for the Irish was part of me . . .
part of . . . my *soul,* I suppose. . . .
and it always put great joy on my heart

to hear the Gaelic being spoken.
Still, in bed that first night,
a bout of grief came over me
at the thought of my poor mother lonely after me.
And sure why wouldn't it, young as I was—
no more than eleven or twelve years old that time?
But indeed and in truth it didn't take me too long
to get the run of the place and know my job:
making meals, getting the children off to school,
teaching them a bit of Irish,
and they teaching me a bit of English . . .
That sort of thing, you know how it is.
Maybe you've done it yourself, indeed.
And in the meantime I was putting down my time:
one day easy, another hard: ordinary life.
Yes, that was the size of it. Ordinary life.
So I didn't feel the time slipping by.
Have I memories of my time there? Well I do. . . .
Oh, God in heaven,
I'll never forget my first Fair Day.
[settling herself for a "story"]
Seamas needed two or three pigs for killing, you see—
to sell the pork to customers for the Christmas.
'Twouldn't be turkeys those days, no.
In the end, he bought four pigs.
The day they were being killed,
God, I was in a right panic.
For I had never seen an animal slaughtered.
Fat Seamas was the pig-sticker:
a stout sallow middle-aged man, and a real bitter boyo,
especially with a drop taken.
You'd not relish it at all
if he looked at you with fury in his eyes.
Well, there was a *table* in the back garden

and didn't the man of the house and Fat Seamus
tie up the pig and land it on top of the table.
"Bring the basin, Peig," they said,
"and hold it under the blood."
I caught the basin so and went to the table.
"Hold it proper now," says Fat Seamas.
Yerra, gentle people, I had the shivers
in all my limbs, and ye would too.
For when he stuck the knife into the pig's throat
she let this unmerciful screech out of her
that knocked the echoes out of the place!
But if she did, I myself let go a screech every bit as loud,
and the basin dropped out of my two hands
and clattered to the ground—
with Fat Seamas letting a great roar out of him:

Overvoice: *[loud, harsh] Hold the vessel right, you thunderin straip,*
           or I'll give you what I'm givin' the pig!

Peig: Oh my dears, gentle people as ye are,
      he put the heart crossways in me—
      with his two wild eyes and his long knife—
      so I did my level best to hold the basin rightly.
      'Twas awful, yes, but awful as it was,
      by the time the last of those pigs was dead
      all my fears had vanished. And that's a fact.
      But now, I hope I didn't shock ye.
      Like I said . . . ordinary life . . . and I got used to it.
      But I remember one Christmas Eve too.
      And a nice memory it is, so it is.
      Not a drop of blood in it at all.
      'Twas paper flowers on the table, and candles lit—
      a red one and a blue one—
      and plenty of jam and butter there too.
      And when all the lamps were lighting
      and the kitchen all decorated

sure I thought I was in the Kingdom of Heaven,
for I'd never before seen such a lovely light.
Of course I was watching everything,
and the family there together—
and I couldn't help thinking of my poor mother at home,
and the kind of a night she'd have—
a nearsighted lonely unfortunate poor woman
without light or joy,
for I wasn't there to raise her spirits
or offer her one scrap of happiness.
Oh it's a strange uneven world I told myself,
and the tears came to my eyes.
But I decided then, I did, I'd take the children
off to see the Crib. Well of course
the night was dark, yes, but you could see—
by the light of all the candles in the windows—
the tiniest object on the footpath, 'twas a wonder.
In the chapel too, such bright lights and candles burning.
Were you even the dullest person living
'twould remind you of the Kingdom of Heaven!
And the nuns were playing sweet music there too,
and my heart filled with joy—
for I'd never heard the likes of that music before.
Well anyway, here's one last story from that time.
Dark enough, but with a happy end to it.
Well, one night
[another "story": quite speedy narrative]
One evening I was trying to let the cow into her cowshed
but I couldn't—for there was something
stretched out on the ground outside the door.
I put my hand on it . . . and . . .
Glory be to God in heaven 'twas a body!
Into the kitchen with me so.
"God, Seamas, there's a dead man

stretched at the door of the cow-shed!"
Seamas got a right fright. "A dead man?" says he.
He took a candle out then,
but he couldn't recognize the body.
"But no matter who he is," says he, "he's finished.
Take you a grip of him."
Well I had the shakes, I did, but in the end
we got a look at the dead man's face.
"Micky Moriarty! dead as a doornail." says Seamas. . . .
"And God in heaven . . . ."
He's been drinking in there in our shop.
Still, we have to do our best. . . ."
Stiff as a poker Micky was, and us tugging away at him,
till we got him inside the kitchen.
I took the boots offa him then
and was rubbing his feet with hot water
with Seamas fingering a cup of whiskey
into his mouth.
'Twas then old Granny Nan walked in.
"Aililiu! what's goin' on?"
So we told her. And says she:

Overvoice: *[old "crone" voice] That way ye're goin' at him's not a bit*
              *   good.*
              But if there's a spark left in his heart at all,
              There's nothin' better than . . . melted butter . . .
              if it could be got back his throat.
              If it's drink he's taken he'll cast it out then—
              that's if he's alive at all.
She got a pat of butter then
and tried shoving it into his mouth with a spoon.
But weren't his teeth locked together,
till Seamas pried them open and then
Old Nan poured the butter back his throat.
"No mercy!" says she. "Give him plenty of it!"

And Lord she was right, for after a quarter hour
up it all came.
"Thanks be to God," says I. "He's alive!"
Well, says Seamas, I can hear him yet,

Overvoice: *[male, strong, normal] you've escaped with your life now, Micky, thank God.*
For we nearly went for the priest as well as the doctor.
But you should have sense from this out
for 'twill be a long day
before you'll drink as much as you did there.

Peig: "Bet your life on that," says me bould Micky,

Overvoice: *[different male voice, higher pitch]*
for as sure as my name is Micky
not a drop o' drink will enter my mouth again
as long as I live. But whisper now,
for the Lord's sake let none of ye tell me wife,
for if she hears a word of it
she'll surely sweep the head offa me.

Well anyway, that was the Death and Resurrection
(may God forgive me!) of Micky Moriarty.
But you know, he kept his promise—
for never again did a drop pass his lips
till the day he died.
I must have been all of sixteen or so
when that happened . . .
for I didn't stay long after
in service with Nell and Seamas—
for I got sick and went home.
But after a while in Vicarstown, then,
'twas back into service again with me.
I'll not tell ye much about that,
though, God's truth, in that thankless house
I often had the rumblings of hunger in my gut . . .
and where Seamas's wife Nell was a great-souled woman,
this one, Brídín, had the . . . the heart of a mouse.

But a great one for loading chores on my back.
'Twas little idle bread I et in that house, I can tell you,
and hardship itself kept a tight grip on me.
Domestic service indeed!
Domestic *servitude* I'd call it.
But, as the *sean-fhochal* has it,
There's no cure for misfortune,
but to kill it with patience.
But listen now: before I was too long there,
didn't I hear from Kate Jim over in America:
and she said she'd send me my passage money,
so I could go and join her over there.
Overjoyed I was then
as I left that house of hard labour
and went home again, and waited.
But God knows, I wasn't long home
when my heart was broken . . .
for didn't Kate take sick, and lost her job,
and couldn't send any money at all.
I got rightly downhearted then, I can tell you.
But sure I just had to make the best of it.
I told no one. That was it. . . .
No hope of America now.
Sure I thought my young life was over.
But ye remember, don't ye,
I said I was born two times over. . . .
Well wasn't the second time just then approaching.
For, by the grace of God, the dark was to turn to light,
and I was to have a new start-over.
Born again, and in a new place, too.
And—though not America—a New World!
A fresh start, aye, and (if ye will believe me)
as a *wedded woman*! In service to no one!
Be easy now, and I'll tell ye how it happened. . . .

But . . . before that, I have a few things more to say.
Just a little *suspense,* so,
till we get to the wedding and all of that.

PAUSE

[little skirl of uileann pipes: the tune "Seán Buí"*]*

Well, I've been rambling on here about ordinary life,
and our own small ordinary lives in our little townland—
and farther afield in Dingle and Dunquin.
Ordinary life, yes, in our own small everyday world.
But now I'd like to make a mention
of a few times when the big world itself
barged in on top of us.
The big world of politics, violence, all of that.
For I remember some of that surely too.
Well now . . . *[breath; "story"]*
I mind the time I was still at school in Vicarstown
and wasn't the Land Question
agitating the whole country.
And there was an eviction locally that time
and it set the whole parish of Ballyferriter up in arms.
Hundreds of men, young and old, I saw on the street,
each with his own weapon on his shoulder:
pikes, furze grubbers, staves
and other weapons that could cause havoc.
And the crown forces—Peelers, Sheriffs, Bailiffs—
drawn up to confront them.
"Fix bayonets," shouted the English captain.
"Fix pikes, boys," cried the Land League captain,
Tomás Martin of Gortadoo.
Rifles, pikes, and cudgels were raised aloft—
God the excitement!—
and all was ready for a royal battle. . . .
And I tell ye no lie,

had the Parish Priest not come between them
and made some settlement—
there would have been blood spilled surely.
But in the end, thanks be to God,
no one was wounded or lost his life.
I was only a child, but the wild excitement of it all—
I never forgot it, and the wild thumping of my heart!
Later, then, and I in service in Dingle,
another such action—only worse—happened.
One day . . . ["story" mode]
I was standing at the door of the shop,
when I saw a crowd shouting and grappling
and running towards the house of Muiris Bán.
Then came a pack of policemen, Peelers in battle dress,
marching down the street at a right get-go.
Each had a helmet on his head
with a spike the length of the leg of a tongs
sticking out the top of it.
Breathing heavily through their nostrils
they came, pushing their way through the crowd.
But 'twas of little use:
for the people fighting were right wicked—
shouting and talking in loud angry voices.
Like a proper pitched battle it was.
"Man alive," calls I to Seamas in the shop,
"there's never been such a set-to
since the time of the Dingle slaughter
as is going on at Muirisin Bán's house this minute.
All the Peelers from Tralee to Dingle are here
and they're making no hand of it at all!"
"Because the country people," says Seamas,
Overvoice: [solid, with feeling] Have no gentle feelings for the Peelers.
For haven't they pitched a poor penniless woman
and her five children

out of her home a few days back.
Her brother swore an oath that day before God
he hoped to get the chance of vengeance—
above board or underhand—and I pity the man
that'd stand in the path of his blow,
for he's a wild man and he's black out against them.
I ran upstairs then and stuck my head out the window.
Still at the lambasting, they were,
and the screeching and commotion going strong.
I saw a Peeler and he grabbing
a big man with a sallow face by the hand
while another one struck him a blow of his fist.
"Let me go," the big fellow told the Peeler,
"or I'll smash your ugly mouth!"
He let fly then, and lifted the Peeler into the air
and stretched him on the flat of his back in the gutter.
Then the big fella was on top of the Peeler.
Uproar and Hullaballoo!
More Peelers crashing in: one got a puck here,
another a push there, or a man
would stick his leg out and trip a policeman,
another give him a belt on the poll,
another send his cap flying. And Lord above,
the Peelers were being hammered and clattered.
But then the barracks got word
and the District Inspector was on his way.
[a brave "speech," rhythmic, half-line by half-line]
East he came riding towards the little bridge:
riding a black gelding, a white star on its forehead.
Reaching the bridge, he blew on a bugle.
There came a roaring from the throng of people.
Oh the District Inspector was a brave young man:
all rigged out on his black gelding,
and bearing his weapons.

Vigour and ferocity he had in his eyes,
A long, wicked-looking spear he carried,
and with the jingle-jangle of his harness bells
you'd think he was the Divil himself.
His intentions seemed . . . anything but wholesome!
A second blast he blew on his bugle
and, God of Miracles! like a flock of small birds
all the people scattered before him.
In five minutes not a solitary Christian
was left on the street.
But the state of things after the fight, is it?
Wicked awful! All in scatter and disarray.
For one of the Peelers was missing his cap,
another bleeding, and bones surely broken.
I heard that horseman was Baby Gray.
And so years later I recalled that
day of disturbance when I heard
Baby Gray, along with his followers,
had fallen in the famous battle of Ashbourne—
at the hands of Dingle's own Tomás Ashe.

PAUSE

[back to normal]

Of course, we all know the *Famine, An Gorta Mór,*
lay behind all that politics and violence.
All that hunger, misery, and death
sticking like a bone in the throats of the Irish.
And not much talk about it after.
Great Famine, Great Silence. That was it.
But 'twas my own father told me once
that when he was sixteen years of age
his own father's brother died of the Hunger.
He had tried to keep his family alive,
but the Hunger got the upper hand of him.

"In those days," said my father,
"there was neither coffin nor sheet
to cover poor people, nor anyone
to shoulder their coffins to the graveyard."
But his own father, he said,
—with a pair of men from the same townland—
knocked boards together to make a class of a coffin,
and put the unfortunate corpse into it.
But listen to my father tell it himself:
"His own father," he said . . .

Overvoice: *[man, normal Kerry accent] young as he was then,*
was the fourth of the coffin bearers
and he was under the front of the coffin.
But there was some misfortune or other
and didn't his heels strike a stone that lay in his path,
and weren't the two legs taken from under him.
And wasn't he capsized below in the dung heap
with coffin and corpse in after him.
And when he lifted his head
the coffin had fallen asunder
and the two feet of the corpse
were sticking out before him. . . .
A terrible sight it was, he told me,
never will I forget it!

Peig: My father went on to say then
that his uncle's wife and family
didn't live long afterwards,
"for their own cabin," he said,

Overvoice: *[man, normal Kerry] was tumbled down on top of their heads.*
And didn't four houses in our townland
meet the same end. . . .
But God grant that Christian people
may never again experience that sort of life.
Those bad times of death, destruction, and emigration

destroyed this land and wiped out the population.
And God help us, isn't that how
some came by the land they have today?
For 'twas easy to get it that time.
Well, that was *my* father's story
of *his own* father's memory of the Famine.
And I'm telling you the same now.
Handed down. Memory by memory. Voice by voice.
Isn't that what they call "tradition"?
And wouldn't it tell you loud and clear,
the poor country was in a terrible state that time and after:
riots, demonstrations, uprisings: all class of violence.
Till in the end came 1916. 1916 . . .
and all the awful, glorious happenings of the Rising and after.
Myself, I was a long time that time living on the Island
when news came to us
of a fierce battle happening
between the Irish and the Strangers
above in the city of Dublin.
At first you'd not believe a word of it.
Gossip, you'd say. But the postman
(may God grant his soul eternal rest)
brought us the story, and 'twas real.
"Dublin city was ablaze," he said: I can hear him yet:

Overvoice: *[male, high and hurried, excited] And the big guns of the Stranger battering it,*
and the fragrant blood of the Irish being spilled.
The Irish are awake again, and the people
stirred to strike a blow on their enemy.
But listen to me now:
Isn't there a warship this very minute
firing on the royal city of Dublin.
Total destruction is done there already.
And aren't the girls of the city
fighting shoulder to shoulder with the lads,

making music to my ears.

Peig: And then, says he, fair play to him,

Overvoice: *May God join strength with the lads,*
and let the King's barracks be knocked down again
and the yeomen be hunted by us.
For our day is after coming at last!
Well 'twasn't long after that—
after the terrible killings and executions and all—
that the battle was all over Ireland,
and nothing to be heard from morning till night
but *War! War! War!*
When a man would get in his door after work in the fields
his first question was:
Is there any story from the War today?
Which side is giving in?
"Well," says I then to my neighbour Nell:
"The blood is being spilt at our door at last.
But sure 'tisn't this war that will end the world,
but God himself, praise forever to Him, will end it.
And sure better people than us, will fall in it."
"That's true Peig," says Nell,
"but that wouldn't take the fear offa me,
knowing a better person than myself would fall in it.
But Dingle," says she, "is to be set on fire,
for madness and anger have a hold on the Strangers
and wholesale plunder is afoot there."
I told her I'd not believe it:
"For aren't we far west from them,
and should have no fear, for 'tisn't worth their while at all
coming out to this sea island."
But says Nell,

Overvoice: *[female, high-pitched, fast] They could come knocking at your*
door in the mid of night.
For they are clean out of their minds

because of how true the Irish are to one another.

Peig: She gave a bit of a speech then:
"But the fools, the fools," she said,

Overvoice: *[rhetorical] they thought they had only to come—*
for they hadn't before them in this little country
but people of no heed.
But they know now 'tis serious soul-gambling
for them to meet the lads.
So I wouldn't be surprised
if they dropped in on us here.
For always the Strangers do have great suspicion of us.
And sure enough, just a couple of days after,
wasn't there a squad of currachs coming in
all full of Stranger soldiers.
The people were frighted then,
thinking the island would be blown up in the sky,
and everything in it burnt, both houses and people.
The end of the world was there that day we thought.
Myself I was sitting then drinking a cup of tea by the fire
when my daughter dashed in—
"Oh God be with us, Mammy," cries she,
"soldiers and guns are all about the village—
and what are you doing?"
"I'm eating," says I.
"If it's death itself for me it's a great thing
to be strong for the long road."
"But everyone and everything
will be burned to the ground," says she.
"Don't mind that, pet," says I,
"we'll all be together in the name of God."
Then in rushed my husband Pádraig.
"For God's sake, Peig," says he,

Overvoice: *[male, strong] have you no anxiety only eating and drinking,*
and your eating and drinking to be ended this minute!

Hurry now and take down these pictures off the wall!
'Twas the pictures of the martyrs of 1916 he meant.
"Musha, defeat and wounding on those who felled them," I said.
"They killed them without mercy and they alive,
and it seems I have to hide their pictures
now they're dead.
But may I myself be dead and dead as stone,
ere I'll take them down in fear of any Stranger wretch!"
"Take it down!" says he. "I couldn't," says I.
"'Twill have to be left . . .
and if it's the cause of our death, 'tis welcome.
They fought and died for our sake.
Heroes they were, and heroic their deeds.
And as for Tomás Ashe's picture:
I can't hide that from anyone, good Kerryman as he was."
But then, before I could say *God with my soul,*
the house was filled up with soldiers.
Such a sight I never saw.
'Twould make anyone tremble.
Especially people the like of us
who never had any experience of military.
But God knows 'twould make you laugh too:
for we had no understanding of each other at all . . .
only deaf and dumb talk and very little of that.
But 'twas God's will they went their way at last
without doing harm or damage. Still,
'Twas a long week before we came to ourselves again.
Says my neighbour, Nell:

Overvoice: *[high-pitched, breathless] Oh weren't they the mob!*
And I was thinking
if one moved an inch he was ready to kill me.
I'd think all the time the iron pistol
would be stuck in my heart.
Were you afraid Peig?

"I suppose I wasn't, Nell," says I,
"For what good was it for me to be afraid!
Fear wouldn't save a person from death, would it?"
Well anyway, that was the big world there
with its troubles and terrors
crashing in on us like that. . . . .
But 'tis time now to leave all that,
and go back to our own small world as I promised.
To the matchmaking, and my wedding and all that.
'Twas one Saturday before Lent, I was nineteen then,
when my brother Sean came home from Dingle with some news.
"What news?" I asked him.
"News of a match, my girl," says he.
"God above," says I, "Who's the man?"
"An Islandman," says he.
"An even-tempered honest boy, and a good man as well.
They'll be coming to visit us some night soon."
Sure enough, three nights after this, 'twas a Tuesday,
three men walked in the door to a hearty welcome.
After a little while, one of them
produced from his pocket a bottle with a long neck.
Bottle followed bottle then
till they had a fair share of drink taken
and then no shortage of talk at all.
Myself, I didn't open my mouth, but I was
peeping from under my eyelashes at the young men.
All seemed fine young men,
but I couldn't decide
which of the three was asking for me.
I knew none of them, though I had seen one
about the town: Peats Guithín—an Islandman
and a class of a hero locally
for having saved a man from drowning.
And if truth be told, I *had* heard he was fond of me.

But as for the others:
well I surely wasn't going to marry
anyone I couldn't love, I knew that—
the way a lot of poor girls do,
only to find out their mistake too late.
Sure hadn't I refused another man one time,
when the sour lady I was in service with suggested him.
"I have no desire, Mam," said I,
"to marry any farmer's son I'd have no feeling for."
Anyway, after the drinking and the chat—
and I still not knowing who was asking—
my father came over to me.
"Will you go to the Island?" says he.
I thought about that for a while. . . .
I had two choices you see:
marry, or go into service again.
But I was sick and tired of that same service,
and I thought 'twould be better for me
to have a man at my back and someone to protect me
and to own a house too,
where I could sit down at my ease
whenever I'd be weary. . . .
Of course I didn't want to go
against my father and my brother, no;
but I wanted to follow my own bent too.
Well you know how it is:
a tangle of things dancing a jig in my mind. . . .
"So what have you to say?" says my father.
"I know nothing at all about the island people," I said,
"but you know them through and through.
So whatever pleases you pleases me . . .
as long as I have some feeling for the man."
"God be with you so," says my father,
while in my own mind, as ye can imagine,

I was sending up a bit of a prayer
for you know what. . . .
Well anyway the bargain was made. It was done.
And it was—*thanks be to God!*—
it was *Peats Guithín* and myself
were to be married in a few days' time—
before Lent started and no one could be married at all.
The following Saturday morning, so,
Sean got the horse ready,
and a crowd of us sat into the cart and off we went.
When we got to Ballyferriter then
the place was black with people—
for seven weddings there were that day.
Then when we left the chapel after all was done,
there was a right tip-of-the-reel and hullabaloo—
for the young people had music and dancing
and the older people were singing and drinking.
My brother Sean called for me then,
and some girls and myself went off home with him.
But Lord above, again: how merriment and melancholy
can jostle each other in the ways of the world.
For when we got home 'twas to bad news—
for we heard a daughter of Sean's
was all of a sudden at death's door
and didn't she die that very night.
We still had wedding visitors of course,
but according as each man would arrive at our house
he'd sit down quietly without speaking a word. . . .
And d'you know, ever afterwards my brother
had great affection for the island people—
for the fine manner
they had condoled with him that night.
So anyway, that's the way my poor wedding went:
a wedding feast and a wake at the one time.

But that wasn't the end of it, no.
For, in the way of the world,
light was to follow dark,
and on the following Tuesday, after the burial,
I went home with the Islanders . . . .
and I suppose you could say 'twas then
my *second life* truly began.

BRIEF PAUSE

Well, come Tuesday
four currachs were launched at the Creek—
one laden with the drinks and eatables
that hadn't been consumed
because of the poor girly dying like that.
I sat in the stern of the currach
my husband was rowing . . .
and as this was my first time ever on the sea
I was terrified out of my wits. Wouldn't you be too!
But the evening was beautiful, the sea was calm,
and we reached the Island's little harbour, no bother.
But I was as amazed then as if 'twas the city of London
I was entering. For the whole place
was black with people gathered to welcome us.
I made my way through the crowds as best I could,
but all the while turning over in my mind
how I'd come to accept this kind of home
without a relation or a friend near me.
For I didn't know one person
among all those shaking hands with me.
I kept asking myself if the day would ever dawn
when I'd open my heart to these people
as I would among the people of Vicarstown.
And I was thinking to myself
How lonely I am on this island in the ocean

with nothing to be heard forevermore
but the thunder of the waves
hurling themselves on the beach.
But then—
with my mind jigging between this and that—
I said to myself:
But sure I have one consolation,
a fine handsome man . . .
and as I can gather now from
the whispering going on around me
I'm not the first woman who cocked her cap at him.
But he's mine now, and Lord—
Hasn't he a fine presentable appearance too!
And his knowledge of the ways of the sea!
For I thought there and we coming over
I would never be in danger of drowning
if he and I were on the same currach.
When we got to the house then
my father- and mother-in-law gave me
a right *Céad Míle Fáilte*
and I was glad indeed, for now
Peats was bound to me by the Church:
we belonged to each other
and all we owned we held in common.
That was the way we promised it would be.
Of course many a person promises
and is sorry afterwards.
But I wasn't sorry, no not a bit—then nor after.
[music—a fiddle jig—she speaks over it]
And at the wedding feast that night
my heart was right and lively—
seeing all the good-looking girls and boys
raising dust from the floor in their dancing.
And there was singing too, and lashings of drink.

And a merry night we had of it, until six in the morning.
. . . And well that was me there at last:
content and settled into my second life.
An Island life. I was nineteen that time. . . .
Young and foolish, as the poem says.
Young yes, but . . . well . . . not *too* foolish.
[lights out: pause; then lights on again]
On the Island, I got to be known
as something of a storyteller.
Taking after my father, I suppose.
Neighbours would come in to hear my stories:
memories, or folktales I knew, that sort of thing.
And strangers would be coming too,
visiting and asking me questions
and listening to my headful of stories—
scholars and teachers interested in folklore and the like,
and in the sweet Kerry Irish I had.
One of them, a lovely man he was—English—
Professor Robin Flower: I called him Bláithín—
he'd be asking me about my life on the island
and my life before it.
Once I told him about the children I had . . .
and their lives too:
there in our small island world,
or them going away from me as emigrants.
For the first birth, I told him, I left the island . . .
for I knew I'd be more at ease
with my own mother and on dry land in Vicarstown—
if I needed a priest, God help us, or a doctor itself.
My husband Peats and another man rowed me over.
There was a swell on the water, but I felt safe there
in the bottom of the currach.
And I felt my baby inside me felt safe too.
Three days after Peats left me there,

I gave birth to a young son, and believe you me
that little stranger was welcome.
When Nell the midwife handed me the child
I could not describe my joy. I did not have the words.
And the very next morning didn't my husband walk in.
"You have a young son since just before daybreak,"
says my mother. "Where's the child?" says Peats,
and he took the babe smartly in his arms and kissed him.
We had a gay day then, and the following morning
brought the baby to Ballyferriter to be baptised.
And we called him Muiris after my husband's brother,
who had gone many years before to America.
That night we had a party, with whiskey in plenty,
and I don't think there was another household
in the parish of Dunquin as gay as we were.
I had more children after that, you know.
Six who lived:
two girls—Cáit and Eibhlín—and four boys:
Muiris, Pádraig, Micheál, and Tomás.
Beyond them I had four more, but they didn't survive.
Common enough that time, but a grief to me yet.
Three swept away in their infancy. . . .
Then the measles took Siobhán,
a fine bouncing girl of eight.
God's will it was. Then, in 1920,
my son Tomás died in an accident—
fell from a clifftop and he pulling a bush of heather.
No words can describe what I suffered then,
when I had to wash and clean
my fine young boy and lay him out in death.
Of course I told Bláithín stories about *emigration* too.
How some of my children emigrated.
'Twas but six months (I told him) after the death of Tomás
that my son Pádraig headed off to America.

And when he'd earned the passage money there
he sent for his sister Cáit, and she went to him.
Then five months after that
my husband, that good man, Peats Guithín,
died from a cold caught while out fishing—
and his heart broken with sorrow and ill health.
His death was the worst blow.
But as soon then as Muiris had turned
the last sod on his father's grave—
he too, though he didn't want to,
had to take to the road like the others,
and his heart laden with sorrow.
I remember the morning he left
he was standing with his luggage,
and his papers on the table beside him,
and unknown to him I was watching.
He stood there stiff as a poker
with his two lips clamped together as if he was thinking.
Then he rounded on me. *Here!* says he,
handing me something wrapped in paper.
I opened it and it was the *Irish flag!*

[Peig listens]

Overvoice: *[dialogue; Muiris, then Peig] Put that away now to keep in*
a place where neither moths nor flies can harm it!
I have no business of it from this out.
Son dear, this will do me more harm than good,
for 'twill only make me lonely.

Peig: *[to audience]* I followed him down to the slip, then,
and what with all the people making their way to the haven
'twas like a funeral that day.
We spoke then, and I can hear us yet:

Overvoice: *[dialogue] Promise me, Mother, when I go you won't be lonely.*
If I promised you that son,
I'd promise you a lie.

But I'll do my best not to be troubled.
I hope mother we'll be together again.

Peig: *[to audience]* God is mighty, I told him, and He has a good Mother—

Overvoice: *[Peig]: so gather your gear, son, and have courage,*
for there was never a tide flowed west
but flowed east again.
And 'twould be a bad place indeed
that wouldn't be better for you
than this dreadful rock.

Peig: *[to audience]* Then off he went.
And I was desolate when he was gone.
Then Eibhlín my daughter went,
and then my youngest, Mícheál, went off too.
And the upshot of all that
was that between dying and emigration,
one by one my children all left me
and I was left alone . . .
without a cow or a sheep or a penny in my pocket. . . .
So there *[deep breath]*—
that's emigration for ye.
How it hurt just one family, my own.
But weren't there thousands like that—
all over our unfortunate country that time, and after?
But isn't emigration a funny mix, too?
Good and bad, I suppose: the good of a new life,
but the loss of the old and all that went with it.

BRIEF PAUSE

Well that's a sad story, surely.
You know, it's my honest opinion
you have to be a bit of a soldier
to get on in this life, ordinary mixed bag as it is.
But I . . . I just went on so I did.
With the help of God and His Mother.

And thinking often of the crosses *she* had to carry.
But I'll tell ye a lighter story now . . .
just to change the music like.
It's about the demon Tobacco.
Oh aye, that same demon, ye know it well.
I think now, there's a curse down on top of anyone
with a mind for tobacco or snuff.
And this is all too true on an island,
for often you have no way to get tobacco at all.
Well . . . *[breath, "story" mode]* . . .
one evening I was all alone,
and I had my old clay pipe ready for a smoke.
So anyway, I put the dudeen down out of my hand
on the flagstone of the hearth and off I went
foraging for any small particle of tobacco I could find.
But I wasn't finding any
and the craving inside me was getting worse.
I searched and searched every hole and corner
where I'd leave a bit of baccy out of my hand
but divil a scrap did I find.
What did I do then but go to the tea canister
so as to put a grain of tea into my dudeen.
But when I came back
not a sight nor a sign of the pipe did I find.
Almighty Father, says I,
What's wrong with me today at all?
No lie but baccy fever has a holt of me.
For by all the brindled Bibles of the Pope
I'd swear I left my pipe down on the hearth there,
and now it's clear as a crystal
and no trace of a dudeen at all.
Why would the dead play tricks on me?
Hadn't they a great mind for tobacco when living?
Well I felt as tormented as a roast herring,

ye know how 'tis.
Going around the floor like a drunken man I was,
but divil a dudeen was there to be found.
In time I looked outside, just in case.
And there in the yard was the trickster of our pup dog
making a knocking noise with something he was chewing.
Of course 'twas my little dudeen,
and it almost ground to powder between his teeth.
"Well the curse of Maghera Mountain
down on top of you, you rascal!" says I.
"Aren't you the boyo, destroying my pipe like that!"
Back I went to the house, so,
thinking it the height of misfortune
ever to have put the stem of a pipe into my mouth.
But then again . . . doesn't everyone have his own weakness?
Sure I knew a woman in Ventry once
and didn't she sell her shawl for a half quarter of tobacco!

PAUSE

Well, what I want to do this minute now
is share something a bit *private* with ye. . . .
Nothing scandalous or bad, nothing like that, no.
But *private*. Nice in its way too.
Then I'll be done,
and after all my talk I'll go quiet.
I heard a poet once—
a fine poet he was, with lovely Kerry Irish—
and when he'd stop saying his poem
he'd say, in English he'd say it, he'd say:
I disappear.
So I suppose when I'm done here talking
and you're done listening so polite-like,
I'll . . . *disappear.* Right so.
Well . . . *[slight pause, breath, then in confiding tone]*

from my early days I had the habit
of looking about me at what I could see
on the land, in the fields, up the mountain,
or at the waves of the great sea itself.
Or up hauling turf with Kate Jim
I'd love the scent of the mountain heather
and I'd pick a bunch of it to tie in my dress.
Very often, indeed, I'd throw myself
back in the green heather, resting.
It wasn't for bone-laziness I'd do that,
but for the beauty of the hills and the rumble of the waves
and the blue sky over me without a cloud . . .
those were always close to my heart.
And I'd be appreciating them
and having feelings about them—
if you know what I mean—
and thanking God for what I was seeing and feeling.
Well, I suppose lots of people do that.
Poets and the like. But *me*?
Sure I wouldn't be writing a poem to save my life.
Not if you gave me gold itself.
But I *could* have those feelings.
Sure maybe at times *ye'd* have the like too.
Of course there were days when the weather
could be wet and sloppy with the rain sloshing down.
But there'd be good days in it too.
Even long summer spells of the finest sunny weather
or fine pet days too, between a pair of bad ones.
Good and bad, so, turn and turnabout,
like all else in this world.
One time, I remember,
I was on my way with my father to Dunquin,
and we both sat down by the edge of the road.
And as far as I could see to the west

the sea was a sheet of shiny glass . . .
and hardly a whisper of wind, just this soft breath
bringing in the salt smell of the sea.
The sun itself was a disc of gold
sliding down towards the ridges of Barr Liath.
And all of a sudden a sort of a
glimmering lance of light shot east across the bay
and broke into tiny bits of silver.
And I said to my father then:
"It's true, there's no place finer than home!"
'Twas then I saw a big ship go by from the north,
and the sea so calm I could see the ship's reflection
as it cut through the water and sailed on.
Praised be God forever! I told myself then.
For the ocean is powerful, surely, to carry a load
as mighty as that great ship on its surface.
I lifted up my eyes then, and what did I see
but hundreds of hills and green fragrant fields
and white seagulls noisy in the sky
or coming down to forage for food.
I could see from Ballynana to Brandon Creek
and north to Kilquane Lake,
and all around to Ballygoleen.
And I had a good view across the bay too, to Iveragh,
and the sunlight painting the water pure gold.
I didn't have the words for such beauty then,
for I was like . . . enraptured, under a spell. The wonder of it!
Though God knows and I myself knew
'Twas a spell (like many another) swiftly broken—
for later that day I had to walk—oh you'd laugh!—
barefoot through a field of heather and furze
and each tiny thorn like a tailor's needle
piercing my bare feet. . . . Ach just so!
And there we are again:

up against life's old mingled yarn,
fine-woven out of good and bad together:
one time the wonder of it, another time the wounding fact.
No mystery there at all . . .
Well, I'll give ye one more example to prove it:
for 'tis one I can never forget. . . .
'Twas on the Island I was . . .
and 'twas the very day I buried my fourth child.
I was troubled in my mind,
and as the evening was fine
I decided to go out and do a bit of knitting
abroad in the open air.
I sat on the bank, so, above the strand,
where I had a splendid view all around me.
Oh dead indeed is the heart
from which the balmy air of the sea
cannot banish sorrow and grief!
Well, I put down my knitting on a bit of grass
and gazed out to sea:
thousands of seabirds were flying around out there
looking for a bit to eat. Every bird—
from the storm petrel to the cormorant,
from the sandpiper to the gannet—
was there, and each had its own call.
Thousands of small gulls there too:
some hovering, casting an eye down
for a little sprat or other morsel.
And whenever one found a mouthful
she'd cry out, and right away
thousands of others were down on top of her.
Such scuffling and pecking—you'd never see the like!
All tangled up in one another they were,
trying to snatch the morsel away from her.
Such *life*!

And I could see the whole bay calm as new milk,
and little bits of silver spray shimmering on the surface.
The sun was brilliant yet, and to the south
Sléa head looking as if 'twould stand forever,
and not a stir out of the water.
And there out before me stood Dunquin,
where I had spent my early days:
fresh summer colours on its fields and gardens.
And away to the north Ferriter's Cove,
and from Fiach to Barr Liath
one great sea harbour—lying like Hy Brasil,
or some enchanted city under a spell.
"God!" says I aloud, for the words were drawn out of me:
"Isn't it an odd person indeed
who would be troubled in mind
with so much beauty around her
and all of it the work of the Creator's hand?"
Yes, I thought 'twas all God's work,
all that splendour you'd not have words for.
And then I thought that I myself too—
in my own ordinary life—
I . . . I was a part of it all.
And indeed, to tell you the truth,
it took my mind for a little interlude
off my great loss. . . .
But of course I had to come back to that too.
For every season in this ordinary life of ours
has its changes, its ups and downs, its griefs and joys,
and I knew both. All in their own time.
And with time passing . . . it just happens.
Grief yes. But joy too. It was just the way it was.
God's will, and no gainsaying it.

Overvoice: *[in Irish, the start of* Peig, A Scéal Féin; *after a beat she speaks over it]*

Peig: And now my own time with all of ye here

has passed, too, hasn't it. Of course it has.
As all things do. Yes.
[pause for a beat, overvoice stops]
But did ye hear that? Do ye know what it was?
'Twas the opening of the book of my life,
Peig, A Scéal Féin. Here's what it says:
[low fiddle accompaniment]
I'm an old woman now,
with one foot in the grave
and the other on its edge.
I have experienced
much ease and much hardship
from the day I was born
to this very day. . . .

                    [music continues, low]

Overvoice: *Many a thing I saw . . .*
           and I never let anything go astray . . .
           for people the likes of us . . .
           will never be there again . . .
           and that old world . . .
           will have vanished . . .
Peig: *. . . for people the likes of us . . .*
           will never be there again . . .
           and that old world . . .
           will have vanished. . . .
           Yes, that was how it started.
           And now ye've heard a bit of both:
           the ease, the hardship . . .
           and a bit of fun too, God knows.
           The same old tangled web of life.
           There were dark parts in it, yes—
           same as everyone's.
           Heavy and hard they were, yes.

But that was then. That was then. Yes.
But I went on, so I did, yes,
in my own ordinary way I went on, yes . . .
And now, *praise be!* Just look at me. . . .
[music stops; she stands]
All my storying done . . . and look! . . . *light as air I* . . .
I disappear!

[Blackout, in which she . . . disappears]

END

Coda

FERRY

A PLAY FOR VOICES

Ferry

Introduction

Ferry is a play for two voices, one male, one female, playing five characters. The title remembers the myths that portray the passage after death to the next world, "the other side," on Charon's ferry. The "passengers" in this case are an old Irishman, once a priest; a younger Irishman, once a fighter in the struggle for political freedom; an old Irish country woman; a younger English woman, whose daughter died young and whose mother was Irish; and a philosopher roughly based on Ludwig Wittgenstein, who spent some time in a cottage in Rosroe, on the coast of Connemara, a place he describes as the "darkest corner" of Europe. These five strangers talk to one another or to themselves, revealing fragments of their lives now left behind them. With the exception of the philosopher, the voices belong to representative characters drawn from various moments in modern Irish history. The philosopher reflects on how we use language to create stories that do, or do not, reflect reality and the connections between thought and language. The plot and development of the play as a whole are of my own invention.

The bits and pieces that emerge in this way form a collage-like meditation on life and death, religion, violence, ambition, body, spirit, language, and memory. What they offer are some random but pivotal moments in these ordinary, or not so ordinary, lives. Between short exchanges and longer soliloquies we get to know a little about these different, wounded lives and, by extension, social and political conditions in Ireland.

Ferry was first performed for the Stonecoast MFA Writing Program in Howth, County Dublin, in January 2013. In this production the staging/set consisted of two tall elevated boxlike constructions, on each of which an actor sat and was contained in darkness, except for his or her head. The actor's face would be illuminated when he or she spoke, making that face alone visible to the audience. The different characters were distinguished by different headgear.

For the original production

SET
    Dark stage. Two spotlights directed at lecterns.
    Two tall, boxlike, enclosing lecterns. Actors sit on high stools, with only faces and torsos visible, the rest of their bodies hidden by the lecterns. Sometimes both lights on, sometimes only one: the speaker's. Where there's a blackout of both lights, it should be very short.

CHARACTERS
    Old Man, Old Woman (country people, slow voices)
    Young Man (Irish accent; speaks fast; worked for a political organisation)
    Young Woman (London accent; mother was Irish)
    Philosopher (foreign, Austrian accent)

TIME
    The Moment

PLACE
    In Between

    Note: In this piece I have left in the various stage directions (mostly these are light cues), since they are so intrinsic to the piece, and the atmosphere of the piece would be less accessible (to a reader) without them. For a radio presentation, more sound effects are naturally possible.

[Music: A minute of "Carolan's Farewell"; *then sound of waves against a boat's hull; lights on Old Man and Old Woman; she wears a headscarf.]*

Old Woman:	So here we are. At last.
Old Man:	True. Here we are.
Old Woman:	They said it'd be crowded.

Old Man:	I've heard 'tis often packed.
Old Woman:	This time, scarce a sinner. Aside from the pair of us.
Old Man:	And that pair sittin' over there. A bit young for this.
	Mostly it's the old. Like ourselves.
Old Woman:	And the odd-lookin' fella on his own by the rail.
Old Man:	But packed, they say, most times.
	Like sardines, I've heard.
	Or the underground in London at rush hour.
Old Woman:	You've been there, so?
Old Man:	Aye. The Metro in Rome too. Packed.
Old Woman:	You've been about a bit you have, lord save us.
Old Man:	Here and there. But settled back over there, in London.
Old Woman:	Myself I've been nowhere. A *lifetime*, as they say,
	on the same windy peninsula.
Old Man:	But you'd see a power of life there too you would—
	in any one small place. Came from one myself I did.
Old Woman:	You might—with your ears cocked, your eyes glued,
	and your nose close to the ground.
Old Man:	And now here we are. All in the same boat.
Old Woman:	'Tis calm anyway. You'd hardly know we were moving.
	I've heard it can be rough enough.
	The journey to "the other side," as they say.
Old Man:	Calm now. No harm. After what we've been through.
Old Woman:	Is that a bird? Lord who'd have thought. A bird!
Old Man:	A cormorant. Only a glimmer in this black they are—
	that little white blaze on the throat.
Old Woman:	The raven now, he's as black. Or blacker.
	You'd not see him at all out here.
Old Man:	The Morrigán they'd call it in my part.
	The same lad as landed on the shoulder of Cuchulain.
Old Woman :	Were you ever in the GPO?
Old Man:	Not for the shootin' I wasn't. Before my time.
Old Woman:	I used to make phone calls there, to my brother in South Africa.
Old Man:	1916 and all that. And look at us now! The cut of us!
	How the mighty are fallen! I've bought stamps there.

Old Woman:	Narrow little cubicles they'd have, with a phone in them.
	And they'd call your number. "Johannesburg, number 5!"
	And there he'd be. *Hello Paddy!* The miracle of it!
	He left when he was twenty and I never did see him again.
Old Man:	Like many another.
Old Woman:	But the telephone was something.
	To stay in touch like.
	Hello Paddy! A miracle.
Old Man:	Far from *miracles* we are now.
	Ourselves alone!
	And all we've left behind us.

[blackout]

[lights on Young Man and Young Woman; Young Man wears wool cap, Young Woman wears no headgear]

Young Woman *[English accent]*: Is that a seagull? Out there. The white
shape.
Wings sort of glittering.

Young Man *[Irish accent]*: That's a seagull right enough. When I was young
I'd believe they were angels I would. *Angels!*
Off the pier there where I used live when I was a kid.
Floatin' on their white wings—
just driftin' and circlin' above the lot of us,
all calm and peaceful like . . . like guardian angels.
Angel of God my guardian dear
to whom God's love commits me here . . .
We'd say that. Kneeling beside the bed—
and I coulda sworn 'twas them big seagulls
was the guardian angels, no lie.
Kids! sure they'd believe anything.
Angels! I have to laugh.

Young Woman: Kids, yeah, they'd believe anything.
Though I only had the one. And with her gone
I had nothing. So I'd go to the music shows.
I liked the songs. Take me out of myself they would.

	All the angels I had time for, I have to admit.

All the angels I had time for, I have to admit.
Ever been to London yourself?

Young Man: I done a few . . . *jobs* . . . over there on and off.
Mailboat there and back in no time.
Spend a few days *reconnoitering*, that's what we called it.
Over I'd go link up do the job get out home again.
Wait for the next call-up. *Marching orders.*
Then same again: mailboat train job . . . train Holyhead
and home sweet home. Oh I've been to London all right.

Young Woman: I suppose you never got to the Palladium?
I remember the stage there. All lit up it'd be—
and the acts, lord the singers! Tom Jones! Lovely voice.
Not an angel mind, but a lovely voice notwithstanding.
"Delilah" that was one of his I remember.
His theme song they said it was.
[sings]

> *My my my Delilah*
> *Why why why Delilah . . .*

And all the young ones and the not so young ones—
they should have known better—all grabbing at him
and snatching their brassieres off (excuse me)
and their knickers too some of them, up they'd fly
onto the stage, crazy sort of carry on it was,
but you'd laugh at it, I would.
The screeches out of them, mad for it they were.
Oh I kept me own knickers on . . .
but don't misunderstand me, I could feel it all I could,
his lovely voice, and the sort of . . . softening inside you'd feel.
But that sort of carry on, it can't last forever can it?

Young Man: Delilah! Wasn't she the hussy
gave Samson the short back and sides?
Women! You'd never be up to them.

Young Woman: True enough. Though I'm one myself.
With my share of it and all, all that sort of larking,

though it didn't last long, and me with the one child,
my little girl, sick first then lost, gone.
Gone into the light, they said.
Isn't she an angel now, they said, *in Heaven?*
Much good to me that was.
Praying? Oh I tried that.
I'd been brought up to that by me mum,
But nothing. Words pouring out of me.
Gushing tears. But nothing. Silence.
Everything turned black on me.
Months and months of it.
Like I was living underground or in a thick black cloud
or off up in Alaska maybe
where there's never a glim of sunlight
from September to March.

Young Man: *Thirty days hath September*
                   April June and November,
                   All the . . .

Young Woman: And every one of them days
                   as dark as what-you-may-call it . . .
                   Hades. Nothing. No light. Not a glimmer.

Young Man: Was there, if you don't mind my asking, a father in the picture?
Young Woman: Not at all. Vanished. Not a trace.
                   Left me dealing with the lot of it. The weight of it.
                   I read once, in a play by Shakespeare it was,
                   in the convent I remember,
                   someone saying over a little dead baby:
                       A terrible childbed hast thou had, my dear;
                       No light, no fire.
                       The unfriendly elements forgot thee utterly. . . .
                   and then something about *Lying with simple shells.*
                   [light out on Young Man]
                   I wept when I remembered it.
                   No light, and me in the dark all that time.
                   No matter how many flowers I'd lay down

where I'd *laid her to rest*, as they say.
Imagine. *To rest.*
But no laying the likes of me to rest, not likely.
Flowers every Sunday it'd be. I'd have a break,
so up I'd go . . . by bus to the cemetery on the hill—
where was it?—up Hampstead way there.
The place . . . dead quiet. . . . Well that was natural I suppose.
Carrying my bunches of flowers.
Daffodils roses irises chrysanthemums carnations—
depend on the season.
You'd get a bunch of them in the flower shop there, by the gate.
Wrapped in newspaper.
I'd arrange them in a little metal thing—
like a tin can it was, and sometimes just that, a tin can—
labels half off, Bachelors Beans, Emerald Peas—
and I'd stick the irises in or the roses daffs chrysanthemums—
and stand a while looking, and feeling—what was it?—
just this big Nothing.
Like I'd been emptied out of myself.
Nothing. *Null and void,* as they say.
Just standing there, without a word.
Then back by bus into the world without her,
always without her, what was the use?
But back I'd go again the following Sunday—
regular as the rising of the sun and the going down thereof, as they say.
Bus up, buy bunch of daffs irises roses mums whatever
depending on the season—pansies even or peonies—
all raging with colour.
And the flowers from the other Sunday where I'd left them,
all withered now—dead brown, dead stalks—
dead as the little one in the ground there,
and drooping all sad-like
the way I was myself in my own chest, all heavy
and near falling over.

So . . . I'd gather the dead in a handful I would,
a bit of wet still stuck to 'em,
and I'd bring them over to the big rubbish barrel
and drop them in, and I'd settle the fresh blooms
(I like that *"fresh blooms"*)
in the rusty can, I would, for the poor little thing
and stand again, same way, empty as . . .
as a stony wreck of a field off there in Connemara
where I used go on holidays with me Mum.
Stand in the middle of that, I would—*null and void*
till I could stand it no more—
silence . . . deep as the ocean . . . and whole wrecks
sunk in it, and one little mite of a child—mine . . .
Lying with simple shells. . . . [light on Young Man again]
Home I'd go then—gas ring, bit of cake, cuppa tea . . .
Times I could only cheer myself up
by singing a song me own Mum taught me.
[sings]

> *I wish, I wish, but I wish in vain*
> *I wish I was a maid again.*
> *A maid again I ne'er will be*
> *'til apples grow on an ivy tree* . . .
> *I wish my baby she was born.*
> *And smiling on her daddy's knee* . . . Oh well . . .

Young Man: Sad song that. But I see the point of it, I do.
But *graveyards* now. I have a different thought altogether.
It's *kissing* I think on, imagine that—
kissing in the cemetery among the tombstones and all.
It's where we went and I a young fella. For a coort.
Safest place on earth, you might say, the graveyard.
Getting a squeeze there or even a tumble among the tombs—
common enough in the place I came from.
Odd when you think of it. Life and death, like.
What was it I heard a fella say one time?

Life, he said, *'tis just like . . . giving birth astride a grave.*
Isn't that a headful to hammer at now?
Though divil a bit of that you'd think
and you in there with a girl.
But sure it seemed right enough at the time.
Not *birth,* mind you, though that's happened too.
Poor things. It'd be in the papers.
But the bit of kissin' and huggin', summertime, no moon,
lyin' down on the grass there.
Often did it myself.
Love? We called it that anyway. Beyond *words* it was. . . .
Words . . . aye. . . .
Columbarium? There's a fine word now.
A tomb it means, in the ancient world.
Where they'd store the ashes of the dead, like.
But *House of Doves,* it means that too.
Odd, that. Death and life like. *House of doves.*
You'd build it up on the roof of your house you would.
A *columbarium.* . . .
Man I knew in London had one.
Kissed his wife there once I did.
She was feeding the birds and I with her.
Most natural thing in the world then.
High up above the world itself,
top of a five-storey house in Hammersmith.
You shoulda heard the humming and buzzing
and little gobblesounds off them birds—
a sort of *music* around the two of us,
like the world was made of wings . . .
and little musical mouths. *[light out on Young Man]*

Young Woman: I suppose it was. . . .
They did little enough *harm* with it anyway.
Makes me sad to hear it, though, and think back. . . .
[light out on Young Woman; light on Old Man]

Old Man: Did you hear all that. The kissing . . . odd . . .

And what that young woman said about her own lost child?

Sad stuff. . . . *[light on Old Woman]*

Reminded me of a poem we had to learn off by heart at school.

Did you ever hear tell of it?

By an English poet 'twas,

about his own daughter that died an infant.

Old Woman: You think you could still say it?

Old Man: I have it still.

[speaks quietly with feeling, but not "poetical"]

> *Here lies, to both her parents' ruth,*
> *Mary the daughter of their youth;*
> *Yet all heaven's gifts being heaven's due*
> *It makes the father less to rue.*
> *At six months end she parted hence*
> *In safety of her innocence;*
> *Whose soul heaven's queen, whose name she bears,*
> *In comfort of her mother's tears*
> *Hath placed amongst her virgin train:*
> *Where, while that severed doth remain,*
> *This grave partakes the fleshly birth;*
> *Which cover lightly, gentle earth.*

Old Woman: Oh that's grand, it is. And very true. True to life.

Which cover lightly, gentle earth. The very thing.

Old Man: Of course we didn't understand the half of it—

ruth, rue, partakes the fleshly birth, virgin train—

sure they meant nothing to us.

'Twas far from virgin anything we were.

Aside from the Blessed Virgin.

Still, 'tis a sad old story, that woman's story.

And no poem would do it for her either.

Her sorrow, I'd say now, was a *passion*, wasn't it?

Trapped in a passion of grief she was.

No consolation in spite of what they'd tell you.

Didn't I learn it all in boarding school myself—
how you were to deal with it all, all the bad stuff, the suffering:
passion, death, and resurrection.
Didn't work for that lady now, did it?
The Passion of Our Lord, they'd say.
Keep it in mind, boys, they'd say.
And then they'd larrup it into you anyway.
You'd have to stare at the crucifix over the prefect's bed
and learn . . . what were we to learn at all? . . .
repentance or something . . . *mortification.*
And we all of thirteen or fourteen years of age at the time.
Then confession time. Sure what'd we have to confess?
God only knows. But isn't that what they told us?
God knows, they'd say.
No hiding from His all-seeing eye, they'd say.
And sure we took it all as Bible we did.
Later then 'twas the crucifixes
all over the walls of the seminary.

Old Woman:	Oh I see . . . the seminary. I didn't know you were a pr—. . . .
Old Man:	Aye. . . .

But no shortage of crucifixes.
That *bruised and bleeding body,* as they'd say.
And naked. A naked body. Or just about.
They'd leave a bit of a togs thing on
so you'd never actually see him naked,
not like Greek statues or Roman statues, pagan stuff like.
Except as a Baby. Lying on his Mammy's breast,
or standing on her knees, maybe hanging onto a bit of a lily, or a bird—
   clutching
a goldfinch maybe in his little babyfist.
Or putting his hand on her breast itself,
like he was wanting a sup of milk.
Later—in Rome that was—I'd see hundreds of them.
Madonnas and Bambinos all over the place. Gorgeous.
Bellini, Botticelli, Raphael, Caravaggio,

and them you'd never hear of. Very *human*, they were.
The crucifixion pictures were that too. Human.
We'd take them in like great gulps of wine.
Vino . . . Oh we had our share of that too.
'Twasn't like being at home at all.
It had a bit of freedom about it, Rome had.
And all the good-lookin' women and the handsome boys
all over the place, running about on the streets of the city.
Just ordinary people, but very lovely they were to look at. . . .
But then . . . back home . . . oh a fair bit later . . .
After things . . . happened . . .
they'd say to me . . . my "superiors" would . . .
Did you do it?
And I'd have to say,
Yes I did it. Did you do it? Yes I did it. Did you do it? Yes. I did it!
Yes, I said Yes! I said Yes! . . . I can hear them yet.
Where was I?
Passion, paintings, the naked little fella. All of that.
Well . . . nothing's forgotten. But is anything *forgiven*?
Tell me this, missus, was there many at your fu—. . . at yours?

Old Woman: A fair share. Friends, neighbours, the parish.
The chapel was full. Cars parked for half a mile.
It was the way, back over there where . . . I lived.
And the family. Six children I had:
three sons and a daughter and the two that died.
And all the kids. Big ones, little ones. Oh a whole squad of them.
And the lot crying as if 'twas the end of the world.
Even the middle lad, though himself and myself
never rightly hit it off, I was never sure why.
Sure that's the way. Maybe that's the why he was crying.
A bit late, but what matter? What can you do?
Then the *words* said. The usual. I'd heard them
a hundred times before. Resurrection and the life. The usual.
And your own, so? Was there many at it?

Old Man:	Divil a one. No family to speak of.
	Brother, sister, gone before. No family of my own of course.
	In England 'twas.
	Chapel empty but for the priest and one altar boy. English.
	A bit bleak, but sure that was the way of it. *[light out on Old Woman]*
	The usual rigmarole.
	Prayers well behind me by then, if truth be told.
	I didn't have much use for them after . . .
	after it all . . . after all that happened.
	[light out on Old Man; light on Young Woman]
Young Woman:	Prayers well behind him, he says.
	Well they might be, by the sound of him. Poor soul.
	But there are lots of ways of praying aren't there?
	It's not all kneel down and bang your breast and bow your head and stuff.
	I remember when my own Mum went off.
	I was fifteen at the time, when my Mum went.
	And her sisters came over from Ireland they did. A while after.
	And they gathered in the little graveyard she was put down in,
	by the stone with her name on it.
	Five of them together. And me with them.
	Dark evening it was too, winter time,
	with a sort of a spitting rain on us.
	The place empty except for my aunties
	with their umbrellas and their Irish accents.
	And they had little candlelight things
	they set around the grave, they did,
	and they sat down then on the curbstone,
	umbrellas up, candlelights flickering.
	Kind of spooky as you might imagine.
	I was a bit scared at first, being young and all.
	But then they just started in talking of her—
	all her little ways, and how she'd been with them
	when they were all kids like, over there at home,
	the mischief she'd be getting into.

And they were laughing quietly among themselves then,
and me looking on at them.
Then . . . they were talking
about their own mother's going, my Gran that'd be,
and the great *wake* they gave her, the whole townland
crowding into the house, and the drink, and the singing,
and the tears, and the laughing.
And here they were for their own sister,
who'd not *had* a *wake*, so they were making a sort of one.
And true enough didn't one of them, my Aunt Delia,
pull out of her handbag a bottle of Irish
and she passed it about. They even let me have a little sip myself.
Then they were sort of crooning to one another.
It's what they'd call keening, but gentle-like,
and I stopped being frightened and I just joined in.
And then I felt reassured somehow,
for I felt my Mum was being as you might say "gathered in."
Taken home again she was. Their voices did that.
We stayed a good hour at it, I remember.
A little band of women under umbrellas,
candlelight flickering in the dark
and a *soft rain*, as *they* said, falling on the lot of us.
Then they went to a pub near there, me too,
and had a few drinks there and talked and talked.
The *craic*, they said:
they were having *a bit of craic* for Anna, me Mum.
I never forgot it.
And not a prayer between the lot of us.
[light out on Young Woman; light on Old Man]

Old Man: She's right of course.
'Tisn't in a church you'd be finding the real prayers often,
but out in the common highways and byways of the world.
People trying to make sense, that's the size of it.
Like those women. More power to them. *[light out on Old Man;*

light on Philosopher; thick brown scarf bundled around his
neck; his accent Austrian, his English carefully enunciated.]

Philosopher: Oh how they talk! To one another. Words.

It seems easy for them. For me no. It is not easy.

And so I must talk to myself again. Or to the dark. Or to the sea.

Or to the birds that come and go.

As I used to do . . . over there . . . in that small cottage-house by the harbour.

The mountain above my head; the sea at my feet.

A pool of darkness I had been seeking and so I found it.

Solitude. Silence. I could think then.

Alone with the birds and the sounds of the sea.

[light on Young Man]

Young Man: And may I ask what was a fella like you at
out there in the back of beyond?

Philosopher: I was a . . . was a . . .

Young Man: I see. You were a wasa?

Philosopher: No. The word is not coming to me.

This is funny, because you see words were my . . . my . . .

Young Man: Yes?

Philosopher: Exactly. My Yes. Also my No. Words were my Yes and No.

Was it in Shakespeare someone who says

yes and no are no good divinity? You want a good word?

I give you *divinity.* That should do, do you think?

Young Man: Go on with you! *Divinity*! Jaysus!

But what *were* you back beyond over there?

Philosopher: I was, I beg your pardon, a philosopher. Of sorts.

Young Man: And what might you mean by that?

Philosopher: A worrier of words. A juggler.

Young Man: Like a poet, is it?

Philosopher: No no. The poet he is the magician.

He pulls the rabbits out of the hat of language.

Young Man: *Rabbits??*

Philosopher: Well, not real rabbits. There was a poet once and she said
poetry was real toads in imaginary gardens.

Young Man:	*Toads?*
Philosopher:	Well, not really. Feelings, thoughts, truths.
	Coaxing the words, you see, to be all that.
	To be real. Always a wrestling match.
Young Man:	*Wrestling match?*
Philosopher:	Well not really, no. But it is all a struggle you see.
	Even now. But all that wrestling
	it was the end, as you say, of my tether.
	And so it was I lost sleep. Yes. Dreams I would have.
	Of knowing. Knowing everything.
	But it was all because I wanted to hold tight on to—
	forgive me I am about to give you another word. . . .
Young Man:	Say it man, it's only a word.
Philosopher:	No. Nothing is only a word. *Love.*
Young Man:	That's it?
Philosopher:	That is the word, yes.
Young Man:	*Love?*
Philosopher:	Yes. There I was in what you call the back of beyond,
	lost in thought—these are nice expressions—
	lost in thought in the back of beyond indeed I was,
	and wanting to be good, and love too.
	Oh such a tangle! *[light out on Young Man]*
	And the birds they would be coming to the window.
	Seagulls. Sparrows. Finches. Blackbirds. Thrushes. Wrens.
	I would watch how they were, each different.
	I'd listen to them talking among themselves. I'd talk too.
	The people my neighbours thought I was teaching the birds to talk.
	But we could not understand each other.
	Once I said *if a lion could talk we could not understand him.*
	We live you see in such different worlds.
	The people my neighbours did not much like me.
	But the birds, I would feed them, and they would like me, I think.
	Myself I used to eat the food in the tins.
	The postman he said that would be the death of me.

I said to him people live too long anyway.
He laughed and asked what sort of meaning had that.
And I said, *Meaning is like going up to someone.*
And so he went away.
And there was one bird I remember well.
A blackbird, and he flew against my window.
And so his wing was broken. He could not fly.
And I took him up and I made a . . . a splint for him.
Four matchsticks and some thread.
I bound the thread around the wing that was broken
with the splint of the matchsticks.
And for more than one week I fed him.
He stayed in the house with me. Such company!
After that I unwrapped the thread and the matchsticks
and he shivered a little and then
he knew he could use his wing again.
And I brought him to my windowsill, where my desk was.
And I placed him there by the window.
And he hopped out and stood there for a little bit of time.
Then he shook his two wings, the way he was testing them.
And then I opened the window. He looked at it,
and he looked at the world out there beyond the window.
Then he made a little hop, tilted his little black head,
opened his golden beak. And then he flew off.
It felt lonely then, the room empty again except for myself.
But in that same night—it was dark, no moon—
I heard bird music. I could hear him
and he was from some hedge in the little garden
singing that beautiful song of his.
And he kept it up and he did not fall silent
until it was a long time after midnight.
It was then I thought could I have perhaps
been a doctor, a surgeon, a simple bonesetter.
Some useful occupation. Something good. *[light on Young Man]*

	But no, I was a philosopher. So what is it I did?
	. . . I tried to help the bee get out of the bottle. . . .
	Or the fly trapped in the closed room.
	That was my philosophy. I tried to open the window.
	And so we would go. Free. Like my blackbird.
Young Man:	And did it all mean something to you,
	all the philosophy? All that thinking you were at?
Philosopher:	Yes. For gradually I came to see that life is not what it seems.
	Once I heard two philosophers arguing.
	And they were arguing about the immortality of the soul.
	It was amusing. I did not understand a word of it.
	It might have been two dogs barking at each other.
	So then I taught school, to little children.
	And I became a gardener in a monastery.
	Just life going on, you see. So . . . *ordinary*.
	So—can I say?—so *real*.
	The most important things, you see,
	just happen to you. . . . Like love.
Young Man:	*Love . . . again?*
Philosopher:	Yes. Love. I discovered that.
	There was one I loved, I think it is right to say that.
	[light out on Young Man]
	But he died young. So bright he was.
	Then he died. I forget it all, all what happened then.
	But I heard that at the, you know, the funeral,
	that I ran around in, as you say, bad shape.
	I heard they said of me—
	He was like a frightened wounded animal.
	I do not remember that, but I feel it must be true.
	Perhaps that is what love is.
	A frightened wounded animal.
	No words . . . how could there be? . . Just that *feeling*.
	[light out on Philosopher; light on Old Man]
Old Man:	Did you ever hear the like of that fella's talk?

It beats Banagher so it does.
If a lion could talk, we could not understand him.
Well there's one thing sure and that's when himself,
philosopher as he may be, when he talks, and he can talk all right,
I don't understand *him!* Not a word. Not a word.
[light on Old Woman]

Old Woman: No more did I myself. Scarce a syllable.
Though he had the words all right.

Old Man: Though I did get that bit about love—
and sure maybe love is like a . . . a frightened wounded animal
like he says. Though it wouldn't be for *me* to say now, would it?

Old Woman: 'Twouldn't then. And what did you do yourself anyway, after . . .
after it all happened—all bad stuff wasn't it?

Old Man: Bad stuff? You might say so.
Sure what could I do? Quit the place.
Change of clothes. Change of address. That was it.
Off I went. Like the thousands heading for the boat, the plane.
My suitcase gaberdine and cap.
And the address of a place off the Kilburn High Road.
'Twasn't much, but sure 'twas a roof and a room
and wasn't that all I was seeking.
Weren't there hundreds of us there that time—
Kilburn, Bayswater, Camden Town, all over London we were,
and in the towns and cities of the north.
I was always fearful I'd run into someone I knew,
from the old place, or the seminary even . . .
someone who knew what I'd done.
Never did. Didn't go near the pubs.
Stuck to the Lyons teashops and the like.
Job? Oh I had a job or two. Stackin' boxes I went,
in a big place, warehouse off Oxford Street. Shoes.
Summers I'd go down to Kent for the canning.
Peas, beans, plums, that sorta thing. Factory work.
The *English*, mind you, the men, and the women too,

they'd be friendly enough.
'owzit, Paddy. Doin' awroigh' are you, Paddy?
Goh a swee'eart have you Paddy?

Old Woman: You stayed away so.
Old Man: I did and all. Had to.
Emigration. . . . Exile. . . .
Never bothered me much I'd have to say.
One place much like another if you ask me.
People. All sorts you'll get anywhere. One is a kind one,
another's a . . . saving your presence . . . a gobshite.
Best come to no conclusions.
All over England we were, the Irish.
Sing out the names and you'd think 'twas weekend football:
Birmingham, Coventry, Leeds, Luton, Manchester,
Sunderland, Liverpool, Sheffield.
It could be rough, though.
I remember in one place I was, early on—
a room out in London somewhere it was, Acton maybe,
and five or six of us in the one room.
Everyone smokin'. And sweatin'. The smell of it somethin' awful.
'Twas there the drunken bowsie of a landlord
(Irish he was too, from the County Cavan, up Belturbet way)
and he near killed a man I worked with.
With a blow of his fist he did.
It took him a week to get over it.
Hard times.
Emigrants the lot of us. 'Twasn't easy. Never is.

Old Woman: And what at all would you live on
and you away alone like that?
Old Man: Toast. God knows I lived on toast. Day in day out.
Morning noon and night. *Toast.* Toast and butter.
The nice warm crunch of it between your teeth.
It kept me going so it did. That and the John West salmon.
And the porridge of a morning. Milk on it and sugar too.

Sure a fella could do worse and him living alone
the likes of me. Like a monk I was.
I thought of it, I did,
after everything that happened you know—
I thought of it as a class of *Purgatory,*
and me living in my little place there,
my own little bedsit.
Just putting things behind me.
A sort of a punishment after what I'd done, but cleansing.
But wasn't the heart gone out of me.
Still, I needed little enough to keep body and soul together.
Body and soul together! That's a good one!

Old Woman: And you had no company at all?
Old Man: Well I had the cat. The queerest wee beastie
that ever you'd see! Such tricks he'd get up to.
Rubbing against your leg one minute,
hissing at you the next. He was "fixed" as they say.
Fixed! Oh aye he was rightly fixed he was.
No carryin on after that. Like myself so, I suppose.
Retired from "the game of life," as they say.
Game of life! That's a good one!
Mind you, I loved that little fella.
Then didn't he fall sick on me.
Took him to the vet but there was nothing to be done.
Kidney gone west, so he had to be put to sleep.
And I with him all through it. And I was thinking,
with his last breath breathed into my face like that,
what teachers these little creatures are, teaching us
about holding on and letting go, the way *they* do.
Quick and bright as light itself when living.
Then in one moment out goes the light, the eyes still open,
but on nothing, and all is dark.
I whispered, as he went, little words of encouragement,
you know the kind of thing you'd say.

Then off he went, breath quiet as a baby's, gone.
But the place seemed very empty to me after,
empty and silent. Full of silence.
I'd get home, no sign of him, nor sound.
No one to talk to. Sure what could you say? . . .
. . . Did you ever have a cat yourself?

Old Woman: No. But we had dogs and I growing up. Always
we'd have a dog, and oftentimes more than one.

Old Man: Oh I had a dog too I had. For a short while.
But it got run over one time. Then I got the cat.
A mongrel the dog was, *[light out on Old Woman]*
like the rest of us. Bit of this, bit of that.
Followed me everywhere. Slept at the end of the bed.
I was safe so. Safe as a house.
Safe as a house? That's a good one!
[light out on Old Man; light on Young Woman]

Young Woman: Did you hear that?
Nice to think of it, though, the poor dog
following that old bloke about the place.
I suppose he's right though.
All sorts of sorrow you can have.
But you can't wallow in it neither.
You've got to pick yourself up, as the song says.
[light on Young Man]

Young Man: And just get on with it.
It's what the *emigrants* have to do isn't it?
All them that goes away, and stays away.
Think of all them pregnant girls
and women with no husbands, or with husbands itself,
heading away over the Irish Sea
and having their babies over beyond.
Or likely as not, not having them, if you know what I mean.
Some couldn't go at all:
Cast out. Disowned they'd be. All alone they'd be.

Young Woman:	Poor things. No one to turn to.
	All they needed was company.
	To be taken in. To belong somewhere.
Young Man:	I know what you mean. The *company*, we all need it.
	I recall my own trips on the mailboat.
	Holyhead in the dead of night.
	The singing. The chat.
	First there'd be the drinking, then the bit of turmoil,
	a fight maybe, then the singing again.
	All the emigrants coming and going.
	Alone as I was I'd be happy enough among them.
	Your own people, like. You'd belong with them.
	Drinking to drown their sorrows leaving home.
	Then drinking and happy, homeward bound.
	Then someone'd break a bottle over someone's head
	and the whole thing goes to bits—
	and you know that's your own crowd too.
	Then more smoking, chattering away, the *craic*, the singing.
	Everybody joining in. Choir of cats!
	But I suppose they had to, mad poor bastards as they were.
	Do you know "Carrickfergus."
Young Woman:	No, I've never been there.
Young Man:	I mean the song. "Carrickfergus." They'd do that one.
Young Woman:	Oh yeah. I know that song. My Mum used to sing it.
Young Man:	Could you give us a bar or two?
	Oh I wish I was in Carrickfergus . . .
Young Woman:	*[sings]*
	But the sea is wide and I cannot swim over
	And neither have I the wings to fly
	If I could find me a handy boatman
	To ferry me over my love and I . . .
Young Man:	Very nice. Thank you. Nice song.
Young Woman:	My Mum used to sing it. Always singing she was.
	Like her own mother before her, she'd say. Always singing.

Young Man:	And would you be singing much, yourself,
	to your own little girl?
Young Woman:	Oh yeah. Lullabies and the like. Course I did.

She loved this one, do you know it? *[sings]*

> *If I were a blackbird, I'd whistle and sing*
> *I'd follow the ship that my true love sails in,*
> *And on the top rigging I'd there build my nest*
> *And I'd fly like a seagull to his lily white breast*

But of course she was taken early.
And the years went by and I'd think of her growing like.
What it would have been like if she'd . . . well . . .
gone on, if you know what I mean.
And I remember once, I was out walking,
near Kilburn it was, just by some school there,
lots of young ones around the place, boys and girls—
black kids and brown, yellow and white,
the lot of them going home.
[light out on Young Man]
And I heard these two young girls, black they were,
West Indian I'd say, walking ahead of me.
School was out, teenagers they were,
in their uniforms, the neat little skirts on them.
In the rain it was, and they were laughing,
talking away twenty to the dozen,
not minding the rain at all,
when all of a sudden one of them lets a great *shout* out of her.
God I got a fright, I didn't know what it was.
But it was only her letting this great big loud *laugh* out of her.
And then the other one started in laughing too,
and the pair of them laughing like that
as if the world was just the best joke ever.
Laughing away and the rain coming down hard on them—
in their navy blue uniforms—
getting soaked and not minding at all—

laughing away, not a bother on them.
And then I thought to myself
she could have been like that:
she'd have been about their age, like them two young ones
—not *black* of course, no, but like, you know, *young*—
and not bothering about the rain and getting wet.
And talking away like that, about nothing I suppose,
or maybe everything. Boys probably. In the rain. Happy.
And then there'd be the sound of *her* laughing
and it rising above the busy world . . . like that.
Afterwards I'd often think
of the sound of them two young girls—
laughing away, not a bother on them, in the rain.
She'd have been like that . . . and isn't it funny to think of it . . .
and think it never happened.
[light out on Young Woman; light on Old Man]

Old Man: You can tell, can't you, that it all meant a lot to her.
Right too. You'd be stopped in your tracks for days
by just some little small thing. Two kids laughing.
'Tis nothing in itself, but it can mean the world.
When I'd be on my own after things happened
just sitting on my own in my little bedsit
I'd often have my head full
of the fellas I was in the seminary with.
Voices in my head.
Just talking away among themselves.
About nothing at all really.
Swapping a square of chocolate for a cigarette.
Even for a small butt of a Sweet Afton or a Gold Flake.
Go on give us one, they'd say. I'm dyin for a drag they'd say.
God I'd gut me oul fella for a smoke, they'd say, and laugh.
I'd be just sitting there, hearing all sorts of their little sayings—
all rattling around in my own unfortunate head.
[light on Philosopher]

Have you ever thought of that, and you a philosopher itself.
All the stuff that'd be going on in your head.
An *infinite* number of things.
Infinity—now there's a notion.
Never got the hang of it.
You'd grab at it, like. Then poof it's gone. Smoke.
Did you ever get the hang of it yourself?

Philosopher: I do not know of the hang of it. But I have thought of it, yes.
Though the ether is filled with vibrations
the world is dark. I said that.
But one day man opens his seeing eye,
and there is light.
And I wondered if that *light* was infinity—
was it how we make sense of the world . . . of what we suffer.
Eternity too. Once I said and I suppose I believed it:
Eternity, I said, *belongs to those who live in the moment.*
I heard that young woman talk of her grief.
That was living in the moment too.
Grief. It is like being in a war.
You must be endlessly . . . vigilant, yes?
And the only thing is to pick up yourself and go on.

Old Man: True for you.
'Twas a war I felt I was in for a long time back over there.
All the time full of fear. And nothing to pray to.
I'd put an end to all that, don't you see,
and there was no way back. Hidden things I'd done—
they were a weight I carried along with me.

Philosopher: I was in a *real* war, yes. The *war to end wars*, they called it.
But they were wrong.
Then I prayed. Or something like praying.
God give me strength, amen, I would say before a battle,
thinking that nearness to death
might bring light into my life.
My life, you see, it was in darkness.

Like you I had hidden things.
Like everyone maybe it is so.
Things that dared not speak their name.
In the War I wrote a book. And I said
What you cannot speak of, you must keep silent about.
Or something like that. But is it not a mystery
that the world *is*, that it exists at all?
Why is there something and not nothing?
So I would feel wonder at the *existence* of the world.
Seeing the world as a miracle, is that what we need to do?
I thought I needed forgiveness.
Because once I hit a little girl, I was her teacher, and I was angry,
and I hit her and I denied it. I have never forgiven myself.
Hitting a little girl. How could I?
You may think it a small thing, but no.
It made me be in bits, as you say, for a long time.
Then it was I had a *desire* for faith.
I would see faith as a . . . a *passion*. *[light out on Philosopher]*

Old Man: I know what he means.
I've known desire myself. Passion too, God knows.
Beyond what they taught us in school or at the seminary.
[light out on Old Man; light on Young Woman]

Young Woman: Did you hear what they were talking about,
them two old ones? *Passion. Desire.* Imagine.
You'd think they'd be past it, wouldn't you?
[Old Man coughs; light on him]
Oh excuse me . . . I thought you'd gone off
with the philosopher chap. No offense.

Old Man: None taken. But sure isn't everything desire?
Everything rushing forward, and no stopping it.
Want this want that. A world of *want*.
Desire at the heart of it all.
Like a fire it is.

Young Woman: Desire indeed. Oh yes, I know all about that.

A lick of flame taking dead leaves all of a sudden.
Turning them to . . . well . . . what? . . .
To smoke, that's what. Smoke. Puff, and gone.
Like my man who left me. Gone.

Old Man: I'd have my own dreams in that direction. Desire . . .
Daydreams mostly. Over my tea and toast
in my little bedsit there. The gas ring lit.
Drop of Power's to go along with it.
I'd buy a Baby Power of a Friday, and 'twould be empty by Monday.
Oh 'twasn't much. Just to add a bit of flavour.
Up on the third floor I'd be.
Chair by the window . . . looking out—
The spires and the rooftops and the people down below.
Noisy lot coming out of the pubs they were too—
a power of Irish among 'em.
But *daydreams*, I'd have *them* all right.
Face of a woman I mighta seen having a cuppa tea in Lyons
would float back into my head and I sittin there.
Or one'd pass me at the newspaper shop
and me coming out with the Irish paper in my hand.
A face, Irish like, that'd stay with me for the rest of the day.
But sure nothing ever came of it.
Daydreams, aye. No harm in them.

Young Woman: You're right. Not a bit of harm in them. Natural really.

Old Man: There *was* one time I remember, though,
and 'twasn't a daydream this, nor a woman neither,
but something more mysterious.
Well 'twas getting on to beyond four o'clock—
the winter near gone—early February it might have been.
I was sitting there *[light out on Young Woman]*
looking out the window, chewin' on a bit of toast, cuppa tea,
the drop of Power's in the tumbler with a splash of water.
The people streamin' by—
men women children—all sorts—all colours.

And the light was quite strange—
a sort of purplish brown in colour, sepia,
and off beyond to the west a sort of rosy colour.
Very striking, I was thinking to myself,
and I watching the people moving through it
on their way from the shops and the offices and the like.
The usual. Then I heard the bells of a church,
church bells ringing out. I don't know
if 'twas a Catholic church, mind you, or a Protestant church itself,
we had both around the place,
but it was making a fine full sound it was.
Not just striking the hour like, but playing
some sort of a tune, some hymn or other I reckon.
And it seemed to me then that all the people
all at once
froze there in that light with the music of the bells,
as if they were all of a sudden caught in it and stopped in it,
and somehow lit up in it.
And it seemed like in that very minute
I was seeing into *the nature of the world.*
'Twas very strange. I thought for the minute or two it lasted,
and it only lasted a minute or two,
that I was seeing into some sort of *meaning* or other,
I couldn't say what. Everything *together* like that, and *illuminated*—
it all made sudden *sense,* if you know what I mean.
And I swear in that minute
I thought I understood *life itself,* and myself a part of it.
And you know
I felt a sort of *happiness* go right through me.
But sure it didn't last more than a pair of minutes, no more,
and then I came back to myself:
and there was the window, and the light outside,
and the sound of the bells, and my cold toast,
and the steam coming off my cuppa tea,

and the glass of Power's still in my hand—

and everything was, you might say, *normal* again.

. . . But I never forgot it I didn't,

though I didn't rightly *understand* it.

[light out on Old Man; light on Old Woman]

Old Woman: Well isn't that the strange story that man told there.

Such odd things can happen, they can,

and in the ordinary world itself.

Out of the blue, as they say, when you'd not be expecting.

[light on Young Man]

Young Man: True enough. I suppose there's something to it.

I mean you'd have strange things happen to you.

You'd see things in a funny light all of a sudden,

and sure it might change your life.

Was the like ever true for yourself?

Old Woman: Yerrah no. It's the ordinary life I led back beyond over there.

Day following day, night following night,

and nothing pass remarkable about any of it at all.

Oh the children being born, and growing, and going off,

and the two that died. There was that.

But sure it all seemed just . . . well . . . part of life.

Normal. I suppose that was it.

No lightning strikes or bright flashes out of the blue,

just sunshine and rain and the rain clearing

and then wind and storm and that clearing too.

The weather never still, and all our lives

just going along the same road.

Though it's fair to say the bad things happened.

Cruel things that'd break your heart.

Some had to leave for reasons not to be spoken.

Some decided—and this would take the heart of you entirely it
    would—

to end things themselves. Straining they'd be

under something sad and dark

till it grew too heavy to bear, poor things.

	And then . . . well you know how such stories end, you do.
Young Man:	Oh I do, I do, no need to tell *me*.
Old Woman:	But thinking of that man's story, now,

I am reminded of one day that seemed to stand out for me.

Oddly 'twas a mix of happy and sad it was. My own wedding day.

Well my husband and myself we were going off on our honeymoon.

We were going up to Dublin to stay in a hotel there.

In Greystones, it was, out on the coast there.

I suppose though 'tis in Wicklow that is.

Near enough the City it was anyway

and we'd heard 'twas the nice place by the seaside,

and we decided we'd spend three days there for a honeymoon,

and home again then. *[light out on Young Man]*

'Twasn't much, but what we could afford.

And it was very nice it was.

The few days of freedom just the two of us ourselves alone.

And once we went into the city. By the train. That was nice too.

The crowds across O'Connell Bridge, the Liffey, and the seagulls,

and the big green double-decker buses and Henry Street and all the
shops.

We had a lovely lunch in Winn's Hotel,

and in Clery's I bought a lovely skirt and blouse. Fancy.

He helped me pick it out, and I thought that was very nice of him,

gentleman-like. And then towards evening

we went back to Greystones by the train, along the coast,

and you could see over Dublin Bay, and the lights coming on

over in Howth. It was a nice day we had of it.

Those three days, yes, they were very nice.

But that wasn't what I wanted to tell. No.

What I remembered

was what happened on the day we left our home place—

after the wedding breakfast, the reception and all,

a small one mind, nothing fancy.

Well my father he drove us to the station.

And we were there, the three of us, standing there waiting for the train.

My father was smoking. We weren't much for talking,
just the usual about the way it had all gone off and all.
Then the train was there
and my husband and I were taking our leave.
And my father, he shook hands with my husband
and wished him a safe journey and God bless.
And my husband he thanked him.
Then my father took hold of me in a way he never had before,
he wasn't one for it, even when we were children.
But a right hug he gave me, nearly desperate you might say,
he held me so tight I near lost my breath.
It was then I could see he was crying,
big tears rolling down his cheeks.
I'd never seen the like of that. He wasn't the type.
But there he was, in public, at the railway station,
crying his eyes out.
And when I said to him, *There now, Daddy,*
it'll be all right, we'll be grand, he looks at me and says he,
But you're going away, you're going away.
But sure it's only a few days, says I.
No, says he, *it's forever, forever it is,* and the tears wetting his face.
I didn't know what to make of it or what to say.
I wondered if it was the drink he'd taken at the reception,
but he wasn't that way given.
No it's forever it is, he kept saying.
Then we had to go, so I sort of hugged him trying to smile,
you know how it is, and my husband
he pushed me up onto the train and jumped in after me,
and I looked out the window and waved as we went off—
with all the noise of the station around us—
and there was my father looking after us:
such a figure he was, his hand in the air,
looking after the train,
but sort of bent and I knew he'd still be crying.

It was the saddest sight I'd ever seen. It stayed with me.

[light on Young Man]

But of course life went on: I was married, we had our children, the
 usual.

But he was right. I *was* going away forever.

We never talked of it again in all the years after.

But I never forgot it either and I knew from that moment,

my father holding onto me at the train station and him crying like that,

that life was all partings.

I *understood* it, if you know what I mean.

Young Man: I understand that, I do.

Sure didn't I have in my own life

a moment in which I saw things

in a new way, saw them in a new light.

And it changed things too, it did, like you say.

Things weren't the same after.

Old Woman: How was that?

Your father, was it, or something like that?

Young Man: Nothing like that. It was just myself.

Over in England I was. On a job.

Passing the time of an afternoon. Waiting for the call—

time, place, weapons, who I'd meet, all the details—

from one of the comrades. *Comrades!*

Just hanging about I was. Out there in a suburb of London it was.
 Wembley,

I think. Where the stadium is.

I was in this park.

Nice place it was, open, with paths for walking.

And I seen a man with a little dog walking ahead of me.

Little furry fella colour of oatmeal the dog was,

and wasn't he pullin' like fury on the lead he was on,

trying to run after a squirrel. Little grey thing with a bushy tail

that scrambled its way up a tree.

And the owner there keepin' a grip on him. And says he to me—

a brown man he was, some class of Indian I'd reckon—

says he, *He likes to kill you know.*
Well it struck me as, like, funny, given what I was about *myself.*
And I was just passing a kids' playground there.
You know the sorta thing: swings and see-saws and slides and the like,
and all the little kids runnin about from one to the other—
and shoutin, such shoutin out of them! Do you good to hear them—
having a great time, free as birds, noisy as a flock of starlings.
[light out on Old Woman]
And the mothers—a couple of dads, but mostly the mothers was in it—
or maybe nannies some of them—
smokin and talkin and keepin an eye on the kids.
Cardigans . . . it musta been early in the summer it was—
arms folded, smoking their fags.
Then there was all of a sudden a bit of a scream
and they all stopped what they were doing—
the kids stopped their runnin and shoutin,
the mothers stopped their chattin,
and they all looked where the scream came from.
And weren't a few of the kids
gatherin around a little fella on the ground there.
I could see his green T-shirt and his white runners,
and wasn't he lying on the ground sort of twisted in his legs
and not a stir outa him.
He'd fallen or maybe jumped off the top of the slide—
and he musta hit his head or something.
But not a stir out of him. Then one woman—
she had a sort of silvery scarf on her head
and I thought to myself . . . maybe she was a Muslim—
and she came rushing through to the little lad and tried to lift him up.
His mother she must have been, crying she was,
and sure I suppose she thought he was dead.
But then didn't he make a little sort of a shiver, and he sat up . . .
White as a sheet he was . . .
and she grabbed him and hugged him

and kept hugging him and wouldn't let go.
That lasted a while it did, and all the parents
talking to their kids, and everyone looking relieved
and then, gradually like, moving away again,
and the kids starting to run around again
and the mothers shouting at them and warning them to be careful. . . .
Well the little injured fella he held tight onto his mother's hand.
And then he was limping away.
And so off home with them. None the worse for wear.
And that was it. Incident over.
But *I swear* the whole thing affected me mightily.
It was the look on that mother's face
when she thought something terrible had happened to her son.
I'll never forget that, it went straight through me
and stayed in me like an arrow in my side.
And then her relief, the look of it.
What was it at all—the sense that
the *bad thing* hadn't happened, they were *spared*.
And I was thinkin of all the bad things that *did* happen,
and sure some of them wasn't I myself after doing—
and I was thinkin there were mothers and kids
hurt and killed in some of them. Of course there were!
So in that moment, and I remember the moment well,
something in me turned, turned away from all that.
Lit out, I did, and made it back home to my own mother's house.
But I knew they'd come looking,
so I moved about a lot, went away, came back,
but always on my guard.
For they don't like anyone saying no to it all—*breaking the oath*—
the way I did. They're vicious about that.
But I never went back on that afternoon,
on what I decided then, seeing how . . .
how vulnerable people are,
how fragile, you might say,

and how the love that woman had for her child was so . . .
such a pure thing . . . I could see it blazing out like that,
like a *light* coming off her. Powerful it was.
Well, powerful enough to turn *me*,
and put me on another road.
Of course I couldn't run forever, could I?
And they never gave up the chase.
It's what they do . . . what they're *sworn* to.
And in the heel of the hunt they caught up with me.
One evening it was, in Dublin I was.
Coming home from the chipper after the pub.
A pub I thought where no one knew me.
In the dark it was. Near the front door of the place I was staying, it was.
I heard someone call my name . . . and I looked about.
And that was it. End of story.
And . . . far as I know . . . they got away with it, they did.
[light out on Young Man; light on Philosopher]

Philosopher: So odd, is it not, to hear such talk. Violence.
Big or small, it has only one ending.
Such strange things it does to our head, is it not so?
It would, would it not, as they say, make the cat laugh.
Can a cat laugh? And would we know why?
All those questions I kept asking!
Like a dog with a bone, as they say.
Once upon a time
I thought I could see the world from above.
Like I was flying. It would be amazing.
The world of dustbins and blackbirds and trousers
and motor cars and children and women's faces.
Wars too. Violence. Everything happening at once.
All the miracles of the world.
I wanted to write a book,
and I would call it *The World as I Found It.*
The way a painter might be seeing what matters—

not all the world, but just what he finds there
in some small corner of it, how it looks to him.
A tree, a woman's hands, light on water.
I always liked when I was travelling on a train
coming out of a long tunnel into the light. That *feeling*.
Maybe that is what will happen.
A room can be empty, you see, yet full of light.
In life one just keeps stumbling, falling, going on.
I remember once one thing very clearly.
It was for some reason a difficult day for me.
And I remember kneeling down, it was odd,
I knelt down, it was in my room and I looked
up above me, at the ceiling, and I said out loud
There is no one here. And I did not know what I meant.
But I said it again. *There is no one here.*
And it gave me some ease to say that.
It was as if I had been *enlightened* in an important matter.
So then in doubtful times I would after that often say
There is no one here and I would look around.
The room was empty, yes, yet it was full of light.
It was as if I could read the darkness, and it became light.
I wondered always at the *existence* of the world.
How it was, well, a miracle.
Was it not in Shakespeare
the old father tries to end his life and fails,
and then his son says to him, *Thy life's a miracle.*
Such a thing to say, it was.
So he could begin again to wonder—
to wonder at . . . the *existence of the world.* The *miracle* of it.
I wanted to be perfect, yes.
It was my *soul* I hoped to be saved.
But body, ah yes, body:
it is the image of the soul, or is it the other way round?
Body. Soul. Such words.

No abode but the body—I heard someone say that once.
No abode (I would think it proper to add) . . . but the
    language.
Body and soul: that is *language* and *silence.*
The *breath* of words. In the beginning
was the *Word,* says the Gospel. Yes. And in the end, also.
It is a world of words to the end of it, says the poet. That too.
But now? . . . . . . Listen. . . . .
Yes. . . .
We have all stopped talking.
[light out on Philosopher; light on Old Man]

Old Man: Well indeed we have not.
World of words, as he says, it is and all, so it is.
Stop talking is it? That'll be the day.
For the likes of him, for the likes of us.
[light on Old Woman]
What do you think, Missus?

Old Woman: Sure I suppose we'll just keep nattering on we will.
Like it always was, back over there.
'Tis hard to silence the likes of us. As it was in the beginning
is now and ever shall be, as they say.
World . . . without end. . . . Amen.

Old Man: I feel like we've stopped moving though.
I suppose we've arrived so.

Old Woman: True enough. We're here. That part's over anyway.
Them two young ones over there, and the foreign fella,
they're lining up to go off. Is it getting brighter it is?

Old Man: Hard to say. What was it that foreign fella said.
Philosopher is right. Hard to philosophy us out of this I'd
    say.
Even an empty room can be full of light.
Well, we'll see.

Old Woman: But I liked when he said a while back, did you hear him—
Eternity belongs to those who live in the moment.
I'll take that as Gospel any day, I will.

For the moment anyway.

[sound of a blackbird]

Old Man: Shush now. What's that sound?

Old Woman: I'm hearing nothing.

Old Man: Listen. There it is again. *[sound of a blackbird continues]*

Old Woman: You're right. Some class of bird it is. Strange.

Old Man: A . . . *blackbird* . . . by the sound of it.

Old Woman: You're right. A blackbird. I'd know it . . . anywhere.

Old Man: Imagine that. What's it saying, I wonder?

Old Woman: God knows.

[Blackout; blackbird song continues]

END

Acknowledgments

My gratitude and thanks go

to my life-partner, Rachel Kitzinger, for her ever-present practical and invaluable editorial assistance with all the plays, especially in their final stages. I could not have completed this collection without her;

to Tegolin Knowland and Seán Coyne, and all their telling voices;

to the owners and management of Renvyle House Hotel, Renvyle, County Galway, where many of these plays were and continue to be often performed;

to Gerard Coyne for the use of the Anna Curley Theatre in his pub, Paddy Coyne's, in Tullycross, County Galway, where a number of these plays were performed and for his design of the posters for J. M. Synge's The Aran Islands, Emigration Road, and Ferry;

to Arne Richards for the music he composed for many of the songs in Hunger! and Emigration Road; and to Shona Flaherty for the music for songs in Emigration Road;

To my daughter Kira Grennan for her design of the posters for Hunger, History!, The Muse and Mr. Yeats, Peig: An Ordinary Life, and The Loves of Lady Gregory;

to Adrian Kitzinger for his invaluable formatting of the typescript of the completed text;

to the Clifden Arts Festival for their support over the years by including productions of many of these plays in their program;

to our friends in Renvyle who have supported us from the start.